JOHN
KING OF ENGLAND

❧ JOHN T. APPLEBY ❧

JOHN
KING OF ENGLAND

NEW YORK: ALFRED A KNOPF: 1959

L. C. Catalog card number: 58–10972

© John T. Appleby, 1958

THIS IS A BORZOI BOOK,
PUBLISHED BY ALFRED A. KNOPF, INC.

FIRST EDITION

PIAM IN MEMORIAM PATRIS MEI

✥ *FOREWORD* ✥

O F ALL *the Kings of England, none, with the possible exception of William Rufus and Richard III, bears a worse reputation than John. How much of that reputation is based on the known facts of his life and how much on Shakespeare's play it is hard to say, but it is safe to assert that many more people have read the play than have read a history of John's reign. The general reader, however, could probably sum up his knowledge of King John in three statements: he ordered Hubert de Burgh to blind the young Arthur, he signed Magna Carta, and he lost all his treasure while attempting to cross the Wash.*

What are called the known facts of his life are largely the accounts given in the contemporary chronicles. These were all written by

monks who were without exception hostile to John, mainly because
of his long struggle with the Pope, and the intemperance of their
language when they speak of him leads one to suspect that they were
far from objective reporters of his actions. Thus, from the very start,
one has to depend upon violently prejudiced writers and to bear constantly in mind a suspicion, to call it no more, that the worst side of
John's character and the worst possible interpretation of his actions
are being given.

Shakespeare's play, from which the popular picture is drawn, is
based on Bishop Bayle's Kynge Johan, a ludicrous attempt to present
John as a thirteenth-century Henry VIII, anticipating the break with
Rome by three centuries. Shakespeare discarded much of the religious
polemics, but he retained Bayle's garbled version of the history of
John's reign.

While I was reading these two plays and attempting to discover
to what degree they followed history and in what respects they di-
verged from it, I realized how little information about King John is
readily available. Kate Norgate's John Lackland was published in
1902, has long been out of print, and is not easily accessible in this
country. Dr. Sidney Painter's The Reign of King John is a book of
profound scholarship, but it does not attempt to present the events
of John's life in chronological sequence. Other than these, I know
of no modern biographies of John.

I turned then to the contemporary chronicles, mainly those of
Roger of Hoveden and Roger of Wendover, and attempted to assemble from them an account of John's life. This book is the result

of my readings in those chronicles, supplemented by occasional information from such other contemporary writers as Gerald of Wales, Richard of Devizes, Ralph of Coggeshall, and the authors of the lives of St. Hugh, Bishop of Lincoln, and of William Marshal. I have also made use of a number of letters from the Close and Patent Rolls. Whenever possible, I have quoted those letters in full, both because they are not generally accessible and because the language of the letters themselves is much more interesting than any paraphrase could be.

This life of King John is addressed to the general reader and not to those having expert knowledge of the history of England during the Middle Ages. It therefore does not have the usual scholarly apparatus of footnotes and bibliography. In the words of one of Miss Compton-Burnett's characters: "I put things from several into another, and then it is called a biography."

Many people have helped me in the writing of this book, and to all of them I am grateful. I am particularly grateful to the staff of the Library of the University of Arkansas, who made their facilities available to me, to Dr. John Clark Jordan, Dean Emeritus of the Graduate School of that University, who suggested the possibility of this book to me and who listened patiently as I discussed the problems I encountered, and to Joseph Michael Lalley, Esq., who offered many helpful criticisms and suggestions.

JOHN T. APPLEBY

❧ CONTENTS ❧

England

During the Reign of
King John

Lindisfarne

BAMBURGH

NEWCASTLE

CARLISLE

Solway Firth

PENRITH

DURHAM

APPLEBY

PALATINE COUNTY
OF DURHAM

WHITBY

SCARBOROUGH

Miles

0   50

LANCASTER

YORK

BRADFORD

SELBY

BEVERLEY

PALATINE COUNTY
OF CHESTER

PRESTON

WAKEFIELD

HULL

GRIMSBY

Humber

Anglesey

CHESTER

High Peak

DONCASTER

Sherwood For.

NEWARK

LINCOLN

The
Wash

NOTTINGHAM

BOSTON

SHREWSBURY

STAFFORD

DERBY

GRANTHAM

LEICESTER

LYNN

GT. YARMOUTH

MONTGOMERY

*Forest
of Arden*

STAMFORD

NORWICH

The Fens

THETFORD

BRIDGNORTH

COVENTRY

HUNTINGDON

W
A
L
E
S

KENILWORTH

ELY

DUNWICH

WORCESTER

NORTHAMP.

CAMBRIDGE

BURY ST.
EDMUNDS

ORFORD

HEREFORD

EVESHAM

BEDFORD

IPSWICH

GLOUCESTER

WOODSTOCK

BRACKLEY

WARE

COLCHESTER

OXFORD

ST. ALBANS

BRISTOL

MARLBOROUGH

WINDSOR

LONDON

Severn

SANDWICH

BATH

DEVIZES

READING

Runnymede

STAINES

BARNSTAPLE

ROCHESTER

GUILFORD

CANTERBURY

BRIDGWATER

SALISBURY

WINCHESTER

HYTHE

SHAFTESBURY

*New
Forest*

SOUTHAMPTON

The Weald

RYE

EXETER

PORTSMOUTH

CHICHESTER

LEWES

Dartmoor

CORFE

HASTINGS

BODMIN

WINCHELSEA

TOTNES

DARTMOUTH

FOLKSTONE

DOVER

English Channel

G. Fleming

France

During the Reign of King John, Showing the Continental Possessions

JOHN
KING OF ENGLAND

CHAPTER I

JOHN,
COUNT OF MORTAIN

✿ 1167–1184 ✿

JOHN'S coming into the world attracted little attention outside Queen Eleanor's bedchamber. As the fourth son of Henry II, with three vigorous brothers ahead of him in the succession, he seemed destined for a life of relative obscurity, with a chance earldom as his highest lot. And for thirty years John remained obscure, almost unnoticed beside his father, one of the greatest rulers England has ever seen, and beside his older brothers, violent, charming, turbulent, bickering, dazzling figures who crowded their youngest brother off the stage. When at last, after almost thirty-two years of dwelling in the shadow, he came to the throne, all Europe still shone with the light from Richard his brother, and in that light John looked dark indeed. In an age when the fighting man was supreme, who could hope to measure up to Richard of the Lion's Heart?

And yet John must have had some small share of the quality that enabled Henry and all his other sons to capture men's hearts and hold their imaginations. Throughout his life Henry loved this youngest son, and John's faithlessness broke his father's heart, whereas the treachery of the other brothers could inspire Henry only to furious fighting and wild curses. Perhaps Henry loved John just because no one else did. Certainly his mother did not, for Eleanor, after Henry turned to other women, saved all her affection for Richard. After their father's death, Richard treated his brother with a half-contemptuous affection and never seemed able to take John and his plottings quite seriously. Henry chose as his friends the best and wisest men of the kingdom; Richard consorted with the bravest of fighting men and the best poets and musicians of his age; but John seems to have had no friends except such dubious characters as were drawn to him through self-interest.

John was suspicious of all men, as well he might have been, for he grew up in an atmosphere of treachery and of internecine warfare in which the sons fought now their father and now each other and transferred their allegiance at a moment's notice. Richard learned from such experiences to be a judge of men; John learned merely to distrust all men.

At the time of John's birth in 1167, his father, Henry II, was thirty-four years old and had been King of the English for thirteen years. He was a man of boundless energy who lived in a whirlwind of activity. He could not bear to be still for a moment, except when he was reading; he sat only when he ate. Even when he was hearing Mass, he spent more time conferring with his officials than in following the service.

Hunting and books were his favorite pursuits, and he is said always to have had either a bow or a book in his hands. He could not endure a settled routine; he dragged his court at breathless speed over the length and breadth of England and of his vast continental domains. This constant moving from one place to another, although not always at the restless pace imposed by Henry, was a normal feature of the royal household during these times, both in order that the

King might hear the more difficult cases and dispense justice in the various courts, and because it was easier for the household to visit in turn the royal manors, which were scattered all over England, and consume their produce on the spot, than it would have been, in an age of slow and laborious travel, when carts could cover little better than ten miles a day, to haul the produce from the four corners of England to some place where the court might be permanently established.

Even when Henry summoned the great men of the realm for a council, he would often ignore their assembly and hunt from morning till night.

His temper was of great vehemence, and he would sometimes fall to the floor in fits of rage and gnaw the rushes in his wrath. All the members of the House of Anjou were subject to such fits of rage and had such violent emotions generally as to lend credibility to the legend that there was a diabolic strain in their ancestry. Gerald of Wales tells the story thus:

A CERTAIN Countess of Anjou, of great beauty but of unknown origins, whom the Count had married solely because of her beauty, rarely went to church, and when she was there she showed little or no devotion. She never stayed in the church till the secret Canon of the Mass but always left immediately after the Gospel. This habit was observed both by the Count and by others with great wonder. At length, one day when she had come to church and was making ready to leave at her accustomed time, four knights, by order of the Count, seized and held her. She quickly threw off the cloak by which they were holding her, and, snatching her two little sons, who were under the right-hand fold of the cloak, under her right arm and leaving behind her two other sons, who were standing on her left, in the sight of all present she flew away out of a high window in the church.

Gerald adds that Richard frequently referred to this legend, saying that it was not to be wondered at that the sons were constantly at war with their father and with each other, since they had all come from the Devil and to the Devil they were all going.

Henry's affections were equally strong. Throughout his life he lavished his love upon his sons, who in their turn did everything in their power to forfeit it. He was loyal to his friends, and it is to his credit that he counted among them the best and most honorable men of his time. He scorned the outward state and majesty of kings; his manners toward his people were of perfect familiarity, and he was accessible to all at every hour of the day and night.

In an age when clothing was simple, Henry was noted for his careless dress. Both men and women of the richer class wore an ample robe, reaching to the ankles, with sleeves to the wrist, and gathered at the waist in loose folds by a belt or girdle. Over this, in cooler weather, they wore a cloak or mantle with a hood, held together at the throat or shoulder by a brooch. Henry was known as "Court Mantle" because he introduced from Anjou the fashion of wearing a mantle reaching only to the knees, instead of the ankle-length one usually worn in England. The dress of the two sexes was differentiated rather by color and ornamentation than by cut, although about this time women began wearing long pointed sleeves, often with close-fitting undersleeves. Men wore green or brown ordinarily; scarlet on great occasions.

When they were riding, men wore a knee-length tunic with a short mantle. The working classes wore a knee-length tunic like the still surviving smock, and ankle-length breeches cross-wrapped to the knee with thongs. What underwear, if any, was worn is not known. Probably women wore a sort of shift and men some sort of drawers.

Keeping warm through the winter was always a problem. The houses, even of the greatest, consisted only of a large, high-roofed hall, rather like a barn or a small church, in which all the life of the household was carried on. Only recently had a separate bedroom for the master and mistress been introduced, and the rest of the household slept on the rushes of the floor. In the larger establishments food was usually prepared in a separate small building. When John had his houses at Marlborough and Ludgershall repaired in 1204, he ordered that a new kitchen be built at each house for preparing his dinner, with a "furnace" in each one large enough to cook two or three oxen in. In the smaller houses the cooking was done over the central fire in the hall. Meals were eaten off trestle tables set up for each meal. Stools and chests, with perhaps chairs of state for the lord and his lady, completed the scanty furniture.

The drafty halls were heated by log fires in the center of the stone floor, with the smoke left to find its way out of an opening in the roof as best it could. Men tried to keep warm by wearing more and heavier robes and fur-lined cloaks. People lived so much out of doors that they were hardened by exposure, and a man like Henry, with his rough, red hands and weather-beaten face, would probably not have looked for much more comfort indoors than could be found under the shelter of a tree in the forest.

The author of the life of St. Hugh, Bishop of Lincoln, tells how Henry, when he was angry with the prelate, summoned him to his presence. When Hugh arrived, he found the King and his attendants sitting in a circle on the ground. Henry had ordered everyone to ignore the Bishop, and his greeting was not returned. Hugh sat on the ground next to the King, who had borrowed a needle and was mending a hole in his glove. Hugh watched him in silence for a while and then remarked: "How like your cousins of Falaise you are!" This was too much for Henry's sense of humor, and he burst into loud laughter, explaining to the circle that the Bishop was referring to William the Conqueror's mother, a woman of low birth from Falaise, a place noted for its leatherworkers.

Henry was as energetic in mind as in body. He brought to his troubled kingdom, which had suffered from the anarchy and civil war of Stephen's reign, a strong central government that proved an effective check to the centrifugal tendencies of the feudal system. Each baron had set himself up as an independent lord, administering his own brand of justice, coining his own money, and waging war on his neighbors when the occasion permitted.

Henry put a stop to all that. He made his own courts supreme in the land and gradually reduced the sphere of influence in which the baronial courts could act; he sternly repressed private warfare and demolished the castles of any barons who tried to practice it; he made himself no mere feudal overlord but in truth King of the English, and he brought law and order back to a land sick of lawlessness. The King's peace was once more supreme in England.

John's mother, Eleanor of Aquitaine, no less strong a character than her husband, was certainly the most remarkable woman of her age. As Duchess of Aquitaine in her own right, she had been married to Louis VII of France in 1137 and had accompanied him to the Holy Land when he went on the Crusade ten years later. Her gay and lighthearted conduct with her troop of women attendants, her frank enjoyment of the civilized pleasures of Antioch, her equivocal relations with her uncle Raymond, Prince of Antioch, which gave rise to ugly rumors of incest, and her Southern zest for life and movement and excitement caused much talk among the crusading host and much burning of heart to the sober, serious, devout Louis. Eleanor, on her side, discovered that she had married a monk, as she put it, and not a man. After they returned from the Crusade, the marriage, which in fifteen years had produced no sons, was dissolved on the grounds of consanguinity. The decree was pronounced on March 21, 1152.

Shortly after the divorce, Eleanor offered herself and her great duchy of Aquitaine, which embraced most of southwest France, to the young Henry, who had recently become Count of Anjou and Duke of Normandy upon his father's death. He also stood a good chance, as the oldest living legitimate male descendant of his maternal grandfather, King Henry I, of succeeding his cousin Stephen as King of the English.

All this made him the most eligible young man in Europe; in addition, he was a gay, handsome, dashing lad of nineteen, with the dazzling reddish-gold hair, the clear gray eyes, and the strong, firm body of the men of the House of Anjou. Although Eleanor was ten or eleven years older than he, and although it was whispered that she had committed adultery with his father, Geoffrey, when he was Seneschal of France, Henry accepted her offer with alacrity. He was not deterred by the example of his father, who had also married a woman ten years his senior and had been forced to drive her from his dominions. Eleanor's age meant little when Henry considered the richness of her dowry.

They were hastily married in May 1152, two months after Eleanor's divorce. In rapid succession, Henry was formally recognized as Stephen's heir, Stephen died, and Henry and Eleanor were crowned King and Queen of the English in Westminster Abbey by Theobald, Archbishop of Canterbury, on December 19, 1154.

Eleanor and Louis had had only two daughters in fifteen years of marriage, but she bore children to Henry with almost clock-like regularity. Early in 1153 (too early for decency, the gossips said) she had a son, William, who lived three years; in 1155, another son, Henry; in 1156, the first daughter, Matilda; in 1157, Richard, the darling of her heart; in 1158, Geoffrey; in 1162, Eleanor; and in 1165, another daughter, Joanna.

John, the last of her brood, was born, probably at Oxford, on Christmas Eve, 1167. There is a tradition that he was baptized in the great black basalt font that is still in the Church of the Preshute in Marlborough. John was handed over to his wet nurse, after which nothing more is heard of him for three years.

Remembering his own troubled youth and the difficulties that beset his succession to the throne, Heny made repeated efforts throughout his reign to assure the orderly division of his domains among his sons upon his death. These efforts led him into great trouble and were the root of the many conflicts of the sons against the father and of the brothers among themselves that intermittently troubled Henry's peace for the last twenty years of his life.

As the first step in this plan, on June 14, 1170, when Henry the son was only fifteen years old, his father had him hallowed and crowned King of the English at Westminster by Roger of Pont-l'Evêque, Archbishop of York, assisted by the Bishops of Durham, Rochester, London, and Salisbury. On the day after the crowning, Henry made his earls and barons pay homage to the new King and renew the oaths of fealty they had sworn to him as Henry's heir as early as 1162.

This act, which was without precedent in England, caused a great deal of trouble, both then and thereafter. It was contrary to all the customs of the English that the reigning king's intended successor should be crowned while the king was still living. Furthermore, the right of the eldest son to succeed his father was not yet fully recognized, and the formality of the election of the new king by the people, a reality until the Norman Conquest, was still observed. Henry's action seemed to imply that the crown was his personal property, to be passed on to whomever he chose. This violation of the ancient customs of the kingdom was highly offensive to many of the English.

Moreover, to hallow and crown the king was the right of the Archbishop of Canterbury alone. The quarrel between Henry and Thomas Becket, Archbishop of Canterbury, was then at its height, and Thomas was sulking in self-imposed exile in Pontigny. From the day of his consecration he had shown himself exceedingly jealous of all the honors and privileges of his position, and this wanton flouting of his most cherished right, demonstrating his pre-eminent place in the Church in England, intensified the quarrel. The presumptuous Roger and the assisting bishops, on Thomas's complaint, were promptly excommunicated by Pope Alexander III, who likened them to "rams having no horns."

The third unfortunate effect of the coronation was that it made an enemy of Louis VII of France. The young Henry, in further-ance of his father's ambitious schemes of marriages for his sons, had been married in 1160, at the age of five, to Margaret, the daughter of Louis by his second wife, Constance of Castille. This was an im-portant union, both because it strengthened the ties between the two rulers and because Margaret brought as her dowry the Norman Vexin, a much-fought-over territory bordering on Henry's Duchy of Normandy, about halfway between Rouen and Paris.

When Louis learned that his daughter had not been crowned with her husband, he interpreted this perhaps as a repudiation of the marriage and certainly as a slight to her. He at once assembled an army and invaded Normandy. The elder Henry thereupon has-tened to Normandy in July 1170 and made peace with Louis by promising that he would have the young couple crowned together in the course of the next year. He fulfilled his promise on August 27, 1172, when they were crowned at Winchester by Rotrou, Arch-bishop of Rouen.

The young Henry, however, was the one who suffered the most, in the long run, from this ill-advised act. Although he was hallowed and crowned King of the English, his father refused to let him exert any real authority in the land whose crown he wore, and kept the reins of government firmly in his own strong hands. During a reign of almost thirty-five years, Henry spent only thirteen years in Eng-land, yet even during his frequent and prolonged absences from the country he entrusted the government to his justiciars rather than to his son.

The young Henry constantly begged his father to grant him real authority over some portion of his inheritance, whether as King of England, Duke of Normandy, or Count of Anjou, in reality and not in name alone, so that he might settle down and gain experience in government, but Henry refused. He preferred to keep his eldest son in leading strings, rich in titles but poor in power and in purse.

Shortly after he had made peace with Louis, Henry became gravely ill while still in Normandy. Fearing that he might die of his illness, he completed the division of his lands among his sons that he had begun with the crowning of the eldest. The young Henry was to receive, in addition to England, Normandy and all the lands that Henry had inherited from his father, Geoffrey of Anjou. Richard received Aquitaine and the lands that had belonged to his mother, Eleanor. Geoffrey, the third son, was given Brittany, which Henry had been holding in trust for Conan the Little and his daughter and heiress, Constance, together with the hand of Constance. Both Richard and Geoffrey were to acknowledge their brother Henry as their overlord. Thus Henry's great empire, which stretched from Scotland to the Pyrenees, would in some measure be kept intact.

Now we hear of the young John for the first time since his birth. To him was given, in contrast to the wide lands granted his brothers, the County of Mortain, in Normandy. Although the title was an important one, reserved for members of the reigning house of Normandy, it conferred more prestige than power, for the lands involved were small in extent. Appropriate indeed was the epithet "Lackland"—"Jean sans Terre"—given him at the time.

Henry recovered from the illness that had occasioned this division of his lands in time to celebrate the Christmas feast at Bures in Normandy, together with his wife and his sons Richard, Geoffrey, and John, the newly created Count of Mortain, then three years old.

The festivities came to an abrupt end, however, at the news of an event that shocked all Christendom. Thomas Becket, with whom Henry had effected a reconciliation of sorts during the preceding summer and who had returned to Canterbury early in December, refused to lift from the Archbishop of York and the Bishops of London and Salisbury the sentence of excommunication laid upon them by the Pope for their share in the crowning of the young Henry. When the three bishops came to Normandy and reported this to the King, he exclaimed in his characteristic headstrong fashion: "What a parcel of fools and dastards have I nourished in my house, that not one of them will avenge me of this upstart clerk!" Four knights of his household took these words literally, crossed over to Canterbury, and murdered the Archbishop in his cathedral on December 29.

Henry professed to be horrified by this barbarous deed, and indeed the brutal murder of a consecrated bishop within the hallowed precincts of a cathedral was an act of savagery and of sacrilege that would chill the blood of the most hardened. The King immediately disclaimed any responsibility for the act. Although they had become bitter enemies of late, Henry could not have forgotten that Thomas had been his most intimate friend and companion during the early years of his reign, and he must have grieved that his friend had met so bloody an end.

Mere professions of grief were not enough, however. The Pope threatened to lay all of Henry's lands under an interdict and to inflict the dread sentence of excommunication upon the King himself unless he did public penance and submitted himself unconditionally to the Church. Before Alexander's legates reached him, however, Henry embarked upon the conquest of Ireland.

He landed there in October 1171, and the stormy winter weather cut him off from all communication with his other domains for six months. When he returned to Normandy in May 1172, he immedi-

ately met the Pope's legates, disclaimed any complicity in the Archbishop's murder, promised to do ample penance, and relinquished
his stand on those points that had been in dispute between him and
Thomas. Something more than remorse drove Henry to this submission; he suspected that a revolt was forming that threatened his
very crown, and he could not afford to be at odds with the Church
at such a time.

Henry's desire to provide further for his youngest son helped to
bring about this revolt, which had been brewing for a long time. It
had many causes, among which were the young Henry's desire for
some of the power to which his titles gave him claim; the enmity of
Louis VII, who lost no opportunity to encourage his young son-in-
law to rebel against his father; and the dissatisfaction of many of the
English nobles with Henry's stern measures to stamp out the lawless
habits contracted during the anarchy of Stephen's reign and to make
all men in England amenable to the law and to the royal authority.
Why Geoffrey and Richard should have joined in the rebellion is
not clear; perhaps they were urged to do so by their mother. The revolt, which spread all over the King's dominions, began as a result
of a marriage settlement that Henry proposed for John.

Shortly after the Christmas of 1172, which Henry and Eleanor
had spent at Chinon in Anjou, a town some twenty-five miles southwest of Tours, and which the young Henry and his wife had spent
in Normandy, the two Henrys went to Montferrat in the Auvergne,
a place about twenty miles east of Grenoble. There they were met by
Humbert III, Count of Maurienne, and his eldest daughter, Alice.
Humbert's territories included the region between Grenoble in
France and Turin in Italy and were of great strategic importance because they held the Mont-Cenis pass across the Alps and hence commanded the entrance into Italy.

A betrothal contract between John and Alice was drawn up, ac-

cording to which Henry was to pay Humbert the sum of four thousand marks—one thousand marks immediately, another thousand as
soon as Henry should receive the Count's daughter to bring up in his
household, as was then the custom, and the rest at the time of the
marriage.

The mark referred to was two-thirds of a pound, or thirteen shillings and fourpence. It was solely a unit of accounting. There was no
such coin; the only money minted in England at that time was the
silver penny. It is almost impossible to translate these sums into modern equivalents. One can best gain an idea of the value of money at
that time by considering some of the current prices for commodities
and services. During John's reign, oxen, cows, and bulls sold for
four shillings, sows and boars for one shilling, coarse-wooled sheep
for sixpence, and fine-wooled sheep for tenpence. The ordinary foot
soldier was paid twopence a day. The knight, armed and mounted
on his heavy war horse, was paid a shilling a day. The knight, a
trained fighter, had of course a heavy investment in his coat of chain
mail and in his horse, which was worth ten marks, or the value of the
knight's wages for more than 133 days, and he therefore commanded
a high wage.

The marriage provided for by this contract between John and Alice was to take place as soon as Alice and John, who was then five
years old, reached the canonical age, or whenever a dispensation
might be obtained for a marriage at an earlier date. Humbert on his
side agreed that if he left no son, John should inherit all his dominions and that if he did have a son, John should nevertheless have an
adequate provision of lands.

All would have been well if the matter had rested there. Humbert, however, after the contracting parties had separated, began to
think things over, and it seemed to him that the wily Henry had got
the better of him. Although it would no doubt be a fine thing to have

a daughter married to a son of the King of England, the son was after all only a fourth son with few possessions in his own right and little prospect of more.

Humbert accordingly, in the following February, went to Limoges, where the two Henrys and Richard had met to receive the homage of Raymond, Count of Saint Gilles, for Toulouse. There he asked Henry how much of his own territories he intended to give his youngest son, to match the proposed settlement of Maurienne upon John. Henry replied that he planned to give John the castles and districts of Chinon and of Loudun and Mirebeau, north of Poitiers.

These important territories, which Henry was now promising to give to John, were a part of Anjou, and Anjou had already been given to the young Henry, if his title of Count of Anjou meant anything. Henry, now eighteen years old, would not consent to this alienation of his lands, and he seized upon the opportunity to press his father once more to assign to him some definite portion of his territories—Anjou or Normandy or England—where he might take up residence with his wife and exercise a real responsibility and jurisdiction. The King again refused to give his heir outright possession of any of his lands. The young Henry, after a violent quarrel, fled to his father-in-law, the King of France, and, with Louis's help and encouragement, declared war upon his father, with the sworn intention of driving him from France.

This was the signal for a general uprising. The young Henry was joined by his discontented brothers, Geoffrey and Richard. Their mother attempted to join them around Easter, 1173. Henry had already grown tired of her. She was past fifty, and her husband did not trouble to conceal his relations with other women. Jealousy no doubt drove her from Henry, and her deep love for her sons, especially for Richard, drew her to their side. She disguised herself as a man, started to flee from Henry, and was captured.

Henry put her into confinement and kept her thus for the next eleven years, while he lived in open adultery with Rosamund Clifford, the "Fair Rosamund" of later legends and ballads. Gerald of Wales says that at this time the King, who had heretofore lived in secret adultery, now engaged in open and shameless relations, not with " 'the Rose of the World,' as she is falsely and most frivolously called, but with the Rose, indeed, of an impure man." His play on the name (Rosa mundi) can leave no doubt that it is Rosamund to whom he is referring.

The rebellious sons were supported by the King of France and his nobles; the King of the Scots joined in; a host of discontented barons in England, Normandy, Anjou, and Aquitaine hastened to overthrow Henry's firm rule, and the King was thus attacked from all sides.

Pausing only to write letters to such of his fellow kings as he thought might be friendly to him, telling of the misfortunes that had befallen him and warning them against exalting their sons beyond their due, Henry attacked the rebels with characteristic energy. By Michaelmas, 1174, he had defeated all his enemies and restored order in his dominions. On September 30, at a conference held at a place between Tours and Amboise, a treaty was drawn up between Henry on the one hand and his sons Henry, Richard, and Geoffrey on the other, that restored everything to the condition in which it had been a fortnight before the outbreak of the rebellion, with a general amnesty on both sides.

One of the articles of this treaty made provision for the young John. He was to have, in England, one thousand pounds of yearly revenues out of the demesne lands, the castle and county of Nottingham, and the castle of Marlborough, which belonged to the royal demesne and was the favorite residence of Henry, probably because of the proximity of the royal deer park of Savernake. In Normandy, John was to have one thousand pounds Angevin (four Angevin pounds were worth one English pound) of yearly revenues and two castles at the option of his father, and in the territory of his brother Henry he was to have a further thousand pounds annually and a castle in Anjou, one in Touraine, and one in Maine.

Although these grants promised John a settled income and position, the county of Nottingham in particular being a prosperous region, they nevertheless would not confer on him power, prestige, or wealth remotely comparable to that of his elder brothers. John at this time was less than seven years old, but his settlement was intended to be permanent and final. The lands and revenues promised to him were the most that he could hope to inherit at his father's death. Barring accidents, the young Henry was to be King of England, Duke of Normandy, and Count of Anjou; Geoffrey would be Duke of Brittany; and Richard, Duke of Aquitaine. Poor landless John, on the other hand, would be merely Count of Mortain and lord of a few scattered castles, dependent upon his brothers' good will for his income.

However, the death of Reginald, Earl of Cornwall, afforded Henry an opportunity to add to John's prospective fortune. Reginald, a bastard son of Henry I and hence an uncle of Henry II, died in July 1175. He had no sons, and this gave Henry a pretext for seizing his lands. Henry kept most of them in his possession, intending to give them to John later. He granted Reginald's three daughters only small portions of their father's estate. Both the title and the lands remained in the possession of the Crown till Richard, shortly after his accession, gave them to John in 1189.

Meanwhile Alice, the heiress of Maurienne, had died, and new provision had to be made for a wife for John. A suitable match closer to home was found for him. William, Earl of Gloucester, the son of Robert of Gloucester, another bastard son of Henry I, had enormous possessions in the west of England and in Glamorgan in Wales, and he had no son to inherit them. Of his three daughters, two had already made suitable marriages. Mabel had married Amaurus, Count of Evreux, and Amicia had married Richard, Earl of Clare. It was now proposed that the third, variously known as Hadwisa, Avice, or Isabella, should be betrothed to John. William of Gloucester, on September 28, 1176, agreed to give his daughter and all his lands to John, provided that a dispensation for the marriage, which was within the degree of kinship forbidden by the laws of the Church, could be obtained. John and Hadwisa were second cousins, having a common great-grandfather in Henry I. In return for the alienation of all their father's land, Henry II agreed to pay each of the two other daughters one hundred pounds a year.

John was in England for the Christmas feast of that year, and this is the first mention we have, since his birth, of his presence in the land over which he was later to rule. Of his childhood and education nothing is known. Two of the King's sons, Geoffrey and John, kept their Christmas with Henry at Northampton. The young Henry and his wife were in Normandy; Richard was in his Duchy of Aquitaine; and their mother was under confinement either at Salisbury or at Winchester for her part in the rebellion of 1173.

In the following May, Henry held a council at Oxford, and there he created John Lord of Ireland. Henry had visited Ireland in 1171 and 1172, while he was waiting for the uproar over the murder of Thomas Becket to die down, and had laid the foundations for the English rule of that turbulent island. At this council at Oxford he divided the Irish lands and established the feudal services due from them. He had all men that held land in Ireland to do homage and swear allegiance and fealty both to him and to John as Lord of Ireland.

Thus John, before he was ten years old, was far from being the landless youngest son of his father's jest. He was Count of Mortain and Lord of Ireland, and when he married he would hold the Earldom of Gloucester, which would place him among the richest and most powerful men in the country. The Earldom of Cornwall was being held for him by the Crown, and he could look forward eventually to enjoying its title. He was still, or again, in England at Christmas 1178, for he spent that period with his father at Winchester.

The Christmas feast, as well as the feasts of Easter and Whitsunday, was always celebrated with great solemnity by the King and his court, and the chroniclers of the time are careful to tell us where the King celebrated the feast each year and what members of his family were with him. Unfortunately, they do not tell us what they had to eat, but we may presume that meat of as many kinds as were available, washed down by great quantities of wine, made up most of the meal. Venison, beef, mutton, pork, chickens, and geese, some boiled and some roasted, much of it served directly on the skewers on which it was cooked, and all eaten with the bare fingers assisted by knives, appeared on the tables of the rich. Except for an occasional fowl or hare, the poor ate meat but rarely, substituting cheese and eggs. Animals were killed in the autumn and salted down for the winter. The wretched state of preservation of the meat accounts for the great value placed on spices that would disguise the taste. Vegetables were few, mostly peas and beans, and fit only for the tables of the poor and the meager diet of monks. What we consider vegetables now would probably have been classed then as "rude herbs and roots," as the author of the *Gesta Stephani* puts it, which only the starving would eat.

The lack of green vegetables and fruits through the winter led to outbreaks of scurvy among all classes. Apples and plums were about the only fruits available. Sugar was rare indeed, and honey was used for sweetening. Fish, both fresh and salted, was a welcome addition to the diet and was of course the main dish on Fridays and through Lent. Salt, procured by drying sea water in pans, was in great demand for preserving meat and fish. The poor had to subsist mainly on peas, beans, and cereal grains in bread and porridge, with very small beer to drink.

The sudden death of the young Henry of a fever on June 11, 1183 moved John one step closer to the throne and also rid the father of a son whose treachery, faithlessness, and lack of principle were a constant grief to him. In keeping with John's increased importance, Henry in the following month made another effort to provide still further for him. Richard was now Henry's heir to England, Normandy, and Anjou, as well as Duke of Aquitaine, and Henry proposed that he give up his Duchy of Aquitaine to John, who was to hold it of Richard and do homage to him for it.

Richard was particularly attached to Aquitaine. He had reduced the rebellious nobles to order and had made his authority felt throughout the duchy. He had just succeeded in driving out the forces of his older brother and his allies, and with this triumph still fresh, he was in no mood to relinquish his duchy to his younger brother. In Richard's fierce clinging to Aquitaine there was something more than the natural desire of a man to hold fast to that for which he had been fighting strenuously for the past eight years. Richard loved Aquitaine, for he was a poet and a Southerner by temperament, and in the highly civilized society of his duchy, where music and poetry were seriously cultivated, he was thoroughly at home. He flatly refused to part with Aquitaine, and Henry, weary no doubt of warring with his sons, did not want to resort to open force. He did, however, give John permission "to lead an army into Richard's land and get what he wanted from his brother by fighting him."

This could hardly have been said seriously, for Richard had already proved himself a highly capable military leader whose prowess his father had good reason to respect, whereas John was an untried fledgling of fifteen. Nevertheless, John, taking the words literally, appealed to his brother Geoffrey for help, and Geoffrey was delighted to have a pretext for attacking Richard and stirring up trouble. He and John collected an army, which would indicate that John already had some money at his disposal, and marched into Aquitaine in June 1184, plundering and burning as they went. Henry, alarmed that his jest should have been taken seriously, at once ordered all three of his sons to come to him in England and forced them to make peace among themselves.

What part John had in this military expedition is not known, but one may assume that Geoffrey was the real leader. At any rate, John gained nothing by it except a certain amount of military experience, from which he would later appear to have profited little, and a more wholesome respect for his older brother.

In the following December he had an opportunity to observe the intrigues that accompanied the election of an Archbishop of Canterbury, when Baldwin, Bishop of Worcester, was elected by his brother bishops. John, who was in London with his father and brothers, followed their example and gave the new Archbishop "the kiss of peace and love." This election was the occasion for the usual squabble between the monks of Canterbury and the bishops of that province, each side claiming the right to elect the archbishop. It was largely owing to Henry, who acted in a manner unusually tactful for him, that the quarrel was composed. Henry ordered the bishops and the monks of Canterbury to meet together in London and elect their archbishop. The bishops, led by Gilbert of London, chose Baldwin, one of their number, and presented him to the King. The monks refused to concur in the election and departed in anger, proclaiming their sole right to elect the archbishop and announcing their intention of appealing to the Pope.

Henry went down to Canterbury and persuaded the monks to hold a separate election and nominate Baldwin. The monks, moved perhaps at being entreated by a King who was more accustomed to command, despatched their prior and the less infirm members of the chapter to London with letters of confirmation. Meeting in the Chapter House of Westminster Abbey, they elected Baldwin as archbishop and then, to avoid the appearance of assenting to the previous election by the bishops, went through the formalities of singing the *Te Deum* and of presenting Baldwin to the King as the newly elected Archbishop of Canterbury. The King again gave him the kiss of peace and love.

Henry was pleased to consider this arrangement, according to which neither the bishops nor the monks relinquished any part of their conflicting claims, as a final reconciliation between them. He solemnly confirmed it in writing and ratified it by oaths on the part of Richard, Geoffrey, and John. Although John took no active part in these negotiations, he could not fail to notice the squabbles, the intrigues, and the jealousies that accompanied the election of the archbishop. He observed the complicated machinery at first hand, and the knowledge of its workings that he thus gained he put to use when Archbishop Hubert Walter died in 1205.

This ratification was made in the presence of a gathering that included Queen Eleanor. She had been released from her captivity in the preceding summer and had joined her eldest daughter, Matilda, and Matilda's exiled husband, Henry, Duke of Saxony. They all celebrated the Christmas feast together at Windsor.

John's childhood and youth may be considered to have ended at about this time. The obscurity that veils these years is only natural, for John, as the King's youngest son, would not be a personage of great importance, and chroniclers were little concerned with such insignificant affairs as the childhood, education, and training of a lad whose portion seemed destined to be such odds and ends of his father's territories as could be wrested from his reluctant brothers. He was brought up partly in England and partly in Normandy; from his earliest years he was a witness to the wars between his father and his brothers and among the brothers themselves, and he figured as a pawn in these struggles. Little is recorded to give us any impression of John as a person in his own right. The one thing that does stand out is Henry's affection and concern for his youngest son. The older brothers, it is true, had already forfeited their father's love by their concerted rebellion against him, and the fact that John was too young to have been involved in it and hence was the only one of his sons who had not borne arms against him probably accounts in part, at least, for Henry's affection for him.

JOHN,
LORD OF IRELAND

❧ 1185-1186 ☙

JOHN was knighted by his father at Windsor Castle on Lætare Sunday, March 31, 1185. The conferring of knighthood had already become an elaborate ceremony, marking as it did the end of a young man's apprenticeship to arms and his entry into the warrior caste. It was given only to those of gentle birth who had completed a rigorous course of training, usually in the household of a great noble. The postulant was given a ceremonial bath, after which he spent the night in the chapel, watching beside his armor. Then he was clad in rich robes, the gift of the man who was to knight him, and the sword of knighthood was girded about his waist.

When John was seventeen, an age at which he should have been ready for the responsibilities of a man, Henry determined to send him to Ireland. The idea of bringing Ireland under English rule occurred to Henry shortly after he had been crowned. He brought the matter up at a meeting of the Great Council at Winchester at Michaelmas, 1155, but his mother, the Empress Matilda, whose opinions on foreign affairs carried great weight with him, had been opposed to an immediate invasion of the island. To be prepared for the future, however, Henry sent John of Salisbury to Rome to get the Pope's approval for the project. The Church in Ireland at this time was sadly lacking in organization and discipline, and the Pope, Adrian IV, himself an Englishman, no doubt welcomed the opportunity to reform it and bring it under more direct control. He accordingly issued the bull *Laudabiliter*.

ADRIAN THE BISHOP, the servant of the servants of God, to his dearest son in Christ, the illustrious King of the English: GREETINGS and the Apostolic blessing.

Laudably indeed and profitably does Your Magnificence contemplate spreading your glorious name on earth and heaping up a reward of everlasting happiness in heaven, since you propose as a Christian prince to extend the boundaries of the Church, to declare the truth of the Christian faith to a rough and ignorant people, and to root out the weeds of vice from the field of the Lord. In order to accomplish this more fittingly you ask for the advice and favor of the Apostolic See. . . .

There is no doubt, as Your Nobility recognizes, that Ireland and all the islands upon which Christ, the Sun of Justice, has shone, and which have accepted the lessons of the Christian faith, belong to the jurisdiction of the Blessed Peter and of the most holy Roman Church. . . .

Since you have made known to us, dearest son in Christ, your desire to enter the island of Ireland in order to make the people subject to the law and to root out the plantations of vice, and to exact from every household a penny a year for Blessed Peter:

We therefore, following your pious and praiseworthy wish with fitting favor and receiving your request with gracious con-

*sent, hold it pleasing and acceptable that you should enter that
island in order to extend the boundaries of the Church, to restrain the attacks of evil, to improve morals and foster virtue, and
to increase the Christian religion, and that you should do whatever concerns the honor of God and the welfare of that country;
and let the people of that country receive you with honor and
respect you as their lord, provided always that the right of the
Church shall be kept unharmed and complete, and saving the
yearly payment of one penny from each household to Blessed Peter and the most holy Roman Church. . . .*

Henry did not make immediate use of this document, but it was
later confirmed by Adrian's successor, Alexander III, and played an
important part in bringing Ireland under English rule.

Henry apparently dismissed the subject from his mind until his attention was called to Ireland by the arrival in Aquitaine of Dermot
MacMurrough, King of Leinster. Dermot, who had been expelled
from Ireland, came to Henry shortly after Christmas, 1166, to seek
his help in regaining his kingdom.

Dermot MacMurrough, destined to go down in Irish history as
"the man who brought the Normans over," was at this time about
fifty-five years old and had led a turbulent life even for a twelfth-
century Irishman. Gerald of Wales describes him as a handsome man
of gigantic stature and with a voice hoarse from shouting war cries
in battle. He had abducted the Abbess of Kildare when he was only
twenty-two, and when the monastic community had tried to prevent
this outrage he had had 140 of them killed. He then set fire to the
monastery. He furthered his reputation for cruelty by blinding seventeen of the chiefs of North Leinster when they attempted to revolt
against his tyrannical rule in 1141.

In 1152 he perpetrated the act that settled his fate and, ultimately,
that of Ireland. While Tiernan O'Rourke, a chieftain in Meath, was

on a pilgrimage to St. Patrick's Purgatory at Lough Derg, Dermot
carried off his wife, Dervorgill, "with all her cattle and furniture."
Dervorgill returned to her husband a year later, but Tiernan was determined to avenge the insult. It is pleasant to record in passing that
after her husband's death Dervorgill entered the monastery of Melli-
font and lived to the age of eighty-four.

After long and bitter struggles, Tiernan O'Rourke, with the help
of Rory O'Connor, the last native High King of Ireland, succeeded
in driving Dermot MacMurrough out of the country in August
1166. Dermot, accompanied by his beautiful daughter Eva, went to
Bristol to secure help in regaining his kingdom. Learning that Henry
was in Aquitaine, he followed him there, swore fealty to him, and
begged for help. Henry was too busy at that time with his continental affairs and with his quarrel with Thomas Becket to spare any
time for Ireland, but he received Dermot graciously and gave him
letters patent authorizing any of Henry's subjects who felt so in-
clined to help Dermot recover his lost possessions.

Armed with these letters and with Henry's expressions of good
will, Dermot returned to Bristol and entered into negotiations with
Richard FitzGilbert, Earl of Pembroke and Striguil, famous in Irish
history as "Strongbow." In return for Strongbow's help, Dermot offered him the hand of his daughter Eva and promised that Strongbow should succeed him as King of Leinster. Strongbow agreed to
these terms, but, since he was out of favor with the King at the time,
he prudently stipulated that he would not go to Ireland till he had
received more explicit permission from Henry. Dermot also succeeded in getting promises of support from two half-brothers, Robert
FitzStephen and Maurice FitzGerald, who were sons of Nesta, the
notorious Welsh princess who had been a mistress of Henry I.

Armed with these promises, Dermot returned to Ireland in August
1167, and spent the winter at the monastery of Ferns, in Leinster.
His old enemies attacked him in the following spring and defeated

him again. This time he was allowed to remain in Leinster, but he was forced to pay Tiernan O'Rourke a hundred ounces of gold as a penalty for having carried off his wife. In 1169 Rory O'Connor began organizing an expedition against Dermot, and Dermot sent letters to his allies in Wales, reminding them of their promises of help. To Strongbow he wrote: "The swallows have come and gone, yet you are tarrying still."

Strongbow was a cautious man. Gerald of Wales says that he was better fitted for the council chamber than for the battlefield, and adds that wherever his standard was displayed on the field, there was a safe refuge for the wounded. Strongbow still preferred to see how the land lay before he committed himself, but Robert FitzStephen assembled a small force and landed near Wexford on May 1, 1169.

The allies succeeded in taking Wexford, which was given to FitzStephen, but Rory O'Connor later defeated them at Ferns. The treaty drawn up after that battle left Dermot in control of Leinster, but he was forced to recognize Rory as High King, to give his son and grandson as hostages, and to promise to bring no more foreigners into Ireland.

Shortly after this, Dermot was strengthened by the arrival of Maurice FitzGerald and a fresh fighting force. He wrote again to Strongbow and began laying ambitious plans to conquer all of Ireland. Strongbow availed himself of a halfhearted permission he had secured from Henry, assembled a force of two hundred knights and a thousand men-at-arms, and landed near Waterford on August 23, 1170. This was the most potent fighting force that had yet come to Ireland, and Dermot and Strongbow succeeded in capturing Dublin within a month. True to his bargain, Dermot gave Strongbow his daughter Eva in marriage.

Dermot and his new son-in-law set out to conquer Meath, to which Dermot had no shadow of a claim, save that it was the lawful possession of Tiernan O'Rourke, his bitter enemy. Rory O'Connor, as High King, warned Dermot not to invade other men's lands and reminded him that he held his son as a hostage. Dermot vauntingly replied that he claimed not only Leinster and Meath but the whole of Ireland as well, and that he did not particularly care what happened to his son. When Rory O'Connor received this insolent message, he promptly had Dermot's son put to death.

Dermot's sordid career was terminated in May 1171, as the Annals of the Four Masters relate, when he died at Ferns "of an insufferable and unknown disease, for he became putrid whilst living, through the miracle of God and the Saints of Ireland, whose churches he had profaned and burned." Strongbow succeeded him as King of Leinster, but his pretensions were opposed by many of the Irish, who united under Rory O'Connor in an effort to unseat him.

Meanwhile, Henry was watching all this with a jealous eye. Whatever the terms of his permission to Strongbow may have been, he certainly did not intend that one of his earls should set himself up as a king in Ireland, and he saw in Strongbow's pretensions a threat to his own designs upon the island. At a council held at Argentan in July 1171, he determined to go to Ireland and assert the authority bestowed upon him by the bull *Laudabiliter*. He collected a fleet of four hundred ships and an army of five hundred knights and four thousand men-at-arms at Milford Haven. As soon as the prudent Strongbow heard of these preparations, he hastened to Henry, laid all his conquests at his feet, and did homage for the lands, embracing most of Leinster, that Henry permitted him to retain.

The great expedition, intended to impress the Irish rather than to overcome them in battle, landed near Waterford on October 17, 1171 and quickly had its desired effect. The Kings of Desmond and of Thomond came at once and did homage, and as Henry proceeded slowly to Dublin many other native chiefs followed their example. Henry built a fine palace in Dublin after the native fashion, and there he spent the winter, entertaining the native princes, receiving the homage of the Irish, and apportioning the land among his English and Norman followers and such of the Irish as were willing to swear fealty to him. The bishops, among whom the bull *Laudabiliter* had no doubt been circulating, were particularly eager to recognize Henry as lord of the land.

The Council of Cashel, held at Henry's instance during this winter, introduced much-needed reforms in the Church in Ireland and brought it into conformity with the discipline and uses prevailing in the Church in England. All this was reported to the Pope, Alexander III, and in due course he confirmed the bull *Laudabiliter* and directed the Irish bishops and princes to be steadfast in their loyalty to King Henry.

Great storms that winter cut Henry off from communication with his other lands. With the spring came ominous news of the attitude of the papal legates who were waiting in Normandy to investigate his part in the murder of Thomas Becket. Threatened with excommunication, Henry made his arrangements for leaving Ireland. Although Strongbow had submitted to him in all things, the King preferred to leave his own man, Hugh de Lacy, as Justiciar and Vicegerent. According to Gerald of Wales, Hugh, who had come over to Ireland with Henry, was a small, swarthy, hairy, ill-made but muscular man, with a flat nose, small, black, sunken eyes, and a disfiguring scar, caused by some accidental burn, running down his right cheek to the chin. Henry granted him the erstwhile Kingdom of Meath and appointed him to rule Ireland in his name when he left the country on April 17, 1172.

Tiernan O'Rourke, of course, had long held possession of most of Meath, and as soon as Henry and his army were out of the way he challenged Hugh de Lacy's claim to his kingdom. Tiernan was defeated in battle, his head was severed from his body and stuck up on a gate of Dublin, and his body was hung by the heels from a gibbet. With his rival thus disposed of, Hugh de Lacy settled down to governing the parts of Ireland under his control. He built castles and established peace and order. He won the good will of the Irish by protecting them scrupulously in the possession of their lands against the rapacity of the Anglo-Normans, and he put himself on a fine footing among them by marrying, in 1181, the daughter of Rory O'Connor, titular High King of Ireland and effectively King of Connaught.

The death of Strongbow of an ulcer of the leg in 1176 left Hugh supreme in Ireland. Henry suspected that his policy of conciliation and his friendly relations with the Irish princes were an indication that he intended to set himself up as king in his own name. He recalled Hugh to England several times for accountings, but the Vicegerent always justified himself and was continued in office.

Partly in order to remind Hugh de Lacy of his subordinate position and partly to give his youngest son experience in handling men and affairs, Henry sent John, in the spring of 1185, to the land of which he had been declared Lord at the council at Oxford in 1177. To prepare the way for him, Henry had, during the preceding autumn, sent over to Ireland his trusted official and former chaplain, John Comyn, whose election as Archbishop of Dublin he had engineered in 1181. Thus an archbishop who had never visited his see was sent as precursor to a lord who had never seen his lands.

John sailed from Milford Haven on the Wednesday in Easter Week, April 24, 1185, with an imposing fleet of sixty ships, in which there were three hundred knights and two or three thousand horsemen and foot soldiers. He landed at Waterford at noon the next day and was welcomed by the Archbishop of Dublin, the Norman and English lords who held land in Ireland, and some of the Irish themselves. These last were well disposed towards the English, and they greeted John with great gladness as their lord and offered him the kiss of peace. The sportive young Normans by whom John was surrounded hooted at the Irishmen in derision and pulled their beards, which after the custom of the country they wore long. The offended

Irishmen withdrew in mortification and went to the Kings of Limerick, Cork, and Connaught to describe their reception by the King's
son. These three, who had been ready to come to John and do homage to him, took second thought, formed an alliance, and swore to
defend their ancient liberties.

From Waterford, John and his company went to Dublin, and
there he completed the alienation of the Irish and of the colonists established by his father. He took away their lands and reapportioned
them among his unworthy companions; he installed as governors of
the castles along the coast men unfit for the task; and he gave no heed
to the counsels of the old and experienced men of the country. He
was accompanied by Ranulf de Glanville, Justiciar of England and
one of the greatest lawyers of his age, but John did not make use of
his wisdom and experience in organizing the strong central government the country badly needed.

John's favorites were the young Normans of his entourage, and he
seemed to consider Ireland a rich prize to be divided among them.
They could not live without the wine on which they had been
brought up; they refused to go inland; and they insisted always on
remaining close to John. Gerald of Wales describes them as boasters,
liars, and lechers, filled with haughty pride and adroit at avoiding any
risks. The little good that was done was done by the English who
accompanied John; they at least were not afraid to fight.

Castles were built at Tibragny, Lismore, and Ardfinnan, to serve
as garrisons for John's forces, and from them they plundered Mun-
ster. The land was thrown into confusion and terror. The governors
that John appointed were concerned only with collecting as much
money as possible, and they made little pretense of enforcing law and
order. The Irish, plundered and oppressed, turned against their governors and roamed the land, burning, slaying, and stealing, while the
English clung close to the castles on the coast, where there was plenty
of wine and women.

The King of Limerick inflicted a crushing defeat on John's forces when they started out from their castle at Ardfinnan to plunder Thomond. Added to these heavy losses were the desertions of John's soldiers, who went over to the Irish in large numbers because John withheld their pay. This was probably the first time in his life that he had had a large sum of money at his disposal, and he saw no reason to spend it on his soldiers' pay when much more pleasant uses could be found for it. What was intended by Henry as the pay of the expedition was diverted into John's private purse, with the result that the army dwindled away.

News of his son's misconduct and defeat of course reached Henry, and in the autumn he ordered him to return to England. John had complained to his father that Hugh de Lacy would not permit the Irish to pay tribute, and Henry accordingly ordered him replaced as Vice-gerent by John de Courcy, who had conquered Ulster. After placing his favorites in positions of power as governors and judges, John returned ignominiously on December 17, 1185 from his first position of trust and responsibility.

This was John's first recorded appearance in public life, and a sorry mess he made of it. He had thrown the land he was supposed to govern into a state of anarchy and had undone all the good work of his father and his father's lieutenants; he had been shamefully defeated in battle; he had shown himself an incompetent judge of men, guided only by foolish favoritism and deaf to the advice of experienced counsellors; he had appropriated to himself the money that had been entrusted to him for the maintenance of his army; he had exhibited an utter lack of responsibility, and he had treated as a pleasure junket his first opportunity to show his mettle and prove himself worthy of his father's trust.

"JOHN, MY HEART"

1186–1189

IN SPITE of the failure of John's first mission to Ireland, Henry determined to send him there again, perhaps in order to give him a chance to redeem himself and perhaps also because Henry was willfully blind to the faults of his youngest son. Hugh de Lacy had been treacherously murdered by the Irish on July 25, 1186. According to the Annals of the Four Masters, he had been building a castle at Durrow, using the venerable stones of the ruined Columban Abbey as building material, and had gone out to see what progress had been made. As he bent over the masonry, "one of the sons of Teffia, a youth named Gilla-gan-inathar Ó'Meyey, approached him and with an axe severed his head from his body." Henry planned to send John back to Ireland to take possession of Hugh's extensive holdings.

While John was waiting for a favorable wind, his father received news of the death of his rebel son Geoffrey, who had gone to Paris, declared himself the man of the King of France, and defied his father. He had died suddenly of a fever on August 19, and his death raised issues more pressing than the disposition of some lands on the outer fringe of Henry's empire.

In the meantime, Henry had sent envoys to the new Pope, Urban III, who had been elected on November 21, 1185. From him the envoys obtained many concessions that they had not been able to get from his predecessor, Lucius III. Among these favors was a bull authorizing the crowning of one of Henry's sons as King of Ireland. The Pope sent Hugh of Nunant, whom he made Legate to Ireland, and Cardinal Octavian to England, bearing a crown of peacock feathers embroidered with gold, with which to crown John. They landed at Dover shortly after the Christmas of 1186, which John had kept with his father at Guildford, and John and the Archbishop of Dublin met them.

Henry had other and more important things to attend to, and he had the crowning, which would have had an ironic flavor in any case, put off. Instead, after sending John ahead of him, he took the two legates with him to Normandy, to lend their weight to a conference with his enemy, Philip of France, who had succeeded his father, Louis VII, in 1180. The differences between them were too great to be composed by peaceful means, and the conference was broken off without any hope of peace or agreement.

In preparation for the inevitable conflict, Henry divided his army into four parts. One part he put under the command of Richard; the second, under John; the third, under William de Mandeville, Earl of Essex, and the fourth, under Geoffrey, his chancellor and bastard son. This Geoffrey, the bastard son, is not to be confused with Henry's legitimate son of the same name. It seems to have been a common practice at this time to give the same name to both a legitimate child and a bastard. John, for instance, had two daughters named Joan, one legitimate and one illegitimate, and William the Lion,

King of Scots, had similarly two daughters named Margaret and two named Isabella. This must have led to a great deal of confusion at the time and still perplexes the reader today.

Philip besieged Richard and John at Châteauroux, seventy miles south of Orléans, in June 1187, and Henry came with a large force to relieve them. Philip raised the siege, and both armies prepared for a pitched battle. Through the intervention of the Pope and of the higher clergy of both countries, who were appalled at the prospect of open warfare between the two most powerful rulers of Western Europe, a two-year truce was arranged on June 23, 1187.

During this uneasy peace, Henry proposed a fresh settlement in a letter to Philip. Let John marry Alice, Philip's sister, he said, and Henry would then give John Aquitaine, Anjou, and all his other lands in France except Normandy, which must remain united with the English crown and would therefore be part of Richard's inheritance. Philip promptly showed this letter to Richard. Alice, whom Henry was now proposing to marry to John, had been betrothed to Richard for the last twenty years, but she was as nothing compared to his duchy of Aquitaine. This evidence that his father intended to take away from him the dearest part of his inheritance filled Richard with rage. He immediately allied himself with Philip, who, like his father, Louis, had always found Henry's sons his most potent weapon against their father. Many of Henry's barons likewise deserted him and, following Richard's example, went over to Philip.

Philip and Richard together, in the spring of 1189, made a hostile incursion into Henry's French territories, and war was again imminent. The papal legate, Cardinal John of Anagni, arranged for another conference between the two kings. They met at La Ferté-Bernard on June 4, when Philip made a fresh set of demands. The first one was that his sister Alice, who was betrothed to Richard and who had, according to the custom of the time, been living in Henry's household since her betrothal, be finally married to Richard. Richard had never shown the slightest interest in her or any desire to marry her, and a sinister rumor had steadily been gaining ground to the effect that Henry had made her his mistress and even had had several children by her. Richard eventually returned the unfortunate lady to her brother in 1191, and some six years later she was at last married to the Count of Ponthieu.

Philip also demanded that Henry's nobles should swear fealty to Richard as Henry's acknowledged heir and that John should set out for the Holy Land. This last condition sprang not so much from Philip's concern for the welfare of John's soul as from a desire to get him out of the way so that Richard might be undisputed heir to Henry. Richard joined in this demand and swore that he himself would not go to the Holy Land, as he had vowed to do in November 1187, unless John went with him.

Henry replied that he would never assent to such conditions, thus showing that Richard's fears were in some measure justified, and proposed instead that Alice be married to John. This of course confirmed Richard's suspicions, and Philip would not agree to the proposal. Henry retired to Le Mans, the capital city of his paternal inheritance of Maine, in desperate straits. Brittany, Anjou, and Aquitaine were all rising in rebellion against him. His barons were deserting him; even his soldiers, now that his treasury was empty, looked for better pay elsewhere.

Sometime during these desperate days John, as a last and crowning piece of treachery, went over to Philip's side, hoping to gain more from his victorious brother than from his defeated father.

Richard and Philip captured Le Mans on June 12, and Henry was forced to flee with only seven hundred knights remaining of his army. Henry had ordered one of the suburbs of Le Mans to be fired, and a sudden change of wind carried the flames to the city itself. When he reached a hill about two miles from the city, he stopped and looked back on the burning town and gave way to wild despair.

"O God," he cried, "since You have today, to heap up confusion on me and increase my shame, so vilely taken from me the city I loved most on earth, in which I was born and reared, where my father is buried, and where the body of St. Julian lies hidden, I shall certainly pay You back as best I can, by taking away from You that part of me that You love best, my soul."

He fled to Chinon and took refuge there. On June 30 his enemies appeared before Tours, and on the same day he was stricken with fever. He retreated to Saumur, and on July 3 Tours capitulated.

Richard and Philip summoned the defeated King, whose cause was now hopelessly lost, to meet them at Columbières, near Tours, on July 4. Henry, so racked with fever that he could scarcely sit his horse, came to hear their demands. Philip was filled with pity at the sight of his defeated enemy in such great pain. He called for a mantle to be folded and placed on the ground, so that his adversary might sit on it, but Henry refused it. As the Kings conferred, a crash of thunder came from the cloudless sky and lightning struck among the host. They fell back in alarm, and when they resumed their conference a second clap of thunder rent the still summer air. Henry was now in such mortal pain that his followers had to hold him on his horse as he listened to Philip's demands. He acceded to them all.

Henry placed himself wholly under the control and at the will of the King of France and did homage to him for all his French possessions. Alice, Philip's sister, was taken from the charge of the English King. Richard was to receive the oath of fealty from his father's subjects in both England and France as the acknowledged heir. Henry agreed to pay Philip twenty thousand marks of silver, and all his barons were to swear that if he failed to make the payment they would go over to Philip and Richard and help them to the best of their ability. As pledges of the King's good faith, Le Mans, Tours, and a number of castles were to be held by Philip and Richard till Henry had fulfilled all the conditions.

Henry gave Richard the kiss of peace when these humiliating terms had been agreed to, but as he drew back he whispered fiercely: "May God grant me not to die till I have revenged myself worthily on you!"

Henry made only one request: that the names of those who had deserted him and gone over to Philip and Richard be written down and given him. He had himself carried back to Chinon, and there that evening the chancellor Geoffrey, his bastard son, who had been faithful to him through all his defeat and humiliation, began to read the list of traitors. The first name was that of John.

"Can it be true," cried Henry, sitting up in his agony, "that John, my heart, whom I have loved more than all my other sons, has forsaken me?

"Read no more," he said, and turned his face to the wall. "Now let all the rest go as it will; I care no more for myself or for the world."

He died on July 6, 1189, crying all the while: "Shame, shame on a vanquished king!" He who had always traveled with two or three archbishops and five or six bishops in his train died without ghostly counsel. His followers plundered him of his remaining treasure and left his body lying naked. A page boy covered it with his own tattered summer cloak, which reached scarcely to the knees of the corpse. Thus Henry Court Mantle was found by Geoffrey, William Marshal, and a few faithful servants, who prepared the body for burial. Henry was dressed in his royal robes, with a golden crown on his head, gloves on his rough red hands, a golden ring on his finger, his scepter in his hand, and slippers of cloth-of-gold and spurs on his feet.

As the body lay with its face uncovered, awaiting burial in the Church of the Nuns at Fontevrault, Richard came to kneel beside the father he had destroyed. At his approach, blood ran from the nostrils of the dead king and continued to flow while Richard knelt before the altar for the space of a Pater Noster. From this men knew that Richard by his treachery had in truth murdered his father.

CHAPTER IV

THE STRUGGLE WITH LONGCHAMP

1189-1192

WHEN Eleanor in England received the news of the death of her husband, she set herself up in the state that Henry had denied her since her part in the rebellion of 1173 and made a queenly progress through the country. She ordered that all captives should be released from prison, since, says Roger of Hoveden, "in her own person she had learned by experience that confinement is distasteful to mankind and that it is a most delightful refreshment to the spirits to be liberated therefrom."

One of Richard's first acts was to dismiss from his service all those who had deserted his father and come over to him, while he retained and showed great favor to those who had been faithful to Henry. He made one exception: he welcomed his brother John and took him back to England with him on August 12, 1189. After they landed, Richard confirmed John's title to the county of Mortain, the county of Nottingham, and the castle of Marlborough, which his father had given him in 1174. In addition he gave him the counties of Dorset, Somerset, Derby, and Lancaster, and the Earldom of Cornwall, which had reverted to the Crown in 1175 upon the death of Reginald; the castle of Ludgershall; the honors of Wallingford, Tickhill, Eye, and Bolsover and The Peak, the high tableland in the northern part of Derbyshire. Finally, Richard gave him the Earldom of Gloucester and the heiress Hadwisa, to whom John had been betrothed in 1176.

John and Hadwisa were married at John's castle of Marlborough on August 29. Baldwin, Archbishop of Canterbury, forbade the marriage because John and Hadwisa were second cousins. John disregarded the prohibition, however, and lodged an appeal to Rome. While the appeal was pending, Baldwin laid John's lands under interdict, but the Papal Legate lifted the sentence in November.

Richard was hallowed and crowned King of England by Baldwin in Westminster Abbey on Sunday, September 3, 1189. Roger of Hoveden describes in minute detail the ceremony, which became the prototype and model for all English coronations since then. In the procession into the Abbey, John walked between David, Earl of Huntingdon, the brother of the King of Scotland, and Robert, Earl of Leicester. Each of the three carried a golden sword from the King's treasury, with a scabbard worked all over with gold. After Richard had been anointed and crowned, the Bishops of Durham and Bath led him to his throne, preceded by John and his two companions, bearing their swords of gold. Mass was celebrated, after which the procession left the Abbey in the same order in which it had entered.

The new King was eager to set out on the Crusade, and his first concern was to raise money for that purpose. As soon as he was crowned and had received the oaths of homage and fealty from all his bishops and barons, he put up for sale everything he had. "If I could find a buyer," he declared, "I would sell London itself." Bishop Hugh Pudsey of Durham, who built the wondrous Galilee

Porch of that Cathedral, bought the manor of Sedbergh for six hundred marks on September 28. John was one of the witnesses to the charter confirming the sale.

With John's marriage and Richard's coronation out of the way, the new King showed his faith in his brother by sending him at the head of an expedition into Wales. Rhys ap Gryffud, Prince of South Wales, had rebelled a number of times against the authority of Henry II, and when he learned that the King was dead he had broken into a fresh revolt. He seized the castles of Llanstephan and Langharne and ravaged Penfro, Rhos, and Gower. As soon as he had landed in England, Richard, with characteristic impetuosity, wanted to go at once and subdue Rhys, but his counsellors persuaded him that the revolt was of no great importance and could be attended to after his crowning.

In October, therefore, Richard sent John into Wales with an army to subdue the rebels and receive the oaths of fealty of the Welsh princes. They came to him at Worcester and made a treaty of peace with him, and when Rhys found that none of the other Welsh leaders supported him he yielded without a battle. Under the safe conduct of John, he went to Oxford to render homage to Richard. Probably because he was too busy with his preparations for the Crusade, Richard declined to come to meet him, and Rhys went back to Wales in great indignation. He did not, however, attempt to break the peace again.

In thanksgiving for his coronation and, no doubt, to beg for the Martyr's prayers for his Crusade, the King made a pilgrimage to the tomb of one of the greatest of the English saints. He kept the feast of St. Edmund at the Saint's shrine at Bury St. Edmunds and stayed at the great abbey from the 18th through the 20th of November.

With Wales now secure, Richard next turned his attention to Scotland. He invited William the Lion, King of the Scots, to meet him at Canterbury, and there, on December 5, they concluded a treaty that brought peace to the two countries for a century to come. The principle article of the treaty was the renunciation by the King of England of any claim to homage and allegiance for the Kingdom of Scotland and his consequent recognition of the King of the Scots as an independent monarch rather than a vassal holding his kingdom as a fief of the King of England. In return, William paid Richard ten thousand marks. This treaty, then, had the two-fold effect of securing peace with Richard's northern neighbor and of providing a large sum for his treasury. John accompanied his brother to Canterbury and signed the treaty as a witness.

Immediately before leaving Canterbury for Dover, Richard confirmed his gifts of land to John and added to them the county of Devon. This gave John complete control of the whole West of England.

Richard had now disposed of most of his affairs in England and had made the Welsh and Scottish borders safe. On December 11, accordingly, he sailed from Dover to Calais to complete arrangements for his continental territories. He summoned a final council in February 1190 to provide for the governing of England during his absence in the Holy Land. Queen Eleanor, John, Baldwin, Archbishop of Canterbury, Geoffrey, the King's bastard half-brother, whom he had nominated Archbishop of York, and the Bishops of Norwich, Durham, Winchester, Bath, Ely, Salisbury, and Coventry crossed over from England and met Richard in Normandy. At this council the King appointed William Longchamp, Bishop of Ely, to be Chief Justiciar, an office for which, according to Richard of Devizes, Longchamp paid four thousand pounds. In order that the administration of his trusted and loyal servant Longchamp might not be hampered by the machinations of John, Richard made his brother swear that he would not go back to England for the next three years without his permission. At the intercession of Queen Eleanor, however, Richard released John from his oath.

William Longchamp, to whom the King thus entrusted the governing of England, had served as Richard's chancellor in Aquitaine. His grandfather was said to have been a runaway French serf. When Richard succeeded to the throne, he made William his chancellor and nominated him Bishop of Ely. Longchamp was consecrated on December 31, 1189 and enthroned at Ely on January 6, 1190. After Richard made him Chief Justiciar, he prevailed upon Pope Clement III to appoint him Legate to England in the place of Archbishop Baldwin, who accompanied Richard on the Crusade.

As delegate of both Pope and King, Longchamp was armed with supreme power in Church and State in England. With the arrogance sometimes displayed by men who rise to positions of power through their own abilities rather than through birth and training, Longchamp, when he returned to England, set himself up in royal state and refused to take counsel with any of the leading men of the kingdom. He traveled about with such a vast retinue of men, horses, hounds, and hawks that a house where he spent a single night was impoverished for years to come. He confiscated lands and other possessions and divided them among his relations and retainers or kept them to pay the heavy expenses his way of living entailed. The sons of the nobles acted as his household servants, serving him on bended knee with downcast eyes, which outraged the English. Longchamp spoke no English, despised the English people, and made no attempt to hide his contempt from them. He set up his household at Oxford and surrounded himself with Normans and Flemings. "He moved pompously along," wrote Hugh of Nunant, Bishop of Coventry, "with a sneer in his nostrils, a grin on his features, derision in his eyes, and superciliousness on his brow."

His heavy exactions, his overbearing conduct, his unscrupulous confiscation of the property of others, and his arrogant conduct toward the leading men of the kingdom aroused a storm of resentment among the people and barons alike. John was quick to seize on this popular feeling and use it to his own advantage. His primary ambition was to be acknowledged heir to the throne. Richard had not done this, and John had grounds for believing that his brother either had named or intended to name the young Arthur, the posthumous son of their brother Geoffrey, as his heir. John began to organize the discontent against Longchamp and to set himself up as the champion and leader of the oppressed nation.

Richard formally set out on the Crusade at the end of June 1190, and he was pursued along the way by messengers from each of the two opposed parties, telling of the troubles that were arising in England. At Messina in Sicily, in February 1191, upon receiving complaints from all the principal men of the kingdom concerning Longchamp's highhanded conduct, Richard determined to curb the power of his chancellor. He sent Walter of Coutances to England with letters to Longchamp ordering him in all business of the kingdom to have him, together with William Marshal, Geoffrey FitzPeter, William Bruyere, and Hugh Bardolph, one of the Barons of the Exchequer, as his associates and witnesses. When he arrived in England, however, the emissary was so intimidated by Longchamp's disregard for the orders and instructions of his master and by his refusal to allow anyone else to share in the administration that he was afraid to present his letters to him and saved them for another occasion.

In the meantime, John had come into open conflict with Longchamp. Gerard de Camville, an adherent of John, was warder of Lincoln Castle and sheriff of the county, offices he had acquired through his wife, Nicholaa de Haia, in whose family they were hereditary. Richard, before his departure, had given Gerard a charter confirming his title. Longchamp, with customary highhandedness, nevertheless attempted to expel Gerard from Lincoln Castle and give his offices to one of his favorites, William de Stuteville. Gerard, however, armed both with his right and with the King's charter, refused to surrender the castle, and Longchamp laid siege to it.

When John learned of this, he started to the assistance of his parti-
san. The garrisons of the royal castles of Nottingham and Tickhill
surrendered to him, and John sent word to Longchamp that if he did
not lift the siege of Lincoln immediately "he would visit him with a
rod of iron." Longchamp capitulated and broke up the siege, recog-
nizing that John had the superior force on his side. John's triumph
was not complete, however, for Walter of Coutances and William
Marshal seem to have told him of their mission and powers and advised him to submit to the arbitration of the leading men of the
kingdom.

John was content for the time being with having checked Longchamp and did not want to push the matter till he was more sure of
his ground. He accordingly met Longchamp at Winchester on July
28, 1191, and an agreement was drawn up between them. John
gave up the castles of Nottingham and Tickhill to be held in trust
for the King by William Marshal and William of Wendenat, respectively, with the provision that if Longchamp were guilty of any
excesses against John and refused to make amends, the castles should
be returned to John. A number of other castles that seem to have
been subjects for dispute between John and the Chief Justiciar were
also given into the custody of various bishops to be held in trust for
the King, thus removing them from the grasp of both John and Longchamp. Gerard de Camville was reinstated as Sheriff of Lincoln but
was to stand his trial in the King's court, on what charge it was not
said.

These provisions restored the conditions existing before the conflict, and neither John nor Longchamp gained anything by them.
The next article of the agreement, however, was a direct slap at
Longchamp and showed to what lengths he had abused his power. It
was agreed that no bishop, baron, or freeholder should be deprived
of his lands or chattels on the mere order of a justice or deputy of the

King, but only by judgment of the King's court, according to the lawful customs of the realm, or by a direct order of the King himself.

The next conflict between John and Longchamp centered in Geoffrey, John's bastard half-brother. Geoffrey was born in England, presumably of an English mother, about 1153, and he was the only one of Henry's sons who might be regarded as English by birth and training. Shortly after Henry became King he acknowledged Geoffrey as his son and had him brought up with Eleanor's children. He was intended for the Church while he was very young and was made a deacon when he was still a boy. He served his father faithfully through the great revolt of 1173, and in that year, when Geoffrey was about twenty, Henry had him elected Bishop of Lincoln. The Pope, in 1175, dispensed him from the impediments of being under the canonical age and of illegitimate birth, and the chapter of Lincoln thereupon received him in solemn procession. However, with characteristic thoroughness, Henry determined that if his son was going to be a bishop he should be a good bishop, and he sent him to Tours to study for several years.

Geoffrey was back in England by the Christmas of 1178, and for three more years he continued to receive the revenues and administer the temporal affairs of his see in an efficient and capable way, while he was still only a deacon. By 1181 the diocese of Lincoln had been without a bishop for fifteen years, and Pope Alexander III accordingly ordered the Archbishop of Canterbury to see to it that someone, either the bishop-elect or another, was consecrated to that see immediately. Geoffrey's long delay cannot be attributed to a cynical desire to eat his cake and have it too. Although he was no saint, he led a good life, and his worst faults were the stubbornness and unmanageable temper common to Henry II and all his sons. Geoffrey seems truly to have doubted his worthiness for the episcopal office, and his delay may be interpreted as proceeding from the struggle between his own honest feelings and the desire of his father to see his most trustworthy son well provided for.

The Pope's letter made a decision imperative, and Geoffrey resigned the bishopric, which was given to Walter of Coutances. Henry, who had learned to trust both his son's character and his abilities as an administrator, made him his chancellor. Geoffrey served his father faithfully till the day of Henry's death. Richard, as soon as he became King, nominated him to the Archbishopric of York in accordance with Henry's last wishes, and he was duly elected by the chapter of York on August 10, 1189.

Immediately everything went wrong. A minority of the chapter of York declared that Geoffrey's election was invalid because the Dean, Hubert Walter, and Hugh Pudsey, Bishop of Durham, a suffragan of York, were not present. They appealed the matter to the Pope. Geoffrey seems again to have been beset by scruples concerning his worthiness. However, he took the first step by being ordained priest on September 23 by one of his suffragans, the Bishop of Whithern. This brought an immediate protest from Baldwin, Archbishop of Canterbury, who advanced the claim that the right of ordaining and consecrating the Archbishop of York belonged to him, and he also appealed to the Pope.

In November Richard sent Geoffrey north to the River Tweed to meet William the Lion and conduct him to Canterbury. On his way, Geoffrey stopped at York, and there the chapter asked him to install some new canons who had been appointed by Richard while the see was vacant. Geoffrey declared that these nominations were not effective without his consent as archbishop-elect, and he refused to install the canons till after his election should have been confirmed by the Pope. By doing this he incurred the wrath of the King and of all the members of the chapter. When he arrived at Canterbury he found everyone against him: Richard, the Archbishop of Canterbury, the Dean and chapter of York, and the Bishop of Durham.

Geoffrey's humility was now replaced by stubbornness. Although Hugh Pudsey, Bishop of Durham, and Hubert Walter, now Bishop of Salisbury but Dean of York at the time of Geoffrey's election, appeared at Canterbury before the Papal Legate, Cardinal John of Anagni, to protest that Geoffrey's election was invalid because they had not been present, and although the Treasurer and the new Dean of the chapter of York also appeared and protested that he was not canonically elected and was a murderer, born in adultery, and the son of a harlot, Geoffrey nevertheless induced the Legate to confirm his election, and he bought back his brother's favor by promising him three thousand pounds for his expenses on the Crusade.

Geoffrey found it impossible to raise the money, and he came to Richard in Normandy in March 1190 with empty hands. Richard, who placed the raising of money for the Crusade above all other considerations, was not pleased when Geoffrey thus failed him. He sent messengers to the Pope to try to persuade him not to confirm Geoffrey's election, and he made Geoffrey swear not to go to England for the next three years. Geoffrey stubbornly refused to accept his brother's nullification of his previous consent and followed him to Vézelay, where the Kings of England and France were to meet for a formal setting out on the Crusade. At last Geoffrey succeeded in influencing Richard to restore his promised office by paying him eight hundred marks on the spot and promising him twelve hundred marks as soon as he could raise the money.

From Vézelay Geoffrey went to Tours, where he stayed for more than a year, waiting for a mandate for his consecration from the Pope. After the agreement at Vézelay Richard apparently did not countermand his request made to the Pope in March that he hinder Geoffrey's consecration, for the Pope made no move till the spring of 1191. In the meantime, in February of that year, Richard had received at Messina the reports of the conflict between John and Longchamp and of Longchamp's arrogant behavior, and it occurred to

him that the presence in England of the Archbishop of York, during
the absence of the Archbishop of Canterbury on the Crusade, might
act as a check on both the Chief Justiciar and John. Queen Eleanor
arrived at Messina on March 30, bringing with her Richard's future
wife, Berengaria of Navarre. On her way back to England, accompanied by Walter of Coutances, now Archbishop of Rouen, the in-
domitable Eleanor stopped in Rome for an interview with the new
Pope, Celestine III, who had been elected on March 30, concerning the affairs of Geoffrey. In Richard's name she asked him to confirm the election and either to consecrate Geoffrey himself or to order
someone else to do so. In May the Pope accordingly sent a mandate
to the Archbishop of Tours, authorizing him to consecrate Geoffrey,
and the ceremony was performed on August 18.

Geoffrey now asserted that at Vézelay Richard had released him
from his oath not to go back to England, and indeed it does not seem
reasonable that Richard would have taken such steps to secure Geoffrey's consecration unless he intended that his brother should return
to England and exercise his office there. When Geoffrey reached
Witsand, in Flanders, messengers from Longchamp met him and
forbade him to come to England. He ignored this order and crossed
over to Dover on September 14. Knowing that the Chief Justiciar's
men would be watching for him, he disguised himself before he left
the ship. When he landed, he mounted a swift horse and rode to St.
Michael's Priory near the town. He reached the sanctuary about
noon, as Mass was being celebrated. He entered the church just
when the Epistle was being read and heard St. Paul's words: "He
that troubleth you shall bear his judgment, whosoever he be," from
which he derived much comfort.

Geoffrey claimed sanctuary, and Longchamp's servants surrounded the priory. After five days of blockade, the Justiciar's men
violated the sanctuary, entered the church just after Mass had been
celebrated, and dragged the Archbishop, still in his vestments,

through the streets and lanes to Dover Castle. There they delivered him to Matthew of Clare, the governor of the castle, whose wife was Longchamp's sister. Matthew immediately put him in prison in the Castle.

John heard of this outrage through his counsellor, Hugh of Nunant, Bishop of Coventry, and he asked Longchamp if it had been done at his order. The Justiciar admitted that it had. John ordered that Geoffrey should be released, and the Archbishop came to London to complain to John, the bishops, and the barons of the disgraceful way in which he had been treated. John then ordered that Longchamp should stand his trial in the King's Court, but the Justiciar, although not refusing to appear before the court, put off his appearance from day to day.

In the meantime a great wave of indignation was mounting against Longchamp. Geoffrey seems to have been popular in England. The men whom Richard had left in positions of trust and power were those who had remained faithful to Henry during his last struggle, and they would of course know of Geoffrey's unswerving fidelity to his father and respect him for it. The barons would resent it that a low-born upstart should thus humiliate the son of a king and the brother of a king. The English people, whom Longchamp heartily despised, would be enraged that a sneering Norman should treat with such contempt the most English of the late King's sons. Finally, bishop and Papal Legate though he was, by violating the sacred rights of sanctuary and by laying violent hands on the highest ecclesiastical dignitary in the land, Longchamp had outraged the religious feelings of the whole nation. He was hated throughout the country, and this piece of highhandedness was the last straw.

John felt that the nation was with him. In consultation with Walter of Coutances, he summoned the bishops and barons of the realm to a council near Reading to try the Chief Justiciar, and he ordered Longchamp to appear before the council. The council assembled, but Longchamp stayed in Windsor Castle and refused to appear. The bishops pronounced him excommunicate, and the council then decided, in order to have the greatest possible authority, to move to London and admit the citizens to their deliberations.

Longchamp got news of this and hastened towards London in order to enlist the support of the citizens before the members of the council should reach there. On the road his party encountered John and the other nobles and their knights. A brisk engagement was fought, in which John's justiciar, Roger de Planes, was killed, but Longchamp's party was greatly outnumbered. He and his supporters fled and took refuge in the Tower of London.

John and nearly all the bishops and nobles of England entered London on that same evening. On the following day, October 10, they met with the citizens of London in St. Paul's Churchyard in a council truly national in composition. Accusations covering all of Longchamp's misdeeds, which culminated in his treatment of Geoffrey, were made. In the words of Hugh of Nunant: "He and his revellers had so exhausted the whole kingdom that they did not leave a man his belt, a woman her necklace, a nobleman his ring, or anything of value even to a Jew. He had likewise so utterly emptied the King's treasury that in all the coffers and bags therein nothing but the keys could be met with, after the lapse of these two years."

The chief men of the kingdom, who should have been associated with Longchamp in the government, testified that he had scorned their advice and had transacted all affairs to suit himself only. Then Walter of Coutances publicly produced for the first time the letters Richard had given him at Messina in the preceding February, associating him in the government and containing the provision that if Longchamp should act contrary to the advice of those appointed to assist and counsel him, he should be deposed and Walter of Coutances made Chief Justiciar.

The whole assembly of bishops, barons, and citizens of London

thereupon deposed Longchamps as Chief Justiciar and elected Walter of Coutances in his stead. Walter agreed to do nothing without
the advice and consent of the Barons of the Exchequer and of those
named in Richard's letters as his associates. John, the new Chief
Justiciar, and his associates then granted to the citizens of London
the privileges of a commune, a form of city government new in England, whereby the whole citizenry were regarded as one person and
this corporate person made a direct feudal vassal of the king, without
the intermediate jurisdiction of any lord. The citizens of London in
turn took oaths of allegiance to King Richard and his heirs and swore
that if he should die without issue they would receive John as their
king and lord. John had thus achieved his purpose and was recognized by the whole assembly as rightful heir to the throne.

John now appears in a better light than at any time in his subse-
quent career. He acted with sound good sense, and he was careful to
associate himself with the leading men of the realm and to act with
their advice. He knew when he had gone far enough and did not
take advantage of a temporary supremacy to make any demands or
claim any rights to which he did not have at least a reasonable title.
For once, he showed himself astute in gauging the temper of those
about him and willing to abide by their judgment. At the same time,
he had enough enterprise to take the initiative and see that those
things were done that cried out to be done.

That this affair of the deposition of Longchamp was conducted in
such an orderly fashion was eloquent testimony to the great advances
England had made under Henry II. By the rigorous training that
monarch had given them, the whole nation, nobles and people alike,
had learned to respect the law and to comply with the orderly proc-
esses of government. The willful selfishness of the feudal nobles,
each acting despotically in his own domain, had been replaced by a
sense of collective responsibility to the king and to the country.

Geoffrey, the original cause of the disturbance, was enthroned in

York Minster on All Saints' Day, 1191. This was not the great cathedral that we know today, but an earlier building, of which only the crypt remains.

The downfall of Longchamp was complete. He immediately surrendered the Tower of London and Windsor Castle to the new Chief Justiciar and promised to give up all the other castles he held, giving his brothers and his chamberlain as hostages. He surrendered some of these castles and then fled to his brother-in-law at Dover. From there he attempted to escape to the Continent, disguised as a woman in a long green gown. Some of the townspeople discovered the ruse and recognized him. Remembering how, only a month before, Longchamp had had Geoffrey publicly humiliated before them, they dragged him through the streets and then shut him up in a dark cellar under guard. All this was reported to John, who forced Longchamp to surrender all the remaining castles and then ordered him to be released.

The fallen justiciar crossed over to Flanders on October 29. There he fell into the hands of some men whom he had injured in England, and they held him until, in the ominous words of Roger of Hoveden, "he made satisfaction to them." From there Longchamp went to Paris, where he paid the Bishop sixty marks to greet him with a procession. Thence he returned to Normandy, but he found scant welcome there, for the Archbishop of Rouen, his successor in England, had had the sentence of excommunication against him published throughout Normandy, and wherever he went the services of the Church were suspended as long as he stayed there.

Longchamp then sent messengers to Pope Celestine III and to the King, telling them how John and his accomplices had expelled him from the kingdom. In December the Pope sent a letter to all the bishops of England, ordering them to find out if it were true that John or anyone else had laid violent hands on Longchamp or had put him in prison or had in any way changed the "state of the kingdom from the

position in which it was placed by His Serene Highness at his departure" on the Crusade. If such proved to be the case, the bishops were
instructed to assemble together and with candles lighted and bells
ringing to pronounce the sentence of excommunication against John
and his accomplices.

Under the authority of this letter, Longchamp, styling himself "by
the grace of God Bishop of Ely, Legate of the Apostolic See, and
Chancellor of our lord the King," wrote to the venerable and great
Hugh of Avalon, Bishop of Lincoln, one of the most saintly men in
England, ordering him to convene the bishops of England and carry
out the Pope's orders. John was to be given a period of grace, till the
next Quinquagesima Sunday, in which to repent. His accomplices,
however, among whom Longchamp named Walter of Coutances,
William Marshal, Geoffrey FitzPeter, William Bruyere, and Hugh
Bardolph, to whom Richard had entrusted the government of the
country in his letters of February 1191, were to be excommunicated immediately.

In addition to these, Longchamp distinctly and especially named
his erstwhile friend, Hugh of Nunant, Bishop of Coventry, to be
publicly denounced. Hugh had written a circular letter describing
Longchamp's misdeeds and downfall, and with malicious glee he had
dwelt upon the spectacle of the fallen justiciar sitting at the seashore
at Dover, dressed in a woman's gown, with a huckster's staff in his
hand and a length of brown cloth, as if for sale, on his arm, and being embraced by a fisherman, cold and wet from the sea, who sought
warmth in the folds of the Legate's dress and, being thus warmed, discovered his sex. This Bishop, directed the smarting Legate, is "to be
strictly avoided by all, that in the future a sheep so diseased may not
be able to blemish and corrupt the flock of the Lord."

Neither the saintly Hugh of Avalon nor any other of the bishops
paid any attention to these letters of the Pope and of his Legate. Instead of pronouncing the sentence of excommunication on Long-

champ's enemies, the bishops met with the justiciars and deprived him of his bishopric. The revenues from the now vacant see of Ely, which in any case would belong to the Crown, they put in the royal hoard to replace some of the treasures Longchamp had taken from it.

The five justiciars, the bishops, and the barons wrote a joint letter to Richard, reporting Longchamp's offenses and telling how they had deposed him. Longchamp on his side warned Richard that John had seized possession of the kingdom and was planning next to seize the crown itself.

John's position was strong. His possession of the counties of Cornwall, Devon, Somerset, Gloucester, and Dorset gave him control of the West of England, and within his domains he ruled with absolute authority and kept kingly state. The revenues from these counties went directly into his own treasury, and he made no accounting of them to the royal exchequer.

He was not pleased, however, with the disposition of the castles over which he had quarreled with Longchamp during the preceding summer. At the same time, he did not dare openly to defy the authority of the new justiciar by seizing the castles of Nottingham and Tickhill, which Walter of Coutances had put in the custody of Roger, the Constable of Chester. Roger afforded John an opportunity to show his discontent when Roger hanged two of the men whom John had placed in charge of the castles, on the grounds that they had consented to the surrender of those castles to John during the past summer. John immediately laid waste all the lands belonging to the Constable of Chester that lay within John's jurisdiction, and his power was so great that the central government seems to have raised no question.

Now that Geoffrey had, at the beginning of November, at last been enthroned as Archbishop of York, he set to work to reduce to order his chief suffragan, Hugh Pudsey, Bishop of Durham, who had led the original protest against his election. He could hardly have chosen a stouter or more wily opponent. Hugh was a grandson of Adela, daughter of William the Conqueror, and hence a second cousin to Henry II. He was made Bishop of Durham in 1153 and thus, as Bishop and Earl-palatine of Durham, had the whole county under his civil and ecclesiastical jurisdiction. He was closely allied with the great families of the North, and during his long tenure of the see had acquired a considerable fortune. He was a great builder of churches, and the Galilee of Durham Cathedral is one of the finest monuments to his zeal in that respect. At this time he had had almost forty years of experience in administering the affairs of his diocese.

Geoffrey ordered Hugh to come to York and make his profession of canonical obedience to him. Hugh refused on the grounds that he had already done obedience to the former Archbishop, Roger of Pont-l'Evêque, and that there was no law compelling him to make a second such profession. Geoffrey then excommunicated him, but Hugh paid no attention to the sentence and continued to celebrate Mass and to cause it to be celebrated in his presence. When he learned of this defiance, Geoffrey caused the altars at which Hugh had said Mass to be demolished and the vessels that had been used in the celebration of Mass in Hugh's presence to be broken.

John incurred his half-brother's wrath by spending Christmas with Hugh at his manor of Hoveden in Yorkshire. This visit to one of the most influential men in the North of England shows John's desire to win the sympathy and support of the leading men of the kingdom, but it served only to get him into trouble. Because he had eaten in the company of the excommunicated Bishop, Geoffrey pronounced sentence of excommunication against him, too. Hugh found that Geoffrey had some power in his province, for most men avoided Hugh's company and refused to speak to him or to eat and drink with him. Hugh then appealed to the Pope, and the Pope decided that the sentence had been inconsiderately pronounced and without reasonable cause and therefore nullified it.

Philip meanwhile had returned from the Holy Land with his small heart bursting with envy and jealousy and spite, leaving Richard in command of the Christian armies there. Philip set to work with plans to injure the English King during his absence. He sent messengers to John in January 1192, asking him to come to France to confer with him. He offered John the hand of his sister Alice, whom Richard had finally and emphatically repudiated by marrying Berengaria of Navarre, and promised that he would help him gain possession of both England and Normandy. John was foolish enough to believe all this and replied that he would come and discuss matters.

Eleanor got wind of the plot and, knowing her youngest son's devious ways and his fondness for double-dealing, hurried to England from Normandy. She found John on the verge of starting for France. The stout-hearted Queen, the Archbishop of Rouen, and the other justiciars forbade John to cross to the Continent and threatened to seize all his lands and castles if he did so. Checkmated by all those in power, John abandoned his plans for the time being.

The new Chief Justiciar and his associates were meanwhile conducting the government of the country in an able manner, and after the oppressions of Longchamp all men seemed satisfied with the new justiciars. It was not to John's advantage that the country should be in a peaceful state; his interests were best advanced amid discord, when he could play off one side against the other. Seeing no hope of getting any support from the faithful servants of Richard who were now in power, and foiled in his design of plotting treachery with Philip, he accepted from Longchamp an offer of five thousand pounds if he could succeed in getting the former Chief Justiciar restored to his office. Longchamp had also given much money to Queen Eleanor and promised to give her still more.

John sent word to him to return to England. In Lent, 1192, Longchamp landed at Dover and remained at Dover Castle with his sister and her husband, but he was afraid to proceed any farther. John in the meantime tried in every way possible to induce the chief men of the kingdom to restore Longchamp to his former position, but they firmly refused. When Walter of Coutances told Eleanor of the excesses of which Longchamp had been guilty, she ceased to plead his cause before the justiciars. They bribed John with two thousand marks from the King's treasury, and he too ceased to champion the exiled Bishop. In general indignation they sent word to Longchamp that if he did not leave the country immediately they would cast him into prison. The former Chief Justiciar returned to the Continent on Maundy Thursday, April 3, 1192.

This episode showed John that his influence outside his own territories was negligible, after all, and that he was not trusted by the nobles, and he seems to have passed the remainder of the year 1192 in a peaceful fashion, looking after the administration of his domains. This peace was interrupted early in 1193 when the news reached England that Richard, on his way home from the Holy Land, had been captured by his bitter enemy, Leopold, Duke of Austria.

CHAPTER V

THE RANSOMING OF RICHARD

1193–1199

THE THIRD CRUSADE had not been a great success. The Christian leaders spent more time in quarreling among themselves than in fighting the Saracens, and against this divided host the infidels had presented an army firmly united in fanatical faith, ably led by their great ruler, Saladin, and accustomed to the climate, the country, and the style of warfare best suited to those conditions.

Richard, indeed, had covered himself with dazzling glory. His daring feats, his reckless heroism, his openhanded generosity, his genius as a military tactician, and his embodiment of all the manly and knightly virtues had gained him the reputation of being the very ideal of Christian chivalry. Nevertheless, when a three years' truce was drawn up between Richard and Saladin, the Christians were not much nearer regaining the Holy Sepulchre than they had been at the start of the Crusade. They were worn out by disease, climate, and constant warfare, and their numbers had been greatly reduced by desertions and by death. Richard had exhausted most of his great wealth, was constantly ill, and had been receiving a series of disturbing reports about John's designs on the throne and about Philip's encroachments on his continental possessions.

Richard arranged a truce with Saladin in September 1192, after he had been in the Holy Land for fifteen months, and started back to England. Why he did not sail directly for his kingdom, going through the Pillars of Hercules with the other returning Crusaders, is not clear; he may have thought that he could go more quickly by land than by sea. At any rate, he attempted to cross through Germany and was captured near Vienna on December 21 by his implacable enemy, Leopold, Duke of Austria, whom he had mortally offended after the capture of Acre. Leopold turned his royal captive over to the Emperor, Henry VI, shortly after Christmas, on condition that he should receive half of whatever sums Henry might get as Richard's ransom.

Philip quickly received the news of Richard's misfortune and sent messengers to John in England, inviting him to join him in invading Richard's French territories. Early in 1193 John crossed over to Normandy, where he was met by the chief men of the duchy. Thinking that he was as much disturbed by his brother's plight as they were, they proposed that John come with them to Alençon to discuss the measures to be taken to secure Richard's release. John replied that if they would receive him as their lord and swear fealty to him, he would come to the conference and would defend them against the French King. The Norman nobles indignantly refused to renounce their allegiance to Richard.

John nevertheless went to Philip in February and did homage to him for Normandy and the other lands that Richard held of Philip. It was said also that John did homage for England as well. Although he was still married to Hadwisa, he swore to marry Philip's sister Alice, and he renounced all claims to the Norman Vexin. Philip in turn gave him the part of Flanders that was then under French control and swore to assist him in every way in gaining England and the other territories belonging to Richard.

This was apparently John's first overt act in his attempt to usurp the throne. He had been suspected of such a design for some time, but he had not hitherto been able to find any person of importance to support his plans. Encouraged now by Philip, he returned to England with a force of foreign mercenaries. The castles of Wallingford and Windsor surrendered to him immediately. Flushed with this success, he went to London and demanded of the Chief Justiciar, Walter of Coutances, and the men associated with him that they turn the kingdom over to him and swear fealty to him. Richard, he declared, was dead, and he claimed the crown as the lawful heir.

The Chief Justiciar and the barons turned down this claim with scorn and indignation, and John withdrew to his own lands. He fortified all his castles and began to attack those belonging to Richard. Many shiftless and discontented people rallied round him, but he could not raise enough of a force to offer any serious threat to the peace of the country. The Chief Justiciar placed strong garrisons at the seaports to make sure that John received no help from his French ally, and Philip gave up the intention, if indeed he had ever entertained it, of sending an army to help him. A few French and Fleming adventurers tried to enter the country to enlist in John's forces, but the Chief Justiciar had them seized and put in chains.

In the meantime, as soon as he had heard of the capture of Richard, the Chief Justiciar sent the abbots of Boxley and of Robertsbridge to Germany to try to find him. After passing through Germany in their search, the abbots found their King in Bavaria, at a town where he had been brought for the purpose of holding a conference with the Emperor on Palm Sunday. They reported to Richard on the state of his kingdom, and he complained bitterly about

John's conduct. He did not see in it any danger to his crown, however, for, he said: "My brother John is not the man to conquer a country if there is a single person able to make the slightest resistance to his attempts."

The abbots returned to England shortly after Easter and brought the news that peace had been made between Richard and the Emperor. Richard agreed to pay a ransom of a hundred thousand marks of silver and to provide fifty galleys, fully equipped, and the services of twenty knights for a year, to help the Emperor in his expedition against southern Italy and Sicily. These envoys were followed by messengers from the King himself, asking for ships and for Alan Trenchemere, the pilot of Richard's own ship. Then Robert of Turnham, one of the King's household, came to England bringing with him Richard's armor and accouterments.

Upon receiving all these cheering indications that Richard was indeed alive and might soon be back in England, the justiciars decided to employ sterner measures in dealing with John. They laid siege to Windsor Castle, and Archbishop Geoffrey, the Sheriff of York, and Hugh Bardolph, one of the justiciars, fortified Doncaster against him.

Philip meanwhile invaded Normandy. He appeared with his army before Rouen and ordered the inhabitants to surrender the city to him, on the grounds that John had done homage to him for England and had surrendered all the English territories on that side of the Channel to him. The stouthearted citizens replied: "See, the gates are open; enter if you like; no one opposes you." The lily-livered Philip, however, took second thought and declined to enter. He burned the twenty-four stone engines with which he had planned to assault the city, broke his wine casks and poured out the wine, and retired with his army.

Time was passing, and still Richard's faithful servants in England had no further word from him as to his return. John was, after all, recognized as heir to the throne in England, and the justiciars and their associates began to doubt the wisdom of dealing too harshly with one who might some day be their king. John in the meantime was predicting that his brother would never return, and the long delay lent some plausibility to his words. Accordingly, the justiciars arrived at a truce with him to last till All Saints' Day, according to the terms of which he retained the castles of Nottingham and Tickhill, but the castles of Windsor, Wallingford, and The Peak were given to Queen Eleanor and men appointed by her, to hold in trust till the expiration of the truce. If Richard had not returned by that time, it was agreed that these castles were to be returned to John. Hugh Pudsey, Bishop of Durham, was engaged in besieging Tickhill at the time the truce was arranged, and it went sorely against the grain for him to abandon the siege just when he was on the point of taking the castle. Bishop Hugh was almost seventy at the time, but his strength and energy were those of a young man.

Richard wrote to his mother and the justiciars on April 19, 1193, informing them that an indissoluble bond of friendship had been formed between him and the Emperor at the price of seventy thousand marks of silver and urging them to raise the money immediately. Eleanor and the justiciars at once set about collecting the tremendous sum. Since money to pay the lord's ransom was one of the three recognized feudal dues, the consent of the bishops and barons was not necessary for this extraordinary levy. All men, clerics as well as lay, were taxed a fourth of the year's income and a fourth of the value of their movables; each knight's fee was assessed at twenty shillings; all the gold and silver of the churches was taken, as the King had specifically commanded; and the religious orders of the Cistercians and Gilbertines, who theoretically had no wealth, contributed all the year's clip of wool. It is an extraordinary testimony to Richard's popularity among a people who scarcely knew him, and to the hold he had secured upon their imaginations and affections by his heroic deeds in the Holy Land that the whole of England turned cheerfully to the task of raising a sum so vast as to be almost beyond the reach of their calculations. Most of the Crusaders had returned from the East by this time, and one may be sure that Richard's exploits lost nothing in their telling of them.

The Emperor wrote to the bishops and nobles of England, urging them in flowery language "to take those steps which are due to the honor of our most dearly beloved friend, your lord Richard." This hypocritical message was delivered by William Longchamp, who had rejoined his master early in the spring. Longchamp landed at Ipswich, spent the night at Hitcham, and sent word to Abbot Samson of Bury St. Edmunds that he would like to hear Mass at St. Edmund's shrine. The Abbot ordered that no one was to celebrate Mass in Longchamp's presence, since he was excommunicated. When Longchamp arrived at the great abbey the next morning and entered the church as Mass was being said, the celebrant, who had already reached the Canon, stood silent till a messenger reported that the excommunicated prelate had left the church. Longchamp in a considerably chastened frame of mind went to St. Albans and was given a frigid reception by Queen Eleanor and the justiciars. He declared that he came to England not as Justiciar, Legate, or Chancellor, but as a simple bishop bearing a message from the King. After delivering that message, he left England immediately and returned to Richard.

Negotiations between Richard and the Emperor were continuing, and by summer they had reached another agreement that Richard was to pay a hundred thousand marks for his freedom. When news of this settlement reached Philip he sent word to John that "he must take care of himself, for the devil was now let loose." John at once crossed over to Normandy and joined Philip as his adherent.

Whilst his brother was engaged in his treachery, Richard sent William Longchamp and William Bruyere to make peace with Philip. Early in July 1193, a treaty was drawn up between them, and one of the provisions guaranteed that John should retain the

lands his brother had previously given him. When his envoys returned to Richard and reported that they had made peace with Philip,
he sent them back to endeavor to win John over to his rightful
allegiance. They persuaded him to leave Philip's court and return to
Normandy, where he took an oath of fealty to Richard. Richard had
ordered that when John had taken this oath the castles in Normandy
that he had previously given him were to be delivered over to John,
but the keepers of the castles, who knew him and suspected more
treachery on his part, refused to relinquish them to him. John was
full of rage at this insult, merited though it was, and went back to
Philip and renewed his allegiance to him. Philip gave him the castles
of Driencourt and Arches, which according to the treaty were to
have been delivered to the Archbishop of Rouen.

The Emperor's messengers came to London and received the
money for Richard's ransom. They expressed amazement at the prosperous appearance of the city and its inhabitants, for the boorish Ger-
mans had supposed that the raising of so large a ransom would leave
the country utterly destitute. Richard summoned his mother, Walter
of Coutances, and many of his nobles to come to him in Germany in
anticipation of his being set free, and in September the Emperor
fixed a date in the following January when he was to be released.

When Philip and John learned that the devil was indeed about to
be let loose, they sent messengers, among whom was Robert of
Nunant, brother of the Bishop of Coventry, to the Emperor, to
make a variety of offers. If he would agree to keep Richard in captivity till the following Michaelmas, they would each pay him fifty
thousand marks; or they would pay him a thousand marks a month
as long as he kept Richard; or Philip would pay him a hundred
thousand marks and John would pay fifty thousand marks if the Emperor would either deliver Richard into their hands or keep him a
full year. These were attractive offers to a man so devoid of scruple
as to lay hands on the person of a Crusader, protected by the laws

of the Church under penalty of excommunication, and they would probably have been even more attractive if they had come from men that might be trusted to live up to them. The Emperor needed time to consider them, and he postponed Richard's liberation till the following Candlemas, February 2, 1194.

On the appointed day, in the presence of his nobles and of Queen Eleanor, Walter of Coutances, William Longchamp, and the Bishop of Bath, the Emperor handed over to Richard the letters from Philip and John and expressed a desire to withdraw from his agreement to free Richard, in view of the tempting terms he was offered to keep him captive. The assembly so reproached him for his intended breach of faith that they prevailed upon him at last to keep his word. He accordingly delivered Richard into the hands of his mother, after he had been in captivity for a year and six weeks.

Whilst Richard and his party were making a leisurely return to England, John sent a cleric of his household, one Adam of St. Edmunds, to England with letters to the keepers of his castles, ordering them to fortify the castles against the arrival of the King. When Adam reached London he had dinner at the house of Hubert Walter, the new Archbishop of Canterbury. He had been elected, not without the usual squabble between the bishops and the monks of Canterbury, to succeed Baldwin, who had died in the Holy Land. Adam boasted loudly about his master's wealth and prosperity and about the intimate friendship between John and the King of France. As proof of this friendship Adam cited the fact that Philip had given John the castles of Driencourt and Arches and would have given him many more if John had had faithful men to keep them for him.

Out of respect for the Archbishop's table, Adam was allowed to leave unmolested, but on his way back to his lodging the Mayor of London arrested him, took all his papers away from him, and turned them over to the Archbishop. On the following day Archbishop Hubert showed John's treasonable letters to the assembled bishops and barons. Since his instructions implied a preparation for civil war, the council decreed that John should be deprived of all his lands in England and that his castles should be seized.

On the same day, Archbishop Hubert, Hugh of Avalon, Bishop of Lincoln, and a number of other bishops and abbots met in the Chapel of the Sick Monks at Westminster and pronounced sentence of excommunication against John and all his abettors and advisors in plotting against the King and the peace of the realm. They also wrote a letter to the Pope, begging that William Longchamp should be deprived of his position as Legate in England.

The principal men of the kingdom immediately set to work with great zeal and laid siege to John's castles. That splendid old warrior, Hugh Pudsey, raised a large army in Northumberland and York-shire and resumed the siege of Tickhill, which he had been obliged to abandon almost a year earlier. David, Earl of Huntingdon and brother of the King of the Scots, and his brother-in-law, Ranulf de Blundevill, Earl of Chester, besieged Nottingham Castle. The Archbishop of Canterbury, who had been appointed Chief Justiciar when Walter of Coutances went to Germany to join Richard, di-rected the operations against Marlborough. This last castle, together with those of Lancaster, which John had entrusted to Theobald Fitz-Walter, Archbishop Hubert's brother, and of St. Michael's Mount, in Cornwall, whose keeper died of fright when he heard that Richard was on his way back to England, surrendered without resistance.

Richard landed at Sandwich on March 12, 1194, and when the news of his arrival reached the members of the garrison of Tickhill they asked leave of Bishop Hugh to send two knights to see if the King had really returned. The knights reported to their comrades that the King had indeed returned, whereupon they surrendered the castle to the Bishop. Nottingham, however, continued to withstand the siege, and the King in exasperation went there on March 25 with such a multitude of men and such a clangor of trumpets that the garrison were greatly disturbed. Still they did not believe that the King had come and continued to resist, thinking that this multitude and uproar were tricks of their besiegers. Richard camped so close to the walls of the castle that the archers killed men at his very feet. He put on his armor and ordered an assault to be made. Although many men fell on both sides and the King himself slew one man with an arrow, Richard succeeded only in driving the garrison back into the castle, taking some defenses that had been thrown up outside the gates, and burning the outer gates. On this day the Archbishops Hubert and Geoffrey joined Richard at Nottingham.

Richard, on the next day, had his stone engines put together so that he might batter the castle into submission. He had gibbets built near the castle, and from them he hanged some of John's men whom he had captured the day before.

Hugh Pudsey and those who had been with him at the siege of Tickhill came to Richard on the 27th, bringing with them the prisoners they had captured. Whilst the King was at dinner, two envoys came from the besieged castle to see if he was really Richard. When they returned to the castle and reported that the King was there and told of the preparations he was making, the two governors of the castle and twelve of their men came to Richard, surrendered to him, and threw themselves on his mercy. The Archbishop of Canterbury on the following day persuaded the remainder of the garrison to surrender to the King.

Richard had now stamped out the last traces of the disaffection stirred up by John, and there was no threat to the tranquillity of his realm. He summoned his bishops and barons to a council at Nottingham, and on the second day of the meeting, March 31, he asked for judgment against John, who was still in France with his confederate, Philip. He charged that John had betrayed his oath to him, seized his castles, invaded his territories both in England and in Normandy, and allied himself with his worst enemy, Philip. In this accusation

he included Hugh of Nunant, Bishop of Coventry, who had aided
and abetted John. The council accordingly decreed that if John and
Bishop Hugh did not appear within forty days to answer these
charges, John should forfeit all his rights in the kingdom and Bishop
Hugh should be tried by a court of his fellow bishops.

Early in May Richard crossed over to Normandy to repulse the
continued depredations of Philip. He sailed from Portsmouth, landed
at Barfleur on May 12, and hastened towards Verneuil, a strongly
fortified town south of Rouen. On the way he stopped to spend the
night at Lisieux, at the house of Jean d'Alençon, the Archdeacon of
Lisieux. There occurred the first meeting between the brothers since
Richard had started on the Crusade.

The biographer of William Marshal says that after he had eaten,
Richard wanted to rest a bit, but he was so uneasy about the situation at Verneuil, where Philip was laying siege to the town, that he
could find no repose. Whilst Richard was tossing on his bed, his
host entered, with a sad and preoccupied expression.

"Why are you looking like that?" the King asked him. "You
have seen my brother John; don't lie to me about it. He is wrong to
be afraid of me. Let him come to me without fear; after all, he is my
brother. If it is true that he has acted foolishly, I shall not reproach
him with it. But as for those who have led him on, they have already
had their reward or will soon have it."

John came in then and threw himself at his brother's feet. Richard
raised him up, saying: "John, don't be afraid. You are only a child.
You have been in bad company. Those who advised you shall pay
for it. Now get up and go eat your dinner."

Richard turned to his host. "What is there to eat?" he asked.
Someone had just brought a fine salmon as a present to the King,
and Richard had it cooked for John.

This homely scene of reconciliation shows how Richard regarded
his younger brother. His attitude toward John seems to have been

compounded of affection, amusement, and contempt, and his great heart was too generous to bear John any malice for his bungling attempts to usurp the throne. Both Eleanor and Richard sincerely loved this youngest son and brother, although at this distance it is hard to see what they found to love in him. Richard's affection, however, did not make him blind to John's utter untrustworthiness. He refused to restore any of John's lands or castles to him, and he apparently forbade him to set foot in England again.

Meanwhile, when Philip learned of Richard's arrival he fled from Verneuil in haste. His strategy, if one chooses to dignify cowardice with such a name, was to avoid pitched battles and to harass Richard with border raids, forays, and tentative thrusts at the weak places along the extensive frontier. The whole military strategy of the time consisted in capturing castles and laying waste the countryside; of battles there were few.

Richard hastened south of Loches, in Anjou, some thirty miles southeast of Tours, to help his brother-in-law, Sancho of Navarre. Whilst Richard was in Anjou, John, Robert of Beaumont, Earl of Leicester, and many other barons met at Rouen to defend that city against Philip, who, as soon as Richard's back was turned, laid siege to a castle four miles from the city. The French forces greatly outnumbered the defenders of Rouen, and without Richard's leadership and example John and his company did not dare attack them. Philip captured and destroyed the castle. As he was leaving that neighborhood, for a direct attack on Rouen was too risky an undertaking for him, Philip captured the Earl of Leicester, who had led his forces from Rouen in an attempt to ambush him.

England lost one of her strongest bishops when Hugh Pudsey of Durham died in the following spring, on March 3, 1195. Although he was in his seventies, Bishop Hugh was in exuberant health, full of strength and vigor, and he had no thought that death was near, trusting, it is said, in the prophecy of St. Godric that he would be blind for the last seven years of his life. After the Bishop's death, men expert in that branch of knowledge explained that St. Godric was referring to spiritual, not physical, blindness. Bishop Hugh ate too heartily of the Shrove Tuesday feast, fell sick, and died at his manor of Hoveden. He was buried in the chapter house of his great cathedral on the River Wear.

John succeeded in winning back his brother's favor to such an extent that in 1195 Richard restored to him the earldoms of Mortain and of Gloucester and the honor of Eye, but he did not give him any of the castles that would normally accompany these grants. In place of all the other earldoms and the vast extent of lands that John had possessed, Richard granted him an annuity of eight hundred pounds Angevin, or two hundred pounds in English money. John's friend, Hugh of Nunant, also regained the King's favor and the Bishopric of Coventry by paying five thousand marks.

John continued to act a minor part in helping Richard with his constant warfare against Philip. In 1196 he captured the castle of Jumièges. In May of the following year he performed a noteworthy exploit. In company with Mercadier, the leader of Richard's Braban-tine mercenaries, he appeared before Beauvais, defeated the Bishop of that city, his knights, and the citizen soldiers in battle. He made prisoners of the Bishop and the knights, and slew most of the com-mon people, as was the custom of the time. Bishops and knights would fetch a good ransom, but no one would bother to buy back a mere burgher.

Flushed with victory, John and his company went on to Milli, the castle of the Bishop of Beauvais, took it by assault, and demol-ished it. Then, "gloriously triumphing," they returned to Richard in Normandy and delivered over their prisoners to him.

John had succeeded in bagging big game, for Philip of Dreux, Bishop of Beauvais, a grandson of Louis VI, was one of the bravest warriors of his time. He had gone on the Crusade twice and had been captured by the Saracens at the siege of Acre. Richard hated him with particular violence, for he had served as one of Philip's emissaries to persuade the Emperor to keep Richard in captivity, and Richard considered him responsible for the prolonging of his confinement. Even though he was a famous warrior, the Bishop had such respect for the canon that made irregular those clerics who shed human blood in violence that he carried no sword. Instead, he armed himself with a heavy mace, with which he could club his enemies to death without shedding their blood.

Richard had him imprisoned in Rouen. The Bishop wrote to the Pope, telling him how, in obedience to the maxims: "It is lawful to repel force by force" and "Fight for your country," he had gone forth to protect his land against Richard, who was raging against Christ Our Lord like a wolf, had been captured, and was now being kept in chains and fetters. His Holiness must have heard of this, said the Bishop, and yet he had done nothing about it. Then he quoted another maxim: "He is not guiltless who, when he can correct a fault, pretends that he can do nothing about it; nor is he free from suspicion of secret connivance who forbears to prevent a manifest misdeed."

To this tactful letter the Pope made reply, beginning: "Celestine the Bishop, servant of the servants of God, to his dearly beloved brother, Philip, Bishop of Beauvais: health and a speedy return from his course of error," and telling him: "Into the pit you have made you have deservedly fallen: where you have been found, there you have been judged accordingly." Nevertheless the Pope promised to write a letter of entreaty, since in this matter he could not command, to the King of England on his behalf, and closed with a comforting quotation from Ovid: "*Leniter ex merito quicquid patiare, ferendum est.*"

When Richard received the Pope's letter on behalf of the Bishop, he sent Celestine the coat of mail, stained with the dust and blood of battle, in which Philip had been captured, with the message: "Holy Father, know now whether it is thy son's coat or not."

The Pope made answer: "He is no son of mine or of the Church; let him be released at the King's pleasure, for he is a soldier of Mars rather than of Christ."

Richard moved the Bishop to closer confinement in Chinon in 1198, and although Philip offered a thousand marks for his release, Richard kept him in captivity as long as the King lived.

Longchamp, like his bitter enemy, John, never succeeded in regaining his position in England, but in Normandy he continued to enjoy Richard's trust. His master employed him on a number of important missions, and at the close of 1196 he sent him to Rome to persuade the Pope to lift the interdict that Walter of Coutances, Archbishop of Rouen, had laid on the country in retaliation for Richard's appropriation of church lands on which to build his fortress of Château Gaillard. On the way to Rome Longchamp fell sick at Poitiers and died there on January 21, 1197. Few in England mourned for him.

Hugh of Nunant, Bishop of Coventry, John's closest advisor, died in Normandy on Good Friday, 1198. Although he had been neither a good man nor a good bishop, he died an edifying death. Knowing that his end was near, he summoned as many of the clergy of Normandy as could come to his bedside, and to them he made confession of all his sins. Chief among them, he declared, was his expelling the monks from the Cathedral at Coventry and installing secular canons in their stead. He begged the Abbot of Bec, who was standing by his bed, to invest him with a monk's habit, "so that he might have as protectors in the life to come those he had persecuted in this." Thus attired, he died "more happily than was expected," as Roger of Wendover remarks.

Meanwhile the indecisive series of battles, forays, counter-forays, and truces no sooner made than broken were dragging on between

Richard and Philip. Richard was exhausting his energy and his treasure without gaining any permanent advantage, and yet if he had relaxed in the struggle Philip would have pushed his frontiers farther into Richard's lands. Philip had not the courage and Richard had not the means for a decisive campaign that would have settled the conflict. Philip invaded Normandy in 1198 and burned Evreux and seven other towns; John in retaliation burned Neufbourg and captured eighteen knights.

Philip sent word to Richard early in 1199 that John had gone over to his side and offered to show Richard the document to that effect, signed by John. It was indicative both of the impetuousness of Richard's character and of the low esteem in which he held his brother that he should have believed this story and deprived John at once of his lands on both sides of the Channel without giving him a chance to answer the charge. When John learned the cause of his brother's anger he sent two knights to Philip's court to prove his innocence or to defend him in trial of battle, as Philip thought proper, but no one at the French court would accept this challenge. This convinced Richard that Philip's charge was false, and he received John back into his favor and restored his lands to him.

Richard heard, in March 1199, of a fabulous treasure-trove on the lands of his vassal Adomar, Viscount of Limoges. Adomar offered to share it with his liege lord, but Richard as lord of the demesne rightfully demanded all of the treasure. When Adomar refused, Richard laid siege to the castle of Châlus, in which he suspected that the gold was hidden. Whilst he and his captain-at-arms, Mercadier, were riding round the castle and looking for the best place at which to attack it, Richard was wounded at the base of the neck by an arrow. The wound became infected, and the bungling attempts of Mercadier's physician to extract the head of the arrow made matters worse. Richard knew that he was dying.

He designated John as his heir and had all those present swear fealty to him. The castle having been taken, Richard asked that the man who had wounded him be brought to him. The dying King forgave him and ordered that he be set free, but Mercadier flayed him alive after his master died. Richard received the Last Sacraments, confessing that through reverence for so great a mystery he had not received Holy Communion for the last seven years because his heart was full of mortal hatred for Philip.

Richard died on April 6, 1199. He ordered that his entrails be buried at Châlus to mark his contempt for the treacherous Poitevins; he bequeathed his heart to Rouen to show his gratitude for the incomparable fidelity of the people of that city, and he directed that his body be buried at Fontevrault, at the feet of his father, whom he confessed he had destroyed.

"With him, in the opinion of many," says Roger of Wendover, "were buried both the pride and the honor of the chivalry of the West."

CHAPTER VI

JOHN, KING OF ENGLAND

1199–1200

JOHN was in Brittany, visiting his nephew Arthur, when he received the news of Richard's death. His first concern, of course, was to make sure of his succession to the throne. The only other prospective heir was this same Arthur, now twelve years old, the son of John's brother Geoffrey. He had been recognized as Duke of Brittany by virtue of his mother's position as only heir of Conan the Little, Duke of Brittany. On Richard's death the nobles of Anjou, Maine, and Touraine, as well as those of Brittany, were disposed to receive him as the rightful heir. In England the principle of strictly hereditary succession by primogeniture did not yet obtain, and little effort seems to have been made there to advance the claims of Arthur to the crown that Richard had bequeathed to John.

The support of two of the most influential men of the kingdom no doubt played a large part in securing John's uncontested succession. Hubert Walter, Archbishop of Canterbury, and William Marshal, the close friend and trusted advisor of both Henry II and Richard, were at Vaudreuil when Richard died. The messenger sent to tell them of the King's death found William Marshal getting ready to go to bed. He dressed again and went to the priory of Notre Dame du Pré, where the Archbishop was staying.

"Ah, the King is dead!" the Archbishop cried, when William Marshal had told his news. "What hope have we now? With Richard dead, there is no one who can defend the realm. The French will overrun us, with no one able to resist them."

"We must make haste to elect his successor," said the Marshal, thus showing that even at this late date the ceremony of the election of the king was no mere empty formality. William evidently thought that he, the Archbishop, and the other leading men of the kingdom were the legitimate successors of the Witenagemot of earlier times.

"I think we ought to choose Arthur," the Archbishop said.

"My lord, that would be a bad choice," objected William. "Arthur has some bad counsellors, and he is haughty and full of pride. If we put him at our head, he will cause us many griefs, for he has no love for the English. But consider Earl John. In truth, he is the nearest heir to his father and his brother."

"Marshal, is that your wish?"

"Yes, my lord, for it is only right. The son is nearer to his father's land than the nephew."

"Marshal, it shall be as you desire, but I tell you that you will be sorrier for this than for anything you have ever done."

John immediately sent these two men to England on his behalf to join Geoffrey FitzPeter, Earl of Essex and Richard's Chief Justiciar. Their mission was to preserve the peace, govern the country, and look after John's interests till he himself could come to claim his crown.

While they set out for England, John went to work to make sure of his possessions. With a few followers he rode to Chinon on Wednesday, April 14, to secure Richard's treasury. The keeper,

Robert of Turnham, delivered it to him, together with the castles over which he had charge. John attached to himself the members of his brother's household, who received him as Richard's lawful successor. Before them he swore that he would faithfully execute his brother's will and would keep inviolate all the legitimate customs and laws of the peoples and lands over which he was to rule.

The great and saintly Hugh of Avalon, Bishop of Lincoln, who had been one of the most trusted counsellors of Henry II, went to Fontevrault for Richard's funeral on Palm Sunday, April 11, and remained there for the following three days to celebrate Masses for the repose of the souls of Richard and his father. Hugh was one of the most respected men in Europe, and John, in order to bolster up his own position by the presence of such a man, immediately sent messengers to the Bishop to beg Hugh to join him.

John went out to meet the Bishop, and at the sight of him he spurred his horse on, leaving his followers behind, and hurried to meet him. He greeted the Bishop effusively and begged him to remain with him and accompany him back to England. Hugh, however, had little liking for royal courts and still less for men of such character as John, and he excused himself from attending him back to England, agreeing only to remain with him for a few days.

They went to Fontevrault together, so that John might visit the tombs of his father and brother. When they arrived at the convent, attended by a crowd of nobles, John himself knocked at the door of the choir and begged admittance, so that he might see the tombs and commend himself to the prayers of the community. Two of the nuns answered his knock and told him that it was forbidden for anyone to enter the convent or the choir in the absence of the abbess, who was expected to return from her journey soon. When John insisted, one of the nuns advised him: "In this matter you would do well to imitate your father of noble memory, who most esteemed those religious who kept the rules of their order with rigid and inviolate devotion."

John turned to Bishop Hugh and asked him to use his influence to obtain the prayers of the nuns on his behalf, promising to give them rich gifts. "You know I hate all lies," the Bishop said; "take care not to make promises that you do not intend to keep."

John swore that he would indeed keep his promises, and the Bishop told the nuns of John's good intentions and commended him to their prayers. Hugh gave his blessing, and they left the church, John assuring him all the while of the good life he intended to lead. He showed him a treasure he valued highly, a stone set in gold and hung about his neck, which he said had been given to one of his ancestors with the promise from Heaven that any of his successors who wore it would never be deprived of the fullness of his ancestral dominions. Hugh rebuked him for this childish superstition.

When they reached the porch of the church, which was decorated with sculptures of the Last Judgment, Hugh called John's attention to the representation of kings wearing their regalia among the damned, waiting to hear the doom: "Go, ye accursed, into everlasting fire," and pointed out to him that it little profited a king to rule over many men if he ruled himself so poorly that he ended in eternal torment.

John, however, drew the Bishop over to the opposite wall, on which were portrayed kings wearing beautiful crowns and being led by angels into the joys of Heaven. "These, my lord bishop," he said, "you should rather have shown to us, for we intend to follow their example and attain to their fellowship."

For these last three days of Holy Week, records the biographer of St. Hugh, John made a great show of his reformed conduct. He was humble and submissive in deeds and in speech; when beggars ran up to him and wished him good fortune, he diligently thanked them, bowing and bending his head low; he humbly returned the salutations of ragged old women by the roadside.

In company with Bishop Hugh, he went to Beaufort in Anjou

to visit his widowed sister-in-law, Queen Berengaria. There he was joined by his mother. On Easter Sunday, April 18, 1199, Bishop Hugh celebrated Mass in the presence of John and the two Queens and the nobles of their households. Three days of exemplary behavior were more than John could endure; at Mass he lapsed into his old habits of irreverence. At the offertory he came up to the altar, as was customary, carrying twelve gold pieces that his chamberlain had given him. He stood before the Bishop, who was waiting for his offering, a long time, gazing at the coins and shaking them in his palm. He kept this up for so long that everyone stared at him in amazement.

"What are you looking at thus?" demanded the Bishop.

"Indeed, I am looking at these gold pieces," John replied, "and thinking to myself that if I had had them just a few days ago, I would not have offered them to you but would have put them in my purse instead; however, do you now accept them."

Hugh was so indignant at this irreverence that he withdrew his hand and would not touch the gold that John offered in such a grudging fashion, nor would he allow him to kiss his hand.

"Throw down what you are holding and withdraw," he ordered, and John cast the coins into the silver offertory dish and returned to his place.

Bishop Hugh then preached a long sermon aimed at John, in which he compared the habits of good and of bad princes and contrasted their future rewards. John was impatient for his dinner, which, after the habit of princes, he took early in the day, and three times he sent one of his attendants to demand that Hugh bring his sermon to an end and conclude the celebration of Mass, so that his audience might go to their meal. The only effect of these messages was to cause the preacher to raise his voice and increase his fervor. All the congregation applauded him, and many were moved to tears by his eloquence.

John did not receive Holy Communion on this feast day or at his crowning on Ascension Day; indeed, the biographer of St. Hugh states that those who knew John best said that he never once received Holy Communion after he reached years of discretion. That a man should go through life at that time without ever frequenting the Sacraments seems almost incredible, unless one reflects on the completely irreligious character of John's life. He was baptized, and that seems to have been his most active participation in the Christian life.

Bishop Hugh left on the day after Easter, and John turned his attention to the city of Le Mans, which had been occupied by Constance and Arthur and their adherents. The nobles of Anjou, Maine, and Touraine were not disposed to accept John as their lord. They argued that Arthur, as the only son and heir of John's older brother Geoffrey, was the legitimate heir and was entitled to all that his father would have received had he been living. In England, on the other hand, William Marshal's contention that John, as a son of Henry II and a brother of Richard, had a better claim than Arthur, the grandson of one king and a nephew of the other, seems to have been generally accepted.

The nobles of these three counties met together, declared that Arthur was their lord, and delivered up the provinces to him. Constance, Arthur's mother, brought the lad to Tours and entrusted him to King Philip. If Arthur were indeed lord of Anjou, Maine, and Touraine, then Philip as King of France was his feudal overlord and had the right to his wardship. Philip had captured Evreux as soon as he learned of Richard's death, and of course he greatly preferred that Richard's continental possessions should pass into the hands of Arthur, a young boy whom he might bend to his own will, rather than into the hands of John, with whose fickleness and treachery he was well acquainted. Philip at once sent Arthur to Paris to his son Louis, as a treasure to be closely guarded, and he took possession of all the cities, castles, and fortresses that had declared for Arthur and placed over them governors of his own appointing.

John and his mother, now in her late seventies, captured Le Mans, the chief city of Maine. To punish the citizens for having accepted Arthur, John leveled the walls of the city and demolished the castle and all the houses built of stone.

He left Eleanor and Mercardier, who had served as the leader of Richard's mercenaries, to ravage Anjou and bring it to submission to him, while he proceeded to Rouen. Arthur had no adherents in Normandy, and there John was received without question as Richard's heir. On Low Sunday, April 25, he was girded with the sword of the duchy of Normandy before the high altar of the Cathedral of Rouen by the Archbishop, Walter of Coutances, who placed on John's head the golden circlet, surmounted by rosettes of gold. The new Duke swore, according to Roger of Hoveden, "in the presence of the clergy and the people, upon the Holy Gospels and the relics of the Saints, that he would preserve Holy Church and her dignitaries inviolate, with good faith and without evil intent, and would exercise strict justice and destroy unjust laws and establish good ones."

The solemnity of the occasion was marred by John's irreverent behavior. He was accompanied by a crowd of thoughtless companions, who applauded, laughed, and chattered throughout the ceremony. When the Archbishop gave him the lance bearing the banner of the Dukes of Normandy, John turned to exchange a joke with his friends and let the lance fall to the ground. This was taken as a presage that as John could not hold the lance neither could he hold the duchy.

John's position on the Continent had now improved greatly. He was undisputed Duke of Normandy; Aquitaine was under the firm hand of its old Duchess, Eleanor; the capture of Le Mans had checked Arthur's party in Maine, and the vigorous exertions of

Eleanor and Mercadier were restoring order in Anjou. John felt that now he could safely go to England.

In the meantime, his envoys had found the majority of the English nobles ready to swear fealty to him without hesitation. Nevertheless, those who had castles were busy stocking them with men and provisions, in anticipation of any civil disturbances that might arise, and an influential party did not at first seem disposed to accept John. This group was headed by David, Earl of Huntingdon; Richard, Earl of Clare; Ranulf de Blundevill, Earl of Chester, who had married Constance of Brittany after Geoffrey's death and hence was Arthur's stepfather; William de Ferrers, Earl of Derby; Waleran, Earl of Warwick; Roger de Lacy, Constable of Chester, and William Mowbray.

Their reluctance could hardly have been due to private grievances, and there is little indication that they thought Arthur the rightful heir, although his stepfather was one of the group. It is more likely that they wanted to seize this occasion, when John needed their support, to exact from him a pledge that he would respect the customary rights of the barons. Henry II throughout his reign attempted to curb the power of his nobles and to substitute a strong central government for the unorganized local liberty of the feudal system. The barons were still smarting from his vigorous curtailment of their irresponsible behavior and from the crushing taxes Richard had levied, and on the occasion of John's accession they grasped the opportunity of demanding an assurance that their liberties and privileges would not be further diminished.

John's three representatives summoned these nobles and others whose fidelity they doubted to a meeting at Northampton, and there they pledged their word to the barons that John would give each of them his lawful rights if they would pledge their allegiance to him and swear to keep the peace.

John crossed over from Normandy and landed at Shoreham on

May 25, 1199. He came up to London on the following day, and on May 27, the Feast of the Ascension, he was anointed and crowned in Westminster Abbey by Hubert Walter. The Abbey was decorated for the occasion with two thousand yards of linen cloth, at a cost of £21 0s. 6d. John took the customary triple oath "to love Holy Church and her ordained priests and to preserve her safe from the attacks of evil designers; to do away with bad laws and substitute good ones in their stead; and to see justice rightly administered throughout England." Not satisfied with this oath, Hubert Walter cautioned him not to accept the crown unless he intended fully to keep the oath he had sworn, and John replied that with God's help he would keep the oath in all good faith.

Matthew Paris, writing in the next reign at least thirty-seven years after the event, says that Hubert Walter made the following address:

"Hear, all of you, and be it known that no one has an antecedent right to succeed another in the kingship, unless he shall have been unanimously elected, under the guidance of the Holy Spirit, on account of the superior merit of his character, after the example of Saul, the first anointed king, whom the Lord set over His people, but not because he was the son of a king or born of royal ancestry. In the same way, after Saul came David, the son of Jesse. Saul was chosen because he was a brave man and suited for the royal dignity; David, because he was holy and humble. Thus those who excel in virtue are elevated to the kingly dignity. But if any relation of a deceased king should excel the others in merit, everyone should all the more readily and zealously consent to his election. We have said this to uphold the cause of Earl John, who is here present, the brother of our illustrious King Richard, lately deceased without heirs of his body; and as the said Earl John is prudent, active, and indubitably noble, we have, under God's Holy Spirit, unanimously elected him because of his merits and his royal blood."

Whether or not such a speech was indeed made, it seems probable that some sort of election by acclamation did take place, in compliance with the old English custom of electing the king from among the members of the royal house. This was the last time that the crowning of an English king was preceded by such a ceremony of election. In any case, whether John was elected or not, the presence and participation of the principal bishops and nobles of the realm attested to the fact that they received him without question as the lawful heir. Of those whom Hubert Walter had conciliated at Northampton, the Earls of Clare, Derby, Warwick, and Chester were present, and Waleran, Earl of Warwick, bore the right-hand Sword of State in the coronation procession. In addition to three archbishops, fourteen bishops, and the aforementioned earls, the Earls of Leicester, Warenne, Salisbury, Striguil, Norfolk, and Arundel, as well as many barons, participated in the ceremony. The Bishop of Durham, Philip of Pictavia, who had succeeded Hugh Pudsey, protested that John's crowning should not take place in the absence of his brother Geoffrey, Archbishop of York, who had gone to Rome, but John would not delay the ceremony till his return.

The crowning was followed by the customary feast. Some idea of the scale of the banquet can be gathered from the fact that twenty-one fat oxen had been bought in Worcester for £6 10s. 6d. and sent to Westminster for the feast. At this time, John girded William Marshal with the sword of the Earldom of Pembroke and Striguil and Geoffrey FitzPeter with that of Essex.

William Marshal enjoyed a reputation for courage, military prowess, knightly virtue, and chivalric honor exceeded in his day only by that of his master Richard. He had covered himself with glory in the Holy Land after the death of the young Henry, whose faithful companion and tutor he had been. He was a man of unswerving fidelity and loyalty, and he had been among the most trusted servants and friends of both Henry II and Richard. He was the son of John Marshal, a distinguished soldier, and his wife Sibyl, the sister of

Earl Patrick of Salisbury. William was a poor and landless knight till his marriage in 1189 to Isabella de Clare, *"la bone, la bele, la sage, la corteise de halt parage"*—"the good, the beautiful, the wise, the courteous dame of high degree." She was the only child and heiress of Richard de Clare, the famous "Strongbow" of Ireland, second Earl of Pembroke and Striguil, and of his wife Eva, the daughter of Dermot MacMurrough. She brought him vast estates in Ireland and Wales, and in her right William assumed the title of Earl of Pembroke and Striguil.

Geoffrey FitzPeter's claim to the Earldom of Essex also derived from his wife, Beatrice de Say. Richard had appointed him Chief Justiciar when Hubert Walter resigned that office on July 11, 1198. Geoffrey was forced to carry out many oppressive measures in order to raise the money that Richard was pouring into his campaigns in France, and his popularity among his fellow barons naturally suffered. He was, however, a loyal servant of the King, and John continued him in his office.

In both these cases John merely confirmed formally the two Earls in the possession of the lands and titles they had been enjoying for the past ten years. Girded with the swords of their earldoms, they waited on the King during the feast.

On this day John appointed as his chancellor Hubert Walter, Archbishop of Canterbury. Hubert, an East Anglian by birth, had served as chaplain or clerk to his uncle, Ranulf de Glanville, Chief Justiciar under Henry II and one of the men chiefly responsible for carrying through the great legal and administrative reforms of Henry's reign. Hubert was made Dean of York in 1186, and when Richard came to the throne he appointed him Bishop of Salisbury. He went to the Holy Land with Richard and acted as a sort of Chaplain in Chief to the English crusaders. He won the respect of the whole army by his zeal, by his practical spirituality, and by his untiring efforts in behalf of the common soldiers. He was made Archbishop of

Canterbury shortly after his return to England in 1193, and Richard made him his Chief Justiciar towards the end of that year. When
Innocent III succeeded to the Papacy in 1198, he renewed the old
decrees forbidding the clergy to hold secular offices, and he ordered
Richard not to allow Hubert to continue in his position as Chief
Justiciar and in the future not to admit him or any other priest or
bishop to a secular office. Hubert thereupon resigned his office,
which was given to Geoffrey FitzPeter.

When John offered him the office of chancellor, Hubert accepted
it, contrary to canon law, the express orders of the Pope, and all
precedents. One of his associates, Hugh Bardolph, a Baron of the Exchequer and a Justiciar of the Curia Regis, warned him: "My lord, if
you really were to consider well the power of your name and the dignity of your position, you would not impose on yourself the yoke of
slavery. We have never seen or heard of a chancellor being made
out of an archbishop, but we have seen an archbishop made out of a
chancellor."

Immediately after his crowning, John visited the shrines of St. Al-
ban in Hertfordshire, St. Edmund at the great abbey in Suffolk, and
St. Thomas at Canterbury. Although at Bury St. Edmunds John and
his retinue were entertained at vast expense with the magnificence be-
fitting the greatest abbey in England, Jocelyn of Brakelond noted
that the King's only gift to the holy Martyr's shrine was a silken cloth
that some of his servants had borrowed from the Sacristan and that,
says Jocelyn sourly, he has not paid for yet, and at the Mass celebrated in the King's presence his offering was thirteen pennies.

No one in England was now disposed to dispute John's title to
the crown, but trouble was threatening in Scotland. As soon as William the Lion, King of the Scots, heard of Richard's death, he sent
envoys to England to demand the counties of Northumberland and
Cumberland. The three men whom John had placed in charge of the

government would not allow the envoys to continue their journey and cross over to the Continent to lay these claims before John in person. Instead they sent David, Earl of Huntingdon, to Scotland to tell his brother the King to wait till John came to England before he took any action. John, when he heard of William's demands, sent word to him that if he would keep the peace till John arrived in England he would satisfy all his demands.

After John was crowned, William's envoys came to him and renewed their master's claims. John said to them: "When your lord, the King of the Scots, my much-loved brother, comes to me, I will do for him what is just, in relation both to this and to his other demands."

He sent the Bishop of Durham to Scotland to escort William into England and went to Northampton on June 5 to wait for him. William, however, chose not to come but sent a message by the Bishop of St. Andrews that if John did not grant his demands he would get possession of the disputed territories by force. He appointed a truce of forty days in which John was to answer, and he set to work assembling an army. John placed the two disputed counties under the charge of William de Stuteville, who had previously shown his loyalty to him at the siege of Tickhill in March 1193. All of William's threats and preparations came to nothing, for he dismissed his army after having, it is said, been warned of impending disaster by a vision at the shrine of St. Margaret at Dumferline.

Since no trouble now threatened in England, John crossed over to Normandy, leaving Hubert Walter as Chancellor and Geoffrey Fitz-Peter as Chief Justiciar. He landed at Dieppe on June 20, 1199 and proceeded to Rouen. There a great number of soldiers, both horse and foot, came flocking to him to offer their services against the French. Philip met him at Rouen on June 24 and had an opportunity to observe the feelings of the Normans. This led him to propose a truce till the day after the Feast of the Assumption, August 15.

On this same day Geoffrey, Archbishop of York, arrived in Rouen from Rome and was honorably and affectionately received by his brother.

Just before the expiration of the truce with Philip, the Count of Flanders came and did homage to John. The adherence of this powerful nobleman strengthened John's hand considerably, as did the news that his nephew Otto, the son of his eldest sister Matilda and Henry the Lion, Duke of Saxony, had been recognized as rightful Emperor by the Pope. Otto sent him word to delay making peace with Philip till he could send his uncle all the help possible.

In the meantime, some knights of Philip's household had captured the Bishop-elect of Cambrai, an adherent of the Count of Flanders, and had turned him over to Philip. Philip put him in prison. Cardinal Peter of Capua, the Papal Legate in France, put that country under an interdict in order to force Philip to release the Bishop. At the same time, in a fine show of impartiality, he declared Normandy under interdict because Philip of Dreux, Bishop of Beauvais, had been kept in confinement ever since his capture in 1197. Philip released his captive, and John his, but not until the Bishop of Beauvais had paid him two thousand marks for his board and lodging while he was in prison. When he was released, Philip of Dreux swore, in the presence of the Cardinal Legate and other ecclesiastics, that he would never again, as long as he lived, bear arms against another Christian.

In order to strengthen his position at the forthcoming conference with John that was to mark the end of the truce, Philip knighted the young Arthur and received his homage not only for Brittany but for Anjou, Maine, Poitou, Touraine, and Normandy as well. On the 16th and 17th of August the envoys of both Kings held a conference at a place between Boutavant and Le Goulet but could come to no agreement. On the third day the two Kings conferred in person. Philip demanded the Norman Vexin, on the grounds that John's grandfather, Geoffrey of Anjou, had given it to Philip's grandfather,

Louis the Fat, in return for Louis's assistance in gaining Normandy from King Stephen. For Arthur he demanded Poitou, Anjou, Maine, and Touraine.

John would agree to none of these terms, and the two Kings parted without having arrived at any settlement. A member of Philip's court asked him afterwards why he so bitterly hated John, who had after all done him no injury and who had been his friend and ally in the past. Philip's answer revealed a feeling of wounded dignity, for he replied that before taking possession of his territories John should have come to him and asked his permission and then done homage for them. Technically, Philip was right, for he was the feudal over-lord of those territories. John, however, knew that the tie binding them to the French crown was a purely formal one, and he had no intention of conceding that the King of France had any voice in de-termining the disposition of the territories that had belonged to Henry and to Richard.

When it became known that there was to be no peace between John and Philip, the French nobles who had adhered to Richard came to his successor and did homage to him. They swore that they would not make peace with Philip without John's knowledge and consent, and John in turn swore not to make any treaties with Philip in which they were not included.

Philip began his campaign with some measure of success. In Sep-tember he took the castle of Conches, near Evreux, and in the fol-lowing month he took Balun. This castle he leveled to the ground. William des Roches, the leader of Arthur's Breton army, protested against this destruction of a fortress over which Arthur, by Philip's own recognition, had jurisdiction, but Philip answered sharply that he would do just as he pleased with any territory that he took from John, whether Arthur liked it or not. This incident opened Wil-liam's eyes to the fact that his young master was a mere puppet in Philip's hands, to give a pretense of legality to his efforts to take

John's territories, and aroused his suspicion that the French King intended to hold as his own all the land he so gained.

Philip next laid siege to Lavardin, on the left bank of the Loire,
near Vendome, but for the first time John scored a success against
him. He and his army surprised Philip at the siege and forced him to
withdraw to Le Mans. John then gave close pursuit and drove him
out of Maine. Philip had entrusted both the city of Le Mans and
the person of Arthur to William des Roches. William now came to
John and arranged a peace between him and Arthur, as a result of
which John took possession of Le Mans and received Arthur and his
mother, Constance, who had lately deserted her second husband,
Ranulf de Blundevill, Earl of Chester, and married Guy of Thouars.

When John entered Le Mans, the Viscount of Thouars, the
brother of Constance's new husband, at John's summons came to him
and surrendered the castle of Chinon and the seneschalship of Anjou.
John distrusted the Viscount, and rightly. On the day of the Viscount's arrival at Le Mans, someone warned Arthur that his uncle,
with whom he had just made peace, intended to keep him in prison
for the rest of his life. That night Arthur, Constance, and the Viscount fled to Angers, which was then in Arthur's possession.

At this point another truce was agreed upon with Philip, and John
spent his Christmas peacefully at Bures in Normandy.

In addition to these spirited doings of great people, the year 1199
was notable in England for the heavy rains and floods, which washed
away bridges and houses. The bridge at Berwick was carried away by
the floodwaters of the Tweed.

The publication of an ordinance regulating the price of wine was
another notable event of the year. John loved wine. When he went
from London to Northampton at the Whitsuntide after his crowning,
fifteen carts were required to haul the wine for the use of the King
and his household. He now took practical steps to make wine available to his richer subjects at a price they could afford to pay. He fixed

the maximum price of red wine at fourpence the gallon and of white wine at sixpence, and he ordered that in every town in which wine was sold twelve inspectors should be appointed to see that the regulations as to price and measure were observed. If anyone was found violating the law, all his goods were to be seized, and he was to be kept in prison till the King sent further orders.

This statute went into effect in December 1199, and the merchants immediately complained that it was ruining them. The price was then raised to sixpence a gallon for red wine and eightpence for white. Even this rate must have been a considerable reduction from the one formerly obtaining, for Roger of Hoveden complains that immediately after it went into effect "the land was filled with drink and with drunkards."

John and Philip met near Les Andelys about the middle of January 1200 for another conference, at which they agreed on terms for a lasting peace. As the cornerstone, the two Kings arranged for a marriage between Philip's only son, Louis, then thirteen years old, and John's niece Blanche, who was of about the same age and the daughter of his sister Eleanor and Alfonso IX of Castile. As dowry John agreed to give her the city and county of Evreux, all the Norman castles that Philip had in his possession on the day of Richard's death, and the sum of thirty thousand marks. In addition, John took an oath that he would not help his nephew Otto with either money or men in his struggle with the Duke of Swabia, the other contestant for the Imperial crown. They planned another meeting in the summer, by which time all the provisions of the treaty were to be carried out.

John entrusted the important mission of obtaining Blanche's hand for Louis and of bringing her to France to his mother. That doughty woman set out, in mid-winter, for the court of Castile, to visit her daughter Eleanor and to bring her granddaughter back with her.

Philip was in the midst of difficulties with the Church, which made him the more willing to come to terms with John. After the death of his first wife, Isabella, the mother of his son Louis, Philip had married Ingeborg, the daughter of the King of Denmark, on August 14, 1193, partly with the hope of thus reviving the old Danish claims to the throne of England. As soon as they were married, Philip conceived an unconquerable aversion, so he said, to his new wife. Three months later he persuaded some of his more pliable bishops to pronounce the marriage void, on the grounds of consanguinity. Ingeborg appealed to the Pope, and in 1196 he nullified the decision of the bishops and forbade Philip to take another wife. Nevertheless, Philip, in June 1196, went through the form of marriage with Agnes, the daughter of Bertold IV, Duke of Meran. In 1199 Pope Innocent III ordered him to put away Agnes and take back Ingeborg, his lawful wife. Philip refused, and Innocent laid the kingdom of France under interdict on January 15, 1200. At first Philip put up a stout resistance. He expelled the bishops and priests who observed the interdict and confiscated their goods, and he laid heavy fines on the laymen who obeyed the papal order.

While Philip was thus engaged, John, accompanied by Geoffrey, Archbishop of York, came over to England to raise the thirty thousand marks for Blanche's dowry. He sailed from Barfleur and landed at Portsmouth on February 27. Immediately he took up the question of raising money. The ordinary unit for purposes of taxation was a measure of land variously called a ploughland, a hide, or a carucate and embracing roughly 120 acres of arable land. John levied a tax of three shillings on each ploughland and apparently encountered little difficulty in raising the sum, except in the archdiocese of York, where Geoffrey would not permit the King's officers to collect the tax from his lands.

John went to York during Lent to meet William of Scotland, whom he had summoned to come to pay him homage, but William again did not come. John spent Easter in Worcester and returned to Normandy towards the end of April.

Queen Eleanor, in the meantime, had been successful in her mission in Castile. She and Blanche arrived in Bordeaux in time for the Easter festival. Eleanor, being understandably "fatigued with old age and the labor of the length of the journey," in the words of Roger of Hoveden, went to the convent at Fontevrault, where her husband and her son Richard were buried. She entrusted Blanche to the care of the Archbishop of Bordeaux, and he escorted her to Normandy and delivered her to John.

John and Philip concluded the treaty of Le Goulet on June 21, 1200. John bestowed the city and county of Evreux on Louis, together with the other territories previously agreed on, as a marriage portion for Blanche. On the following day the young couple were married by the Archbishop of Bordeaux, in the presence of the French court. John had intended that the ceremony should be performed by his brother Geoffrey, but the Archbishop of York refused to come when John summoned him. Blanche was already distinguished by the beauty that made her one of the most attractive figures of her age. At a time when few royal marriages turned out happily, on this day Blanche and Louis began a married life that lasted for twenty-six years without their ever being parted for as much as a day.

On the day of the marriage John and Philip held another conference, this time at Vernon, in Philip's territory. Philip recognized John's title to his continental territories, including Brittany, and Arthur, on Philip's advice, did homage to his uncle for Brittany. Arthur remained, however, in Philip's charge.

John might well congratulate himself on having concluded the treaty of Le Goulet, arranged the marriage of his niece with Philip's son, and gained an undisputed title to all the territories of his predecessor. In a little more than a year he had won more from Philip than his brother had in the ten years of his reign, and prospects may have seemed fair to him for a lasting peace with France. Even a superficial knowledge of the character of Philip, however, would indicate that he would observe the treaty only as long as it suited his convenience to do so. Philip's boundless ambition, his faithlessness and duplicity, and his unceasing efforts to strengthen in every way possible the power of the French throne were assurances enough that there could be no lasting peace between France and England so long as the English king had jurisdiction over any of the lands belonging, if only nominally, to the French crown. Although a situation in which the King of England, as Duke of Normandy, Duke of Aquitaine, and Count of Anjou and of Maine, owed feudal homage and service to the King of France as his overlord was a logical development of the feudal system, the practical consequences of the situation involved many contradictions. Only a weak overlord, such as Philip's immediate predecessors had been, who refrained from exacting his full dues, would tolerate a vassal who was stronger than his lord, and, on the other hand, the King of England, one of the most powerful monarchs of Europe, could not well brook being a vassal of a lord less powerful than he himself.

Even strong and capable kings like Henry II and Richard found that it took unceasing efforts and the expenditure of the greater part of their time and treasure merely to keep their continental possessions from open revolt and Philip of France at bay. As Philip consolidated his position and grew in strength, such a task became increasingly difficult. Although John no doubt hastened the process, no English king in these circumstances could long have retained Normandy, the territory for which Philip struggled the most persistently.

THE LOSS OF NORMANDY

~ 1200-1205 ~

IMMEDIATELY after the conference at Vernon, John set out on a progress through his continental territories. He took a large army with him into Aquitaine, a territory he had not visited since his accession to the throne, but the nobles there offered no resistance to his claims, thanks to the energetic measures of their old Duchess, his mother. For once, all of John's territories were at peace.

Such a state did not last long. John himself took the first steps toward stirring up trouble by alienating the loyalties of many of his continental vassals and of a powerful party of his English nobles. He had been married to Hadwisa of Gloucester for over ten years and had had no children by her. The Archbishop of Canterbury had forbidden the marriage and laid John's lands under interdict when his prohibition had been disregarded. The Papal Legate, however, had lifted the interdict pending an appeal to Rome. This appeal had been decided in John's favor, and a dispensation was granted.

During the summer of 1200 John submitted the question of the validity of his marriage to the Archbishop of Bordeaux and the Bishops of Poitiers and Saintes. That John had any scruples about his marriage is hard to believe; it is more probable that he had grown tired of Hadwisa and had given up hope of having any children by her. It is significant that he did not ask the Pope for a decision but instead referred the matter to bishops of his own lands. These prelates obligingly pronounced the marriage invalid on the grounds of consanguinity, in spite of the dispensation granted by the Pope, if indeed they knew that such a dispensation had ever been granted.

John parted from Hadwisa but kept her dowry. He used part of it to satisfy the claims of his vassal Aumary de Montfort, Count of Evreux, the son of Hadwisa's older sister Mabel. The county of Evreux had been ceded to Louis as part of Blanche's dowry, and John made restitution to Aumary by giving him, in place of Evreux, the county of Gloucester, which Hadwisa had inherited from her father. Hadwisa is heard of no more till in 1214 she married Geoffrey de Mandeville, the son of John's Chief Justiciar, Geoffrey FitzPeter.

John immediately cast about for another wife and sent an imposing group of ambassadors, both English and Norman, to Sancho I, King of Portugal, to ask for the hand of his daughter, whose reputation for beauty had interested John. While the embassy was on its mission, John's fancy was suddenly taken by Isabella, the twelve-year-old daughter of Aymar, Count of Angoulême, and he immediately married her. Roger of Hoveden says that he did this on the advice of Philip. The French King could not well be considered a competent advisor in such matters, for his own matrimonial difficulties had caused his lands to be under interdict at this very time.

In any case, in view of the trouble this affair stirred up, John could hardly have chosen worse. His repudiation of Hadwisa offended many of his English barons; his marriage with Isabella was equally offensive to many of the French nobles. On the advice of King Richard, Isabella had been solemnly betrothed to Hugh of Lusignan, Count of La Marche and a member of the most powerful family of Poitou. Because of her youth, she was living with the family of the Count of La Marche till she should reach marriageable age, when the contract with Hugh would be completed. When her father learned that John had conceived a passion for her, he gained possession of her by trickery and gave her in marriage to the King, who was twenty-one years her senior. They were married by the Archbishop of Bordeaux at Angoulême on August 26, 1200. The Lusignan family were of course highly offended by this violation of contract and became John's implacable enemies.

After his marriage John went to Anjou and took a hundred and fifty hostages from among the members of the leading families. These hostages he caused to be kept under guard as pledges for the good behavior of the Angevin nobility.

In the meantime, Philip's difficulties with the Holy See were increasing. The interdict under which his kingdom had been laid suspended all public religious services, and the dead had to be buried along the lanes, in unconsecrated ground. In spite of the pleading of numerous emissaries sent to him by Philip, Innocent III refused to lift the interdict unless Philip submitted to the Church and put away Agnes of Meran. At last, on September 7, 1200, Philip made his submission. In the presence of the Papal Legate and the archbishops and bishops of France, he publicly repudiated Agnes and took back Ingeborg. The Legate then lifted the interdict, the bells rang again after their long silence, and there was general rejoicing among the people.

Although Philip thus effected a formal reconciliation with the Church, his matrimonial difficulties were by no means ended. Agnes was pregnant at this time. She retired to the Chateau of Poissy and died there in giving birth, early in 1201, to a child who survived her by only a few days. Philip meanwhile applied again for an annulment of his marriage to Ingeborg. When it was denied, he had her put in ignominious confinement, without the companionship of a single friendly person, with little opportunity to practice her religion, with scraps for food, and without even the common decencies of life. Thus she remained for the next thirteen years. Philip, needless to say, did not lack for feminine companionship during this period.

Ever since Geoffrey of York had returned to England with John in February 1200, his troubles and difficulties with his brother had been increasing. He had purchased the office of Sheriff of York from Richard for three thousand marks but had not yet paid the money. John pressed him for it, apparently during the time when he was raising the money promised to Philip at the conference at Les Andelys, but Geoffrey either could not or would not pay the sum.

John accordingly deprived him of his office as Sheriff and gave it to Geoffrey FitzPeter, who appointed James of Poterne his deputy. James seems to have entered upon his new duties with more force than tact, for he immediately evicted Geoffrey's servants by violence and laid waste his property. Geoffrey, with bells ringing and candles burning, excommunicated James and his followers. He also excommunicated the townspeople of Beverley because they had broken into his park and damaged his property, and he suspended the town from the celebration of divine services and from the ringing of the church bells. While he was at it, he excommunicated all those who had stirred up or who wished unjustly to stir up the King's anger against him.

As a result of Geoffrey's failure to pay the three thousand marks he owed the King, of his refusal to allow the King's officers to collect in the Archdiocese of York the tax of three shilling on each ploughland that had been levied in the spring, of his having refused to cross over to Normandy to officiate at the wedding of Blanche and Louis, and of his having excommunicated the King's officer, the Undersheriff of York, John in the summer of 1200 ordered him to be deprived of all his manors and estates.

John and his young bride crossed over to England and landed at Dover on October 8, 1200. They proceeded to London and were crowned in Westminster Abbey by Hubert Walter, in the presence of the nobles of England. On this occasion, the King's singers, Eustace and Ambrose, sang the *Laudes Regiae* and were paid twenty-five shillings. The *Laudes* were sung only before the King on the most solemn occasions. After the antiphon, *Christus vincit, Christus regnat, Christus imperat,* and a prayer for the Pope, the singers continued antiphonally:

Regi Anglorum a Deo coronato:	*Salus et victoria.*
Redemptor mundi:	*Tu illum adjuva.*
Sancte Ædmunde:	*Tu illum adjuva.*
Sancte Ermingilde:	*Tu illum adjuva.*
Sancte Oswalde:	*Tu illum adjuva.*
Christus vincit, Christus regnat, Christus imperat:	
	Exaudi Christe!
Reginae Anglorum:	*Salus et vita!*
Redemptor mundi:	*Tu illam adjuva.*
Sancta Maria:	*Tu illam adjuva.*
Sancta Felicitas:	*Tu illam adjuva.*
Sancta Ætheldrida:	*Tu illam adjuva.*
Christus vincit, Christus regnat, Christus imperat:	
	Exaudi Christe!

There followed prayers for the clergy, nobility, and army of England and a set of variations on the theme *Christus vincit, Christus regnat, Christus imperat.*

Geoffrey of York attended the ceremony, and it was probably at this time that he effected a reconciliation with his brother. John restored his lands and appointed a day for him to appear in the King's Court and answer the charges against him.

Soon after this, John sent an imposing delegation to William the Lion. The Bishop of Durham; the Earl of Norfolk; William's nephew, the Earl of Hereford, and his brother David, Earl of Huntingdon; Roger de Lacy, Constable of Chester; Eustace de Vesci and Robert de Ros, who had married William's bastard daughters Margaret and Isabella, and the Sheriff of Northumberland presented to William letters from John giving him safe conduct and asking him to meet the King at Lincoln in order to perform the homage he had so long delayed.

Hugh of Avalon, Bishop of Lincoln, was at this time on his deathbed in London. John came to pay his respects to this great ecclesiastic, who had been one of the principal advisors of his father and whose reputation for great piety, profound moral courage, exemplary purity of life, and heroic sanctity had spread over all of England and France.

During the preceding summer Bishop Hugh had revisited the Grande Chartreuse, where he had served as a monk in his youth, before Henry II had called him to England. On his way back to England he fell sick of a quartan ague and was with difficulty brought to London, to the Old Temple, the residence of the Bishops of Lincoln. He lay ill there for several months. John visited him, confirmed his will, and promised that in the future he would ratify the reasonable wills of all prelates instead of confiscating all their personal property, as had been the royal custom.

From London John went to Lincoln to meet William the Lion. On November 22, 1200, in the presence of the bishops and barons of England, on a lofty hill outside the city in the sight of all the people, William did homage to John and swore fealty to him "for life, for limb, for earthly honor, against all men." He then renewed his demand for Northumberland, Cumberland, and Westmorland, which he asserted were a part of his patrimony. The two Kings could come to no agreement concerning these counties, whereupon John asked for a truce till the following Whitsuntide to deliberate on the matter.

Bishop Hugh, meanwhile, had died on November 17. On the 20th the citizens of London began their procession to Lincoln with the Bishop's body. The journey occupied four days, and Roger of Wendover records that although the procession was made through winter winds and rains, they were never without the light of at least one candle. When the procession arrived at the outskirts of Lincoln, the two Kings, the Archbishops of Canterbury and York, thirteen bishops, and all the earls and barons went out to meet it. John helped carry the bier on his shoulders to the door of the Cathedral.

Lincoln Cathedral, except for the West Front, had been almost wholly destroyed by the great earthquake of 1185, and Hugh had begun the rebuilding. The Choir known now by his name was his work, and he had helped carry stones and mortar on his own shoulders to build it. His body lay in the Choir through the night of November 23, whilst the Office of the Dead was chanted. A Requiem Mass was celebrated on the following morning in the presence of the two Kings, the Archbishops and bishops, and many of the nobility of England, and Hugh was buried in the Chapel of St. John the Baptist, in the northeastern transept. Miracles of healing were reported immediately, and he was canonized twenty years later. When work on the great Angel Choir, to the east of St. Hugh's Choir, was sufficiently advanced, the body was moved to a shrine there in 1280.

While John was at Lincoln, twelve Cistercian abbots came to him and complained that his foresters were destroying their cattle and driving them out of the royal pastures and forests and that they and the poor for whom they were responsible were being ruined. John fell at their feet and begged forgiveness. He promised them his protection, confirmed their right to graze their cattle in the royal forests, and vowed to build for them an abbey "for the good of my soul and the souls of my parents, and for the security of my kingdom." He kept this promise by building the abbey at Beaulieu in Hampshire, probably in 1204. He gave it a rich endowment of land in the New Forest, a hundred and twenty cows and twelve bulls, a golden chalice, and a yearly tun of 250 gallons of wine. Thirty monks from Citeaux moved into the new abbey.

John spent the Christmas of 1200 at Guildford in Surrey. He distributed a number of rich garments among his knights at the Christmas feast. Hubert Walter, not to be outdone, did the same thing at Canterbury. John, thinking that his chancellor was trying to put himself on the same level as the King, was greatly annoyed by this.

John returned in January to Lincoln, where the question of Bishop Hugh's successor was being discussed. John wanted the chapter to elect Roger, the brother of Robert FitzParnell, Earl of Leicester, who was then Bishop of St. Andrew's and the chancellor of William the Lion, but the canons insisted on their right to elect their bishop freely, without dictation from the King. Since neither side would give in to the other they could arrive at no agreement, and the see remained vacant.

John went next to Cottingham, where he was entertained by William de Stuteville, into whose charge he had given Northumberland and Cumberland shortly after his crowning. He had also given him leave to build a castle at Cottingham, and it was probably there that the King was entertained.

On the next day he went to Beverley. The canons wanted to receive him with a procession and the ringing of bells, but the Archbishop would not allow this, for he had excommunicated the townspeople of Beverley and specifically had forbidden the ringing of bells. A certain John le Gros, who also had been excommunicated by Geoffrey, offered John a sum of money to induce the King to visit him, and this John did. Geoffrey had a manor at Beverley, and John tried to take from it some of Geoffrey's wine. Henry des Chapelles, the Archbishop's servant, would not allow the King to have any of the wine, and John had him thrown into prison. He also ordered that all of Geoffrey's servants should be arrested, wherever they might be found.

The King and Queen were at Scarborough on Candlemas Day, February 2, 1201. John and his court then made a progress through the North, as far as the Scottish border, and wherever he went he laid heavy fines on the people, on the grounds that they had laid waste the royal forests. John and Isabella visited York at mid-Lent, and there Geoffrey arrived at an understanding with his brother. In return for the sum of a thousand marks, which Geoffrey undertook to pay within a year, John restored his manors to him, released his servants from prison, and gave him a charter confirming the liberties of the Church of York as they had been in the days of Geoffrey's predecessor. Geoffrey, on his side, absolved William de Stuteville and James of Poterne from the sentence of excommunication he had laid on them.

The royal couple spent Easter, March 25, at Canterbury, and John revived the old English custom of wearing his crown in solemn state at the celebration of the feast. On the three great holy days of the year, Christmas, Easter, and Whitsunday, it had been the custom for the Archbishop of Canterbury or, in his absence, the ranking prelate, solemnly to place the crown on the King's head in his private apartments. Then the King, the clergy, and the barons walked in procession into the church for the celebration of the Mass. At the Offertory the King made his offering in the same solemn form that was observed at the Coronation Mass. After Mass, the procession returned to the King's apartments, and he exchanged the heavy crown and ceremonial robes for lighter ones, which he wore during the feast that followed.

This custom had been discontinued by Henry II when he and

Eleanor had laid their crowns on the tomb of Bishop Wulfstan in his Cathedral of Worcester at Easter, 1158 and had vowed not to wear them again. When Richard had returned from his captivity and was crowned again at Winchester on April 17, 1194, it is probable that, instead of re-enacting the coronation ceremony itself on that occasion, he revived the old ceremony of the wearing of the crown, which had been half-forgotten in the previous thirty-six years. The coronation ceremony, with its anointing and hallowing of the king, was regarded as quasi-sacramental in character, and it is not likely that it would have been repeated.

On this Easter Day of 1201 Hubert Walter, Archbishop of Canterbury, performed the ceremony of placing the crowns on the heads of John and Isabella, with five bishops and many barons in attendance. The Archbishop entertained the King and Queen and their court in a magnificent, not to say ostentatious, fashion that attracted much comment.

While John was thus occupied in England, the members of the house of Lusignan were taking energetic steps to avenge the insult they had received from him. They were the most powerful family in Poitou, and they set to work to stir up disaffection and open revolt among the Poitevin nobles. They invaded the Norman border and laid siege to a number of John's castles. In retaliation John ordered the Seneschal of Normandy, Guarine de Clapion, to take the castle of Driencourt, which belonged to Ralph of Issoudon, Count of Eu, the brother of Hugh of Lusignan. Philip, ever eager to take advantage of any opportunity to harass John and promote discord in his dominions, hastened to help the Lusignan family, and with his assistance the Poitevins soon captured all the castles they had been besieging.

To meet this new threat to his continental possessions, on Ascension Day, at Tewkesbury, John issued orders to his earls and barons and to all others who owed him military service to meet him at Portsmouth on Whitsunday with their horses and equipment ready for service overseas. When they received these orders, the earls and barons assembled at Leicester, compared their grievances, and sent word to John that they would not go with him unless he would first redress their wrongs and restore their rights.

What these grievances were is not stated in the chronicles of the time. There is no record as yet of any of the acts of gross injustice that disfigured John's later years, and the taxes levied up to this time, although heavy, were not unduly so. One may be justified in thinking that the chief cause for complaint at this time was not specific abuses, acts of injustice, or violations of the barons' rights, but rather that the meeting at Leicester was a general protest by the baronage against the continuing curtailment of their feudal privileges through the operation under Hubert Walter and Geoffrey FitzPeter of the legal and administrative system devised by Henry II.

The barons' ideal was a feudal system carried to its ultimate development, in which each baron, in return for his military service and the payment of the established dues, held a territory over which he exercised complete control, even to the extent of trying all offenses in his own courts. Such a system was not English in either its origins or its practical effects, and it carried with it, as was demonstrated during the reign of Stephen, the seeds of anarchy. Henry II curtailed the irresponsible power of the barons by taking the administration of justice from their hands and their whims and putting it into the charge of the Curia Regis and the itinerant justices, working under a uniform system of clearly defined law and through and with the help of the freemen of the hundreds, the citizens of the towns, and the knights of the shire.

Thus the administrative, the legal, and, through the Exchequer, the financial machinery of the country, in its continued operation through the reigns of Henry II and his two sons, tended constantly to deprive the barons of their special privileges, to take from them their absolute and irresponsible powers over their territories, to make them and their followers amenable to the same code of laws by which the whole country was governed, and, by substituting for the old feudal services a regular system of taxation based on assessments made by the sheriffs and by jury inquests, to remove their financial exemptions. To this whittling away of their powers and special privileges the barons did not take kindly, and their revolts and disaffections under Henry II are ample evidence of the vigor with which they tried to defend the old order. Their vigor was more than matched by the energy and determination of the King, but neither he nor his successors could succeed in stamping it out entirely, till the virtual extinction of the old nobility in the Wars of the Roses enabled Henry VII to institute a system of government bordering on tyranny, in which the nobles had no effective part in the governing of the country.

In the meeting at Leicester it was no doubt the vague sense of being deprived of their old powers by the continued operation of the ordinary mechanism of government that led the barons to present their demands to John. His reply was quick and decisive; he threatened to deprive them of their castles if they did not obey. He began with William of Albini and demanded that he surrender his castle of Belvoir. William offered to give John his son as a hostage to guarantee his fidelity and thus made peace with him. When the other nobles saw that the King was in grim earnest, they capitulated without further talk of their rights.

The army assembled at Portsmouth by the appointed day, May 13, 1201. In a sudden change of plans, however, John allowed many of the barons to go back home, after taking from each one the money he had brought with him for his expenses. A number of explanations for this change are possible. It may be that the force that assembled was larger than John thought he would need for the quelling of the disturbances on the Norman border and of the Lusignans who had inspired them. Again, it may be that he distrusted those whom he let return and preferred to hire mercenaries in the place of the disaffected barons who had voiced their grievances at Leicester. Finally, it may well have been one of those impulsive, inexplicable acts that occurred throughout John's life. Be all this as it may, John nevertheless sent two strong detachments of a hundred knights each ahead of him into Normandy, one under the command of William Marshal, Earl of Pembroke and Striguil, one of the most capable military leaders of the time, and the other under Roger de Lacy, Constable of Chester. John assigned a third force of a hundred knights to his Chamberlain, Hubert de Burgh, and made him Keeper of the Welsh Marches.

Before he left England, John made a gift of fifty marks to "Philip, the son of King Richard," as the entry in the Chancellor's Roll for the third year of the reign reads. This royal bastard was apparently Richard's only child.

The same Roll provides the interesting information that "the men of Gloucester render account of forty marks to have the King's good will because they did not furnish him with his lampreys." They paid twenty marks and owed a further twenty. Gloucester was famous for its lampreys, and John, like his great-grandfather Henry I, seems to have been particularly fond of them. In 1207 he issued a letter fixing the price of these delicacies:

THE KING ETC. to the Sheriff and Burgesses of Gloucester and his other faithful subjects ETC. *Let it be known that it is ordered by our command and by the advice of our barons that at the time when lampreys are first caught in the year, none shall be sold for more than two shillings, until February, and thereafter they shall be sold at a lower price. And therefore we prohibit you under pain of forfeiture and of our amercement from doing anything contrary to this.* WITNESSED BY G. FITZPETER ETC. at Reading on the 12th day of January in the 8th year of our reign.

After keeping the feast of Pentecost at Portsmouth, John and Isabella sailed to Normandy. The Poitevin nobles would seem to have been checked for the time being by William Marshal and Roger de Lacy, for John soon went to meet Philip near Les Andelys for a friendly conference. There were no witnesses to the agreement between the two Kings, but that it was an unusually amicable one is attested by the fact that three days afterwards, on July 1, John went to Paris and was magnificently entertained by Philip, who moved out of his own palace in order that John and his court might stay there.

From Paris John went to Chinon and made his headquarters there for the struggle against the Poitevin nobles. Queen Berengaria, Richard's widow, came to John and asked for a settlement of her dowry. Philip of Pictavia, Bishop of Durham, who had been present at her marriage, was with the King at Chinon, and he testified as to what the marriage settlement had been. In accordance with its terms, John gave her the city of Bayeux, two castles in Anjou, and a yearly income of a thousand marks.

Instead of subduing the rebellious barons of Poitou with the force and energy that his father or his brother Richard would have displayed, John summoned them to appear before him and defend themselves and their causes by doing battle with his champions. He had selected an especially tough and capable group of men to act as his hired champions, so that it was no reflection on the valor of the Poitevin nobles when they declined to submit themselves to such an ordeal. They claimed the right of being tried by a jury of their peers but, since no jury of their fellow nobles would convict them, John in turn declined to settle the matter in such a fashion. He had committed a gross violation of feudal honor when he had taken his vassal's intended bride away from him, and the sympathies of his fellow nobles lay with Hugh of Lusignan and his party. After thus failing to arrive at any solution of his difficulties in Poitou, John returned to

Normandy, leaving "his beloved and faithful" Robert of Turnham as Seneschal of Poitou and Gascony.

Ralph of Issoudon, Count of Eu, the brother of the wronged and insulted Hugh, formally "defied" the King, thus renouncing his allegiance to John and leaving his conscience clear to make war against him, as the King reported in an open letter to Ralph's vassals:

THE KING ETC. to the men of Eu: *Well do you know that you were the men of Richard our brother of happy memory and of the Lord Henry our father and of our ancestors, and that you are and ought to be our faithful subjects. And because we know well that you will ill abide any injury to us, we inform you that Ralph of Issoudon, Count of Eu, defied us last Sunday, not through our fault but through his fault and his pride. Wherefore we command you and yours, as soon as you receive this letter, to do to him and his all the harm you can. And henceforth do not obey him or his in any matter, and keep your town well and safely, and receive into your town those whom we shall send to you to harm the aforesaid Count and his followers, knowing most certainly that if you do this, as we well know that you will, we will uphold and defend you as our faithful subjects, and we will cause you fully to have those liberties that you ought to have throughout our lands. Otherwise have no trust henceforth in us or in any of ours in any place in which we or ours can harm you.*

During this year Hugh Bardolph, a member of the Curia Regis and an itinerant justiciar, went to St. Botolph's Fair with some of his fellow justices to hold the assize of cloth. This assize, established under Richard, empowered the justices to seize all woolen cloth that was less than two ells wide. The clothiers persuaded Hugh not to enforce this regulation or the one establishing a uniform measure for corn, and for this corruption they paid a large sum of money to the King. This transaction prepared the way for much swindling in the sale of cloth and of grain, two of the principal commodities of trade.

John spent the Christmas of 1201 at Argentan in Normandy. During the holiday season, he made a graceful gesture to a lady who shared his love of good food:

> JOHN, by the grace of God, ETC., to all men ETC. *Be it known that we have given leave to Samson, the bearer of this present, to go to Nantes and buy there some lampreys for the Countess of Blois. And this letter is good for only one trip and no more.* MY-SELF AS WITNESS, *at Baugé, on the 12th day of January.*

He also laid in a supply of wine against his return to England:

> THE KING ETC. to all men ETC. *Be it known that the six score casks of wine that the bearers of this present are bringing to England are for our royal use. Whence we command you to allow them to pass freely and without hindrance and to protect them from all harm.* MYSELF AS WITNESS, *at Chinon, on the 18th day of February.*

During the following Lent, on March 25, 1202, he and Philip had a conference at Le Goulet, in the course of which Philip demanded that John surrender all his continental possessions to Arthur. John of course refused, and he asserted his feudal authority over Arthur in the following letter:

> THE KING ETC. to his beloved nephew Arthur ETC. *We order and summon you to come to us at Argentan during Easter Week to render to us that which you are bound to render to your liege lord. And we will gladly render to you that which we are*

bound to render to our dear nephew and our liege man. MYSELF
AS WITNESS, *at Andely, on the 27th day of March.*

War broke out again. On the day after the conference, Philip
seized the castle of Boutavant and leveled it to the ground, and he
captured a number of towns on the Norman border. On July 8 he
laid siege to Radepont, but after eight days John came with a superior
force and drove him away. Philip went next to Gournay, which he
captured by the expedient of breaching the dam that retained the
lake above the town. When the town was thus flooded the garrison
fled, and Philip marched in and took possession without any opposition.

Having thus secured the border, Philip returned to Paris and sent
Arthur into the field with two hundred knights. As they were marching along with a fine braying of trumpets, they learned that Queen
Eleanor, Arthur's grandmother, was in the castle of Mirebeau with a
small company of soldiers. Arthur, who had embarked on the conquest of Poitou, laid siege to the castle, and all the nobles of Poitou,
led by John's chief enemy, Hugh of Lusignan, came to lend Arthur
their help in capturing their Duchess. They succeeded in breaking
through the outer walls, and Eleanor and her small force fought val-
iantly from one of the towers.

The aged Queen sent word of her predicament on July 30 to
John, who was then at Le Mans. He hastily collected a large force
and by riding night and day reached Mirebeau on August 1. The
besiegers went out to meet him, but John and his force attacked with
such energy that they put the enemy to flight. Arthur's army dashed
back to the castle for shelter, but John's knights were pursuing with
such speed that they reached the castle at the same time. John rescued
his mother and captured Arthur, Hugh of Lusignan, two hundred
French knights, and all the knights of Poitou. He loaded his prisoners
with fetters and shackles and had them ignominiously hauled away in

wagons. He treated them not as honorable prisoners of war but as rebellious knights who had made war against their liege lord, and who as such deserved all the harshness with which they were treated. He sent them off to prison, some in Normandy and some in England. Savaric de Mauléon and twenty-five others were sent to Corfe Castle, where most of them died of starvation. Savaric, however, made his guards drunk and escaped. He later made his peace with John and returned to France, where John made him Seneschal of Poitou early in 1206. John kept Arthur under close custody at Falaise.

While John was thus occupied at Mirebeau, Philip laid siege to the castle of Arques, which Richard had acquired from him in 1196. The garrison held out stoutly against a greatly superior force for a fortnight. When he learned of Arthur's defeat and capture, Philip hastily lifted the siege and fled to Paris, burning and plundering the Norman countryside as he retreated.

Later in the year John came to Falaise and ordered Arthur brought before him. He tried to induce his nephew to separate himself from Philip and return to the allegiance he had pledged at Vernon on June 23, 1200, immediately after Blanche's marriage to Louis, but Arthur answered in an insolent and threatening manner and demanded that John surrender all his continental possessions to him. He swore that unless he gave these territories to him John "should never enjoy peace for any length of time." John had the obstinate lad removed to Rouen, to be kept under close guard in the new tower there.

"Shortly afterwards the said Arthur suddenly disappeared," records Roger of Hoveden. Exactly what happened to Arthur after his removal to Rouen is not known with certainty. The writer of the *Annals of Margam*, a contemporary chronicle, states categorically that on April 3, 1203 John, in a drunken rage, killed Arthur with a huge stone and threw his body into the Seine. Ralph, Abbot of Coggeshall, writing shortly after John's death, says that John ordered Hubert de Burgh to blind and otherwise mutilate Arthur so that he would be incapable of making any more trouble. Hubert, according to Abbot Ralph, spared Arthur but told John that he had carried out his orders. This account was embodied by Holinshed in his Chronicles and thus furnished the basis for the touching scene in Shakespeare's play, but it does not explain how Arthur met his death.

Whether or not John killed Arthur with his own hands, it is at any rate certain that Arthur died about this time and that John was responsible for his death. John would have been justified, according to feudal law, in putting Arthur to death after a legal process as a sworn vassal who had made war against his lord. Such a sentence would have been of extreme severity, but it would not have appalled and horrified his contemporaries nearly so much as did the suspicion that John had done the deed with his own hands and without any sort of a trial. This suspicion spread quickly throughout England and France, and because of it some of John's subjects began to feel a deep hatred for him.

In this year, Geoffrey FitzPeter, the Chief Justiciar, established a legal assize of bread that embodied the prevailing idea of the just price. According to the ethics of the time, merchants were not justified in charging all that the traffic would bear or in taking advantage of local or temporary shortages in order to raise their prices. Each article had its just price, which was arrived at by computing the cost of the materials and the labor involved and by adding to it a reasonable sum for the profit of the merchant. Thus, in establishing the price of bread, the Chief Justiciar took into account the wages of the baker's servants and boys, the salt, the yeast, the candle to light the bakery, the wood to heat the oven, and the baker's profit. Then he fixed a sliding scale according to which the price of bread varied in proportion to the cost of corn.

John had now been absent from England for well over a year, and the Chief Justiciar, for whom John had little affection but whose great administrative abilities and experience made him the obvious man for the post, seems to have acted as though he were independent of the King. Geoffrey and the Archbishop of Canterbury got themselves involved in a long-drawn-out dispute over the custody of Windsor Castle, which John had awarded to the Archbishop but which the Chief Justiciar refused to surrender to him. At last John sent his Justiciar a sharply worded rebuke:

> THE KING ETC. to Geoffrey FitzPeter ETC. *You well remember, we believe, how we ordered you by our word when you were in Normandy and how we afterwards commanded you by our letters to give our venerable Father in Christ, the Lord Archbishop of Canterbury, possession of the Castle of Windsor with its defences and forest, and how we ordered John FitzHugh by our letters patent to surrender it to him, and he [John] replied to our letters that he would not surrender it to him until he had first come before us. Whence we are greatly astonished that he did not surrender it to him at our order, nor did he come to us afterwards, nor did you give him possession of it as we ordered you. And therefore we firmly repeat our command to you, that as soon as you see this letter you give him possession of the castle with its defences and forest without delay, for it is our will that he have it and we have the power to accomplish this.* WITNESS MYSELF *at Cailly, on the 11th day of June.*

John kept the Christmas of 1202 at Caen in Normandy in a most carefree manner. The holidays were given over to sumptuous feasts with his Queen and court, and the royal couple stayed in bed till dinner-time, around noon, every day.

Philip, meanwhile, was preparing for renewed assaults on Normandy. Shortly after Easter he took to the field again and attacked

John's castles along the Norman border. The smaller ones he demolished, but the larger castles he preserved and stocked to serve as advance bases for further operations.

Messenger after messenger came to John to report that Philip was seizing his castles and carrying off the governors shamefully bound to his horses' tails, and, in short, proceeding through Normandy unopposed. John lay idle all the while at Rouen, feasting, drinking, entertaining Isabella, and displaying no concern over the threat to his power. To all who objected to his inaction or reported fresh acquisitions by Philip, John languidly replied: "Let him do so; whatever he takes I shall regain in a single day."

Such of John's English nobles as were in Normandy with him were so disgusted and baffled by his foolish words and frivolous conduct that they asked permission to return to England to look after their estates, pretending that they would come back to him when he should feel the need for their services. John readily granted the permission, and thus he was left in Normandy with only a few soldiers.

Seeing that no help was forthcoming from the King, the men he had placed in charge of his castles began to surrender them to Philip without offering any resistance, and as the news spread of John's strange apathy to his losses and of his cheerful demeanor as one by one his castles fell into Philip's hands, men began to say that Isabella had infatuated him by sorcery or witchcraft. The King did indeed seem bewitched by this fifteen-year-old girl from whom he apparently could not be parted for a day.

Hugh de Gournaye surrendered the castle of Montford to Philip, admitted the French soldiers into it by night, and, renouncing his allegiance to John, adhered to Philip. Robert FitzWalter and Sayer de Quincy had been made joint governors of the castle of Vaudreuil, an important fortification near the mouth of the Eure, and they too delivered up the castle to Philip without the slightest show of resistance. Even Philip was so disgusted by their cowardice that he had them put in chains and kept in close confinement at Compiègne till they were redeemed for a ransom of five thousand marks.

Roger de Lacy, Constable of Chester, alone of John's lieutenants showed the energy and courage in which his master was so notably lacking. He had been given command of the great fortress of Château-Gaillard, which Richard had built on the Rock of Andelys to defend the lower valley of the Seine and the approaches to Rouen. Richard embodied in this castle some novel ideas of military architecture he had acquired in the Holy Land, and it was considered the strongest fortress in the country. Part of this strength it owed to its situation, for it was built on a rock whose perpendicular sides were continued in the walls and to which access could be had only by a narrow and easily defended bridge of land, and part to the admirable construction of the walls, of a strength and thickness not seen before. Battering rams and scaling ladders could not be brought to bear against it, and stone-throwers and other engines of war could not make the smallest breach in the walls. All that Philip could do was to blockade the gallant and faithful Constable of Chester and his company and prevent them from getting fresh supplies.

Some of the common soldiers, at any rate, were not afraid to follow Roger's example and fight for their King, as the following letter shows:

THE KING ETC. to all men ETC. *Be it known that Robert, the son of Robert the Mercer, not because of any felony on his part but in our service at Chateau Neuf sur Sart, lost his ear. And we tell you this so that you may know it.* MYSELF AS WITNESS, at Montfort, on the 23rd day of July.

At last the defection of many of his Norman nobles, who, seeing that they could hope for no help or protection from him, deserted him, roused John to action. He had few men at his command, for he had allowed his English knights to return to England and his Norman nobles to leave his service, and his money had been exhausted in feasting and indolence. He took ship and landed at Portsmouth on December 6, 1203. When he confronted his earls and barons, he accused them of having deserted him in the midst of his enemies and demanded from them a seventh of all their movable property. Geoffrey FitzPeter collected this tax from the lay barons, and Hubert Walter commanded the clerics that were tenants-in-chief of the Crown to pay it. The administrative machinery of the Exchequer functioned smoothly and efficiently, so that no one escaped paying the tax.

Philip, when he learned that John had left Normandy, went all over the district, telling the citizens and the governors of the castles and other administrative officers that John had deserted them. Philip said that since he was the overlord of the duchy it reverted to him when John thus abandoned it, and he threatened that if they did not submit peacefully to him he would take the country by force and hang or flay alive all who resisted him. No French king had asserted his authority in Normandy since Charles the Simple had ceded the land to Rollo in 911, and there was much discussion before a compromise was reached. A truce was declared, to last for a year, and the Norman nobles gave hostages to Philip. They agreed that if by the end of the year John did not assist them and re-establish his sovereignty they would acknowledge Philip as their lord.

Meanwhile, John kept the Christmas of 1203 at Canterbury as the guest of the Archbishop.

Innocent III in this year canonized Wulfstan, Bishop of Worcester, who at his death in 1095 was the last of the Anglo-Saxon bishops. The decree of canonization was issued through the efforts of Mauger, one of Wulfstan's successors, who stood high in the Pope's favor. He was of illegitimate birth, and when he was elected Bishop in August 1199 Innocent annulled the election on that ground.

Mauger went to Rome to plead his cause in person, and the Pope was so impressed by him that he dispensed him from the impediment and consecrated him with his own hands. When Mauger returned to England, he caused the remains of Bishop Wulfstan to be reverently replaced in his cathedral. The cathedral was destroyed by fire on April 17, 1202. In order to stimulate devotion and to raise funds for the rebuilding, Mauger requested the canonization of Wulfstan and submitted instances of the many miracles that had occurred at his tomb since the reburial.

Innocent also in this year sent a long letter to John, complaining of his treatment of the Church. He accused the King of interfering with the courts christian, of applying the revenues of the Church to his own uses, of attempting to prevent the election of bishops to vacant sees or at least of postponing indefinitely the elections, which were supposed to take place not later than three months after the see became vacant, so that he might enjoy the revenues of the vacant sees, and of forcing the electors to choose in accordance with his own arbitrary decisions. Specifically, the Pope accused John of having expelled the Bishop of Limoges from his see, of having appropriated its revenues, and of having oppressed and insulted the Bishop of Poitiers and almost completely destroyed his church and diocese.

John summoned the Great Council to meet at Oxford on January 2, 1204, and he asked and received a grant of two and a half marks on each knight's fee for the prosecution of the war in Normandy. This tax, like the seventh levied the month before, applied to bishops and abbots as well as to lay barons.

Philip's forces had meanwhile been battering away at Château-Gaillard for almost a year without having reduced it. At last, on March 6, 1204, when all their supplies were exhausted and they were faced with starvation, Roger de Lacy and his men armed themselves and stormed forth in a desperate attack on their besiegers, preferring a speedy and glorious end in battle to slow death from hunger.

After a fierce fight in which they succeeded in killing many of the French, they were with difficulty captured and made prisoners. To the credit of Philip's chivalric feelings, which were generally pretty well in abeyance, he made Roger a prisoner on parole, out of admiration for his courage and ability. His ransom was set at a thousand marks, and John helped raise the sum.

Shortly after this, on April 1, 1204, Queen Eleanor died. She had lived into her eighties, a fabulous age for those times, and had been the wife of two kings and the mother of two kings. She had been to the Holy Land as a crusader; she had ruled her great Duchy of Aquitaine; she had stirred up a revolt of her sons against their father, and she had suffered long in prison for it. Then, at an age when most women would be content to sit by the fire, she had emerged from prison full of life and energy and had ruled as Queen of England for the ten years of Richard's reign. She had traveled into Navarre in quest of a daughter-in-law, into Germany in search of her son, and into Castile to fetch her granddaughter. She was buried at Fontevrault beside the husband she had hated and the son she had most dearly loved.

A fortnight after her death, John made a handsome gesture in memory of her:

THE KING ETC. to the Sheriff of Dorset ETC. *You are in-formed that for the love of God and for the health of the soul of our very dear mother who has died, we have set free and quit claim, on the Wednesday next after Palm Sunday, that is, on the 14th day of April, in the 5th year of our reign, all prisoners in-carcerated for whatever cause they were detained, whether for murder or felony or theft or for forest offences or for any other of-fences whatever, except the prisoners captured in our war and ex-cept those whom we sent from Normandy to England to be im-prisoned or kept in custody, and except our Jewish prisoners.*

*And therefore we order you that as soon as you see this letter you
set free all the aforesaid prisoners that have been incarcerated or
detained except the aforesaid ones. So do this that those prisoners
who are to be set free find in the full county court a pledge that
henceforth they will live as faithful subjects, and thus they may
remain in our land. Otherwise, make them abjure our land before
the full county court so that they acknowledge their guilt and
that they go out from our land within forty days after the abjura-
tion. Make those, however, who were taken for homicide find a
pledge in the same county court that they will stand for their right
or that they will make peace with the parents. If they will not or
cannot do this, make them, like the others, abjure our land and
go out from our land within the aforesaid period, unless they want
to return to prison and stand for their right. Those who are accused of forest offences and detained in our prison we wish to be
entirely set free, except those who were caught with venison and
convicted of having killed a deer. Concerning these, we will that
they find a pledge that henceforth they will commit no offence in
our forest. If they will not or cannot find a pledge, let them abjure
our land like the aforesaid offenders who have fallen into our
mercy and let them go out of our land within the aforesaid period.*
MYSELF AS WITNESS, *at Freemantle, on the* 15th *day of April.*

When a member of his household was knighted during this summer, John gave him rich gifts:

THE KING ETC. *to the Sheriff of Southampton:* GREETING.
*We order you to give Thomas Esturmy, our valet, a scarlet robe
with a fine linen cloak and another robe of green or brown, and
a saddle, and a pair of reins, and a rain-cloak, and a couch, and a
pair of linen sheets, for he is to be made a Knight. And what you*

spend for these things will be accounted to you at the Treasury.
MYSELF AS WITNESS, *at Bristol, on the 17th day of July.*

The fall of Château-Gaillard left the way to Rouen open to Philip, and the keepers of the Norman castles in great alarm sent messengers to John to explain their perilous situation to him and to warn him that the end of the year's truce was drawing near, at which time they would have either to surrender the castles to Philip or forfeit the hostages they had given him. John replied that they were to expect no help from him, but that each one must do what seemed best to him. The Norman nobles interpreted this as a tacit renunciation by John of the Duchy of Normandy and as freeing them from the allegiance they had sworn to him, since the feudal bond included not only the obligation of the vassal to serve his lord but also the duty of the lord to defend his vassal.

Without meeting any resistance, Philip took possession of the whole of Normandy, Touraine, Anjou, and Poitou except for the castles of Rochelle, Thouars, and Niort. John received the news of these shameful and staggering losses with inexplicable equanimity; of all the great continental possessions that he had inherited, only his mother's portion, shorn of most of Poitou, remained to him. Roger of Wendover tells how John bore his losses: "When this was told to the English King, he was enjoying all the pleasures of life with his queen, in whose company he believed that he possessed everything he could desire; moreover, he felt confidence in the immensity of the wealth he had collected, as if by that alone he could regain the territory he had lost."

Normandy and England had been united under the same crown for a hundred and thirty-eight years. The free intercourse between the two countries was now cut off, with the result that the upper classes became more thoroughly English in character and feeling.

From the English point of view, the loss of Normandy was a good thing. The English had never derived any profit from the duchy; on the contrary, the King's efforts to keep it had meant a constant drain of men and treasure that would better have been employed at home. Many nobles had estates in both countries; now a division was necessary. Some houses divided their holdings between two branches; others who had the greater part of their land in one of the two countries chose to forfeit the smaller estates in the other. John made an exception in the case of William Marshal and allowed him to do homage to Philip for his lands in Normandy, although that meant that William could not thenceforth bear arms against Philip.

"I know you are so loyal," John said to him, "that nothing could turn your heart from me. Do homage to him, then, for the more you have the better you will be able to serve me."

John spent the Christmas of 1204 at Tewkesbury. This was a winter of exceptional severity, and the ground was frozen so hard that all agricultural operations were suspended from January 14 till March 22. This resulted in a scanty harvest. The price of corn increased greatly, and there was much misery in the land. The King ordered Hugh Neville to feed a hundred poor men at Marlborough and directed the Barons of the Exchequer to reimburse him.

John's last decisive military operation had been the relief of Mirebeau, on August 1, 1202. After more than two years of inexplicable lethargy, he suddenly roused himself to action and set about raising an army. On April 3, 1205 he ordered all the sheriffs to proclaim the summons throughout their bailiwicks. All the knights of England were to be divided into groups of ten, of whom one would serve "in the defence of our realm for as long as necessary," and the other nine were to see that he was well provided with horses and arms and two shillings a day for his expenses. If any knight failed to comply with these orders, he and his heirs were to be deprived of all land forever, beyond any possibility of regaining it.

John brought together a great fleet and army at Portsmouth at Whitsuntide and ordered his barons to join him there. Hubert Walter and many others of his council tried to dissuade him from this expedition, probably because they thought that it was now too late to regain the territories in which Philip was well entrenched. It may be, too, that the mysterious degeneration of the King's character during these years, when he was sunk in a listless slothfulness quite foreign to the wild energy and turbulent restlessness that marked both his father and his brother Richard and that reappeared in John later in his life, led them to distrust him and to doubt both his determination and his ability to drive Philip out of his acquisitions.

William Marshal also tried to dissuade John, and this led to a painful scene between them. John was sitting on the shore at Portsmouth with his entourage, looking out to sea. He summoned William Marshal to him and in the presence of his court accused him of having made an alliance against him with the King of France.

William, wounded to the quick, replied that he had made no alliance against John, and that what he had done, in doing homage to Philip for the lands he held of him, had been done with John's permission.

John proposed that the barons judge the matter, and William, in great grief, took off his cap and repeated solemnly that he had had John's permission to do homage to Philip.

"I deny that!" John cried. "But I shall be patient with you. You shall come with me to Poitou to fight the King of France, to whom you did homage, and help me conquer my inheritance."

William protested: "It would be an evil thing, since I am his man, for me to fight against him."

"Hear, my lords," John cried in triumph, "he cannot deny this. Now you can see the work that is being so vilely disclosed. He says that he is the King's man and that he will not go with me!"

William denied again that he was being false to John by observing his sworn obligations to Philip, and he offered to prove it by combat.

"By God's teeth," John swore, "that is nothing! I appeal to the judgment of my barons."

William Marshal raised his head and put his finger to his forehead. "Look at me, my lords, for by the faith I bear you I am this day an example and a mirror for all of you. Pay good heed to the King: what he is trying now to do to me, he will do to all of you, if he gets the upper hand."

John in great anger demanded again the judgment of the barons. They looked at each other and fell back; no one was willing to speak a word against William Marshal.

Finally Baldwin of Bethune, Earl of Aumale, said: "It is not for us to judge in court a knight of the Marshal's worth. In all this army there is no man rash enough to assert that William Marshal has been false to the King."

Seeing that his barons were all on the side of William Marshal, John arose and went to his dinner without further words. Later he dismissed the host, and in a bitter rage he embarked with a small company on July 15 and put to sea with all sails spread, as though he intended to defeat Philip alone and single-handed.

He landed on the third day at Wareham, by which time his anger had cooled somewhat. He immediately accused the barons of having refused to accompany him to the Continent to recover his lost territories, and on these grounds he exacted heavy fines from them.

The castle of Chinon had been surrendered to Philip on June 23, and he made it his headquarters for bringing the whole of Poitou to submission.

THE CANTERBURY
ELECTIONS

❧ 1205-1207 ❧

HUBERT WALTER, Archbishop of Canterbury, got along unusually well with the monks of Christ Church in Canterbury. He was, of course, their titular abbot, and he greatly enjoyed visiting them when his many duties as Primate and Chancellor allowed him a little leisure. He was enjoying such a visit with them early in July 1205, when he was called upon to settle a quarrel that had arisen between Gilbert de Glanville, Bishop of Rochester, and his monks. Reluctantly, Hubert left his friends, promising to come back again and stay with them longer than usual. He set out for Boxley Abbey, but on July 10 he fell sick of a fever and a carbuncle and turned aside to Teynham. He died there on July 13. Ralph of Coggeshall says that his happy death was a fitting close to a good life. He was an energetic and courageous man, deeply versed in the law, and one of the best administrators of his time. That England enjoyed a capable and tranquil government during the early years of John's reign was in large measure due to the firmness and probity of Hubert Walter, assisted by the experience and legal knowledge of Geoffrey FitzPeter.

John gave way to indecent joy when he learned of the death of one of the two men who had been able to exercise a restraining influence on him in his governing of the kingdom. "Now for the first time am I truly King of England," he declared.

He hurried to Canterbury on July 15 and induced the prior and the monks to promise him that they would wait till after St. Andrew's Day, November 30, before doing anything about the election of a new archbishop. Hubert Walter had left the costly and elaborate furnishings of his chapel to the Cathedral, and John expressed a wish to see them. He was so taken with their beauty that he had them carried to Winchester, where he presented them to the Bishop-elect of that city, Peter des Roches, one of his favorites.

The election of the new archbishop was a matter of the greatest importance, for the Archbishop of Canterbury was not only Primate of All England but also by long custom one of the King's closest advisors. One of the characteristics of the Church in England was that many of its episcopal sees were monastic in origin. The abbot of the monastery was also bishop of the diocese, and the monks of the monastery, or the minster-men, to use the Old English term, formed the chapter of the cathedral, their conventual church. Canterbury was one of these foundations, and the monks of Christ Church Priory had by long custom the right of electing the archbishop, who was also their abbot.

Since, however, the Archbishop of Canterbury was also Metropolitan of the dioceses south of the Trent, the bishops of the Southern Province had long claimed the right of assisting in the election. Finally, inasmuch as the archbishop was one of the greatest tenants-in-chief of the Crown, the holder of a great temporal barony, the leader of the influential body of bishops, and entitled to a prominent place in the king's councils, the king also was interested in the election of a man who held such great power in the realm. When the king was strong and the minster-men were weak, the king nominated the man of his choice and the monks forthwith elected him. The ideal situation, of course, occurred when the minster-men, the bishops, and the king could all unite in choosing the same man; such a situation, however, rarely presented itself, and the election was usually marked by a great deal of friction among the interested parties.

Before Hubert Walter had even been buried, a number of the younger monks, secretly and by night, without asking the King's permission to proceed with the election and in violation of their promise to him, chose one of their number, the Sub-Prior Reginald, as their Abbot and Archbishop. They immediately chanted the *Te Deum*, vested him at the high altar, and seated him on the Archbishop's throne. On that same night Reginald took an oath not to mention his election to anyone till he reached Rome, and, taking some of the monks with him, set out immediately, with the hope that the whole matter might be kept secret, above all from John, till the Pope should have confirmed the election.

No sooner had Reginald landed in Flanders, however, than he began to boast that he was the Archbishop-elect of Canterbury, on his way to Rome to receive the pallium from the Pope. To confirm his boasts, he displayed the letters from the minster-men, reporting his election and begging for its confirmation. When he reached Rome, he presented his letters to the Pope and asked for the Apostolic blessing. The letters must have raised doubts in the highly trained legal mind of Innocent III. Having been hastily written by a group of younger men, they probably had such deficiencies in the customary forms that a Pope who was accustomed to counting the dots in the papal seal to make sure that all one hundred and seventy-seven were there would have no difficulty in realizing that there was something wrong with the election. Innocent, therefore, instead of

giving Reginald the immediate confirmation that he apparently expected, told him that he would take time to consider the matter and
assure himself of the validity of the election.

The news of Reginald's boasting in the meantime reached England and threw the minster-men of Canterbury into a panic. They
hastily sent a deputation to John to repudiate their loose-tongued and
indiscreet Sub-Prior and to beg the King's permission to proceed
with the election of their archbishop. This permission John graciously granted, and he hinted to them that John Grey, Bishop of
Norwich, was joined to him in great friendship and knew all his se-
crets. The monks, he let it be known, would be doing a great service
both to their king and to their country, as well as to the Church and
the Province of Canterbury, if they would elect John Grey as their
archbishop, and John asked them to present his request to the community. He sent some clerics of his household to Canterbury with
the returning deputation to make known his views and to promise
many honors to the monastery if they did as he requested.

When the monks returned to Canterbury, they told the community of their interview with the King. John himself came to Canterbury for the election, and on December 11 the whole chapter
unanimously chose John Grey. The Archbishop-elect was a native
of Norfolk, of the same sturdy East Anglian breed that had produced
Ranulf de Glanville and Hubert Walter. He had been consecrated
Bishop of Norwich on September 24, 1200. He was a man of great
learning, well versed in administrative matters, and endowed with a
pleasant and agreeable disposition that made his company particularly welcome to the King. At the time of his election he was in Nottingham looking after the King's affairs, probably as an itinerant
justiciar.

On the day of the election, John sent a letter to the Pope that was
intended to remove any doubts from Innocent's mind as to the legality of the proceedings. He informed the Pope that after Hubert

Walter's death both the bishops of the Province and the monks of Canterbury had lodged appeals before him, affirming their respective rights to elect the archbishop. The bishops, however, fearing that an involved dispute might leave the see vacant for a long time, with great harm to the Church and the realm, renounced their appeal in his presence on St. Nicholas's Day, December 6.

"We therefore," John continued, "went to Canterbury on the following Sunday," (December 11) "where the Lord John, Bishop of Norwich, with our consent was elected Archbishop of Canterbury by the Prior and Convent of Christchurch in Canterbury. We therefore affirm by this our letter patent that from the death of the aforesaid Hubert, Archbishop of Canterbury, until this day the aforesaid bishops have made no election of an archbishop with our knowledge or consent."

Around Christmas, 1205, John sent a deputation made up of Master Honorius, Archdeacon of Richmond, Master Columbus, Master Geoffrey of Dereham, and six monks of Canterbury, to Rome to inform the Pope of the election of John Grey and to secure his confirmation. Before the delegation left, John, on December 20, wrote to all the bishops of the Province, requesting them to affix their seals, as the Bishop of London had already done, to the letter they were bearing to the Roman Curia. John gave these messengers large sums of money to be distributed as gifts to members of the papal court to make sure that his friend was confirmed.

At the same time, the suffragan bishops of the Southern Province, who had had no part in either election, sent agents to complain to the Pope that they had been grossly wronged by the minster-men, who had presumed to elect the archbishop without their assistance. They sent witnesses and documents to prove that in three cases in the past they had had a share in the election, and they made no mention of the renunciation that John had reported in his letter.

Innocent now presumably had three separate delegations before him: Reginald and his companions, to ask the confirmation of the Sub-Prior; the monks sent by John, to request the confirmation of John Grey; and the deputation from the bishops, to protest both elections. After hearing all of them and examining the documents and the witnesses, the Pope declared that he would deliver his decision on December 21 of the following year and ordered those present to return at the appointed time to receive his pronouncement.

Why Innocent should have introduced almost a year's delay into the matter is not clear. No intricate or knotty problems of canon law were involved. All the witnesses, with the relevant documents, were at hand, and it was not a question of summoning new witnesses from England. The Papal Curia, to be sure, was a busy place, but it is not likely that any of the cases before it could outweigh in gravity and importance the matter of the election of the Archbishop of Canterbury. The Pope may have hoped that a long delay might give heated tempers an opportunity to cool, but if such was the case he showed himself a poor judge of men and of English tempers.

After keeping the Christmas of 1205 at Oxford, John turned his thoughts once more to France. The projected expedition of 1205 had been abandoned largely because of the opposition of Hubert Walter and William Marshal. Now that his Chancellor was out of the way, John revived his plans for an attempt at regaining some of his continental territories.

In preparation for his return to Poitou, John made an effort to recall his Poitevin barons to his allegiance:

THE KING, to all the barons and knights of Poitou: GREET-INGS. *Be it known to you that if you return to our fealty and service, we will dismiss all ill will that we have conceived against you and pardon you wholly, in such a way that henceforth we will do neither evil nor harm to you on account of any fault that you have committed against us up to this time. And we will and concede that you hold of us surely and in peace all lands and tenements that you held whether by gift of King Henry our father or of King Richard our brother.* MYSELF AS WITNESS, at Beer-Regis, on the 5th day of January, the 7th year of our reign.

John assembled a large army at Portsmouth and sailed on June 25, 1206, landing at La Rochelle on July 9. He was greeted with great enthusiasm, and the inhabitants flocked to him with promises of money and help. Philip's rule had evidently not been popular.

John subdued the region around La Rochelle and then marched southeast to Montauban, where a number of rebellious Poitevin barons were assembled. John's forces made breaches in the walls with their stone-throwers, and the English soldiers, "who," says Roger of Wendover, "were greatly renowned in that sort of warfare, scaled the walls and fought hand-to-hand with the enemy." John captured the castle in a fortnight, and this was a source of great pride to him and his soldiers, for no less a person than Charlemagne had laid siege to this same castle for seven years without success.

Montauban surrendered on August 1, 1206, and John then turned to the northern part of Poitou, where Philip had established his outposts. Some of the Poitevin nobles joined John, but when Philip and his forces drew near, again neither side was willing to fight the matter out. It was one thing for John to overcome some of the rebellious barons and reduce the fortresses in which they had taken refuge, but it was quite another thing to meet the King of France in a pitched battle.

Pitched battles in the open were rare at this time, although it was one of almost constant warfare. The opposing forces bent all their efforts towards capturing castles. A modern and well-stocked castle like Château-Gaillard was almost completely impregnable against the offensive tactics of an enemy as long as its provisions held out. He might batter away indefinitely at its stout stone walls with battering rams without making an impression on them. He might hurl huge boulders against it with his stone-throwers and catapults, and if the walls were thick enough they would suffer little damage. A rain of arrows and stones into the courtyard would harm only those rash enough to be caught unprotected in the open. At best, a skilled archer could hope to pick off now and then an unwary foe who showed himself at the narrow embrasures of the parapet.

The attackers might try to scale the walls with ladders, after they had first crossed the moat, but such an attempt was usually suicidal, unless, as was apparently the case at Montauban, they had a great advantage of numbers and could attack from several points at the same time. They might try to undermine the walls by digging a tunnel from a protected place, sinking it under the weakest part of the walls and shoring it up with timbers as they proceeded. Then they would set fire to the timbers and, when they were burned through, the walls would collapse, if all went well. A well-built castle, however, would rest on the solid rock or have its foundations so deeply laid that mining would be impossible.

As a last desperate resort the attackers might build a tower as high as the castle walls, mounted on wheels and covered with green hides to make it fireproof, fill in the moat, roll the tower across the moat and up against the walls, mount by ladders inside the tower, and thus come to grips with the defenders. All this called for a great deal of preparation and work, and it was costly of the lives of the attackers. Richard used this daring expedient in the Holy Land, but neither John nor Philip was desperate enough to attempt it in their chronic warfare.

The defenders, on the other hand, if their walls were stout and their provisions ample, could let the attackers batter away to their hearts' content, picking them off with arrows, stones, and molten lead whenever they were rash enough to come within range. The older and weaker structures, such as the one at Montauban presumably was, could eventually be battered into submission. Finally, as was the case with many of John's Norman castles in 1205, the treachery of the defenders themselves might lead to their surrender.

Once the castle was captured, the garrison, or such members of it as were of sufficient rank and fortune, would be held for ransom. What happened to the ordinary foot soldiers and men-at-arms no one bothered to record. Indeed, it was a misfortune both for the victim himself and for the victorious attackers if a defending knight were killed, for then the knight lost his life and the victor lost his ransom. Consequently, most of the warfare of these times was not a bloody affair. The chief sufferers were the wretched townspeople, if the castle were surrounded by a town, and the miserable peasants of the adjoining countryside. Houses were demolished or burned, growing crops trampled under, vines and fruit trees hacked down, and the country laid bare.

It is difficult to detect any strategy underlying this apparently random attacking, defending, and seizing of castles. Each side remained in a state of watchfulness, ready to seize a castle whenever it had a momentary advantage. Eventually, of course, if one side seized a sufficient number of castles, as Philip did in Normandy, it would gain possession of the territory the castles dominated. Few of the campaigns of this time, however, show any systematic attempt to penetrate into enemy territory according to a prepared plan, and nothing makes drearier reading, even if one follows them on a map, than the lists of castles attacked, defended, and captured, with which the chronicles of the time abound.

On November 1 the two Kings agreed to a truce for two years, with the border to be left as it was, along the northern confines of Poitou.

Before he left Poitou, John had his Queen recognized as Countess of Angoulême, as the following letter to the knights and free men of that County shows:

> WE command you to swear an oath of fealty to your lady, the Queen, our wife, in the presence of our beloved and faithful Seneschal, Savaric de Mauléon, that you will bear fealty to her as your liege lady against all mortal men, saving your fealty to us while we are alive, and that you will deliver up no city or castle or fortified place to anyone except to her or at her command, if we should die. MYSELF AS WITNESS, at La Rochelle, on the 4th day of November, in the 8th year of our reign.

John went back to England and landed at Portsmouth on December 12. This expedition had not been entirely fruitless. He had made his hold on Aquitaine more firm and had investigated and improved the administration of the duchy. If he intended to hold Aquitaine rather than to cede it supinely to Philip, such a visit served a useful purpose in reminding the nobles that he was still their lord and in showing Philip that he did not intend to abandon his rights.

The Pope, in full Consistory, on December 21, 1206, delivered his decisions regarding the Canterbury elections. Innocent III was one of the greatest Popes of the Middle Ages. He was born Lothario of Segni in 1160 or 1161, and he studied theology at Paris and law at Bologna. His uncle Clement III, who was Pope from 1187 to 1191, made him a Cardinal in 1191. When Clement's successor, Celestine III, died on January 8, 1198, Cardinal Lothario was elected Pope that same day. He at once set about ruling the Church with vigor and ability. Innocent was guided by two great aims: to reform, restore, and unify the Church, giving it a universal discipline expressed in the Canon Law and removing more and more of its administration to the Papal Curia in Rome; and unceasingly to assert the supremacy of the spiritual over all temporal powers. Innocent's conception of the role and duties of the Papacy was a most lofty one, and in putting it into execution he displayed great ability and remarkable tenacity. He kept his primary objectives clearly in mind and suffered nothing to deflect him from his pursuit of them.

His knowledge of the law was the admiration of his contemporaries. He personally heard cases in Consistory three days a week, and lawyers crowded to hear his summaries of the cases before him and to wonder at the wisdom of his decisions. His knowledge of the law, unfortunately, was not balanced by an equal understanding of men. He tended to be rigid and uncompromising, sacrificing to the letter of the law the possibilities of accommodations and adjustments that might have made his rulings more generally acceptable. Even the most learned legal decision is of little value if it cannot be enforced, and there are many occasions when a strict adherence to the letter of the law might well be tempered by a consideration of the human elements involved in the case. In the Canterbury affair, which grew from small beginnings into a monstrous scandal, Innocent may have adhered to the strict Canon Law, but he showed himself woefully ignorant of the power of custom and tradition in England and particularly ill-informed concerning the character of the English King.

In the first place, the Pope decreed, the right of electing the archbishop belonged to the minster-men of Canterbury alone, and the suffragan bishops, in spite of having assisted at the election of three archbishops in the past, had no legitimate claim to participate in the election. The Pope then declared that both of the disputed elections were invalid: the first because it had been made surreptitiously and by a minority of the chapter, the older and wiser monks not having participated; and the second, that of John Grey, because it had been made before the first had been annulled.

Because the Sub-Prior Reginald and Bishop John Grey had been

parties to these irregular proceedings, the Pope disqualified both of
them from ever holding the Archbishopric in the future. This was
the normal practice in the case of disputed elections. When the Pope
quashed a man's election to a bishopric, he almost always added a
prohibition forbidding that man to hold any episcopal see in the
future without a direct dispensation from the Pope. Men usually
were nominated bishops because of the king's influence. If they were
denied a particular see by the Pope, the king's favor would assure
them of election to the next suitable vacancy, unless such a disquali-
fication were enforced.

A deputation of sixteen monks from Canterbury had come to the
papal court to hear these decisions. Twelve of them, before they left
England, had sworn a solemn oath to the King that if they were required to participate in an election, they would cast their votes for
John Grey. Innocent told them of his great solicitude for the See of
Canterbury, which now, thanks to his delaying tactics, had been
without a head for a year and a half. To fill that vacancy, the Pope
asked them to proceed therewith to elect Cardinal Stephen Langton,
who was present at the Consistory. Innocent praised his learning, his
virtue, and his discretion, and he assured the monks that the election
of Cardinal Langton would be of great advantage not only to the
Church in England but also to the King, who would benefit from so
wise a counsellor.

The monks, having just had a good lesson in Canon Law, replied
that they could neither elect an archbishop nor consent to an election
unless they first had the King's permission and the authorization of
their chapter. Innocent, who did not know John as well as did the
monks, assured them that the King's consent was not necessary for
elections made at the Apostolic See. The Pope informed them that
they were of sufficient number and of such character, being of the
older and wiser part whose votes counted for more than did those of
the younger and more foolish monks, as to be able to make a valid

election, and he ordered them, by virtue of their vow of obedience and under threat of excommunication, to elect as archbishop the man he had just named to them as a father and the shepherd of their souls. The twelve who had sworn to John that they would vote for John Grey told the Pope of their oath, and he dispensed them from it therewith.

The monks, under the eyes of the Pope and the assembled College of Cardinals, "reluctantly and with murmuring," says Roger of Wendover, gave their consent, with the exception of Master Elias of Brantfield, who considered himself bound by his oath to the King. The other monks chanted the *Te Deum* and carried Cardinal Langton to the altar.

The man thus elected was indubitably of English birth, although he had not lived in England, apparently, since his early youth. He had gained the degree of Doctor of Theology at the University of Paris and had continued to live and teach there. Whilst he was at Paris he conceived the idea of dividing the text of the Bible into chapters for easier reference, an arrangement that is followed to the present day. He was also the author of the great hymn, *Veni, Sancte Spiritus*. He had quickly won a reputation for great learning and holiness of life, and he had become a friend and trusted advisor of King Philip. He had been made a prebend of York and of the Cathedral of Our Lady in Paris. Innocent III had summoned him to Rome and had created him Cardinal in 1206, and Matthew Paris remarks that he was equal if not superior to any one at the papal court in probity and learning.

John meanwhile kept the Christmas of 1206 at Winchester. Twenty oxen, 100 pigs, 100 sheep, 1,500 chickens, and 5,000 eggs were consumed at the feast, at a cost of £11 16s. 6d., and 500 yards of linen were used for table napery.

At Candlemas, February 2, 1207, he summoned his council and ordered that a tax of a thirteenth or, more exactly, a shilling on every mark (13s. 4d.) of the value of all movable property be laid on both laymen and clerics. John was usually in need of money, both because his foreign expeditions were expensive affairs and because the ordinary income of the Exchequer was not sufficient to provide for the increasing cost of the governmental administration. In earlier times, the king had been expected to "live of his own": that is, the income from his extensive lands, from the royal manors, and from the fines levied in the royal courts was supposed to provide not only for the maintenance of the royal household but also for the expenses of the whole legal, financial, and administrative system of the country. No line was drawn between the personal expenses of the king and his court and the cost of the official administration. For the last fifty years, as the organization set up by Henry II had become increasingly complex, the expenses of such an organization increased accordingly, without a corresponding increase in the revenue of the Crown.

The feudal dues were no longer a dependable source of income sufficient to meet the emergencies for which they were originally intended or to form a substantial part of the income of the Exchequer. The king's tenants-in-chief paid reliefs on the occasion of their taking possession of their fiefs and aids at the knighting of the king's eldest son, for the marriage of the king's eldest daughter, and to make up the king's ransom if he were captured. Their obligation to military service was gradually being transformed, beginning in the reign of Henry I, into the payment of a fee known as scutage in commutation for the service, with which the king could hire mercenary soldiers to fight in their stead. Scutage could normally be levied only in time of war, and it was a disputed point as to whether either military service or scutage was due when the war was being fought overseas. John, however, levied scutages regularly and successfully on lay and ecclesiastical lands alike to pay for his foreign wars.

By John's time the pressing need was for a regular system of taxation that would yield a certain sum annually to defray the expenses of the government, that could be collected without undue trouble, and that would bear more or less equitably on all his subjects in proportion to their ability to pay. Two methods of taxation most nearly met these qualifications: a land tax and a tax on movable property. The land tax, under the old name of Danegeld, had been levied principally before the Conquest; it had long ceased to be a regular source of government income. Hubert Walter, the financial and administrative genius of the time, revived the land tax, or carucage as it was now called, during the reign of Richard, and John had frequent recourse to it. The tax on movable property normally took the form of a grant of a certain proportion of property made by the Great Council for a specific purpose.

Although there was a great deal of murmuring against the tax John levied in the spring of 1207, the money was collected with speed and vigor. Special assessors went all over the country to estimate the amount each man was to pay, and the sheriffs collected the money. Those who tried to list their possessions at less than their real value or to conceal their property were heavily fined, and those who sought to avoid paying had their goods seized and in some cases were thrown into prison. The tax yielded almost sixty thousand pounds, a handsome sum indeed.

The only one to oppose it openly was Geoffrey, Archbishop of York. He claimed that the King had no right to tax the movable property of the clergy, ordered his clergy not to pay the tax, and excommunicated all the officers who tried to collect it. John was too strong for him, however. Geoffrey launched a final anathema against the agents of this robbery, as he termed it, and fled to the Continent. He appealed to the Pope, and Innocent, in December 1207, laid the whole Province of York under an interdict, which had no effect and was generally disregarded. This protest was Geoffrey's final act in English affairs; nothing more is heard of him till his death in 1212, still in exile.

John sent a graceful letter to his brother-in-law on May 6:

THE KING, to his beloved brother Peter de Joigny: GREET-ING. *We command you to come safely to England until the feast of St. John Baptist, in the 9th year of our reign, to see the Lady Queen, our wife and your sister, who greatly longs to see you, and we much entreat you thereto.*

Innocent III wrote to John in the spring of 1207 to inform him of the election of Stephen Langton as Archbishop of Canterbury. His Holiness greatly praised the learning, the virtues, the life, and the morals of Cardinal Langton and pointed out to John that a man of such exemplary piety would be of great advantage to the welfare of the King's soul, as well as, through his learning and skill, to the temporal affairs of the kingdom. The Pope also ordered the minster-men of Canterbury to receive Stephen as their pastor and to obey him in all things, both temporal and spiritual. Without waiting for a reply to these letters, Innocent consecrated Stephen Langton at Viterbo on June 17, 1207.

When John received the Pope's letter, he fell into one of the violent rages to which the members of the House of Anjou were particularly prone. His wrath was aroused on two counts: that the election of John Grey had been annulled, and that Stephen Langton had been elected. He vented his anger first on the minster-men of Canterbury, whom he accused of having crowned their perfidious conduct with treachery. First they had elected the Sub-Prior Reginald to be Archbishop, without even having notified John of the fact, much less having asked his permission to hold the election. To redeem this fault, they had then elected John Grey, who they knew would be acceptable to him. The King had given them money from his own purse to pay the expenses of their journey to Rome to secure the confirmation of John Grey. When they had arrived in Rome at his expense, however, they had proceeded to elect Stephen Langton, who was known to be an open enemy of the King, to the highest ecclesiastical position in the realm.

Furthermore, the whole miserable business had begun with their childish attempts to hold a clandestine election without consulting him, as though they were electing the prior of the most obscure convent in England instead of an Archbishop of Canterbury. That piece of folly had thrown the election into the Pope's hands and given him the opportunity to try to foist his own nominee on the King. If they had behaved like grown men, worthy of the King's trust, instead of like a parcel of mischievous and irresponsible children, John Grey would have been consecrated as Archbishop of Canterbury long before now and the ecclesiastical affairs of the kingdom would be in capable hands and at peace.

John's anger against the minster-men of Canterbury knew no bounds. On July 14 he sent two knights of his household, Fulk de Cantelu and Henry of Cornhill, to Canterbury. With drawn swords they entered the monastery and ordered the Prior and his monks, as traitors to the King's Majesty, to leave the country immediately. Unless the monks obeyed forthwith, the two knights threatened to set fire to the monastery and roast the monks alive in their buildings. Faced with such threats, sixty-seven monks fled to Flanders and took refuge in friendly abbeys there, leaving behind thirteen monks who were in the infirmary and too ill to walk. John installed some monks from St. Augustine's in the monastery to take care of the Cathedral services and put Fulk de Cantelu in charge of the Cathedral properties. The revenues from the rich lands belonging to the Archbishop and to the monastery, amounting to almost £1500 a year, reverted to the Crown.

Stephen Langton meanwhile remained on the Continent, fearing to come to England while the King's anger was so hot against him. He stayed at the Cistercian monastery of Pontigny, where Thomas Becket, too, had lived in exile. The Archbishop's father, Henry Langton, fled to Scotland in fear of John's wrath. The King ordered all his possessions confiscated, and Henry died in exile around 1210.

In his reply to the Pope's letter, John stated explicitly the grounds for his objection to Stephen Langton. Not only had the Pope annulled the election of John Grey, whom the King had particularly recommended for the position; he had also consecrated Stephen Langton, a man who was quite unknown personally to John and who had been for many years the trusted advisor and friend of John's bitterest enemy, Philip of France. John considered it a direct personal insult that Innocent should attempt to foist on him as Archbishop of Canterbury and Primate of All England, the cleric who by the very nature of his office was entitled to share in the King's closest councils, a man who had spent his adult life in Paris and had been on terms of intimate friendship with a king whose greatest ambition was to accomplish John's destruction. That in itself was a slap in the face to John personally; what turned a personal affront into an attempt to deprive the Crown of its just and customary rights and privileges was the fact that neither the monks who performed this election, if one could call it that, nor the Pope who consecrated Stephen had troubled to ask his permission for the election or consulted him in any way as to the acceptability of the man so elected.

John expressed his amazement that the Pope, before he treated him with such studied contempt, had not recalled how much the friendship of the King of England had hitherto meant to the papal court, inasmuch as more money had poured into the papal coffers from England than from all the other countries on that side of the Alps combined. The King declared that he would stand up for the rights of his crown and defend them with his life, and he expressed his firm intention to insist upon the election and promotion of John Grey to the Archbishopric, because the Bishop of Norwich was a man whom he knew and trusted. If his wishes were not attended to, John declared that he would cut off all traffic with Rome and thus keep in England the treasure that had formerly poured into Rome and that he might better use to defend his territories from his enemies. There was no need, he added, to extol the learning of Stephen Langton; in England there were plenty of clerics of every degree who were well versed in every branch of knowledge, and John did not have to beg for justice or judgment from strangers and foreigners.

Innocent's reply to this intemperate letter must have seemed to John full of legalistic quibblings and evasions. The Pope began by reproaching him for his rebellious and stiff-necked attitude. "Whereas We defer to you more than We ought, you show Us less consideration than you ought; for if your devotion is very necessary to Us, still Our regard is no less advantageous to you." To John's objection that Stephen Langton was a man unknown to him, Innocent replied that it was strange that the King did not know a man of such widespread fame for virtue and knowledge, a man to whom John had written three times to congratulate him on his having been created Cardinal, telling him that he had wanted to summon Stephen to his service but was now happy that he had been raised to a higher office. Furthermore, wrote Innocent, Stephen's loyalty was proved not only by his having been born in England of parents loyal to John but also by his having accepted a prebendal stall at York.

As to the matter of John's consent, Innocent affirmed that although it was not the custom to wait for any prince's permission when elections were made at the Apostolic See, he had nevertheless sent two monks to John for the express purpose of asking his consent, but the monks had been detained at Dover and had not been able to reach the King. The Pope asserted that he had full authority over the Church of Canterbury. The election had been made, and he did not intend to be diverted from seeing this matter through to the end. Innocent advised John to acquiesce and commit himself to the Pope's good pleasure, warning him that otherwise "you may bring yourself into difficulties from which you will not easily be extricated."

John's first son, meanwhile, was born in the autumn of this year, on October 1, 1207, at Winchester. He was christened Henry, after his grandfather. John kept the Christmas of 1207 at Windsor, and during the festive celebrations he distributed rich cloaks among his knights. He seems to have been in a benevolent frame of mind, as the following letter suggests:

> THE KING ETC. to William of Albini ETC. *Be it known to you that we have granted to Robert de Ros that his son, who is in your custody, may be with him and his mother this winter. And the same Robert has agreed that he will return him to us at Easter. And we therefore command you to deliver him to Robert.* WITNESSED BY THE LORD PETER, BISHOP OF WINCHESTER, at Guildford, on the 28th day of December.

When Innocent realized that John had no intention of relaxing his opposition to Stephen Langton, His Holiness wrote to William of Sainte-Mère-l'Eglise, Bishop of London; Eustace, Bishop of Ely; and Mauger, Bishop of Worcester, ordering them to try to reason with the King about the Canterbury affair and to induce him to yield to the Pope. If they found him still obdurate, however, Innocent directed them to lay the whole kingdom under interdict and to tell John that if the interdict failed to bring him to submission the Pope had even more severe punishments in store for him. Innocent also wrote to the suffragan bishops of the Southern Province and again commanded them to receive Stephen Langton as their father and pastor and to obey him as their rightful Archbishop.

The three bishops came to John and with tears begged him to recall the minster-men of Canterbury to their monastery and to receive Stephen Langton as Archbishop of Canterbury. They implored him not to expose the kingdom to the shame and humiliation of a general interdict. God would reward him with honor on earth and glory in heaven, they assured him, if he would but submit himself in this matter to the Supreme Pontiff.

When the bishops tried to reason further with him, John became almost mad with rage. He broke into wild blasphemies against the Pope and the College of Cardinals and swore "by God's teeth" that if the Pope or anyone else dared lay his kingdom under an interdict he would drive every clerk, priest, and prelate out of England and confiscate all their property. Furthermore, he declared, if he found any Roman clerks in any of his territories he would pack them off to Rome with their eyes gouged out and their nostrils slit, so that men might know who they were. And if the bishops valued their own safety, he added, they would get out of his sight immediately.

The bishops left the royal presence in haste and reported the results of the interview to Innocent.

One last attempt was made by Simon Langton, Stephen's brother, but the interview led to nothing, as John reported in the following letter:

THE KING to all the men of the whole of Kent ETC. *Be it known to you that Master Simon Langton came to us at Winchester on the Wednesday next before Mid-Lent and in the presence of our bishops asked us to receive Master Stephen Langton, his brother, as Archbishop of Canterbury. And when we spoke to him of preserving our dignity in this matter, he told us that he would do nothing concerning that unless we threw ourselves wholly upon his mercy. And we tell you this, so that you may know the evil and the injury that has been done to us in this affair, and we command you to believe what Reginald of Cornhill*

will tell you on our behalf about the aforesaid happenings be-
tween us and the aforesaid bishops, and that same Simon, and to
obey our orders in this matter. MYSELF AS WITNESS, at Winchester, on the 14th day of March.

John sent Reginald of Cornhill to Canterbury as the bearer of this
letter and to take over the custody of all the lands and treasure belonging to the Archbishopric and the monastery.

CHAPTER IX

THE INTERDICT

1208–1209

WHEN Innocent III learned that John had no intention of submitting to him and of receiving Stephen Langton as Archbishop of Canterbury and when the Bishops of London, Ely, and Worcester reported that their expostulations and entreaties did not move the King, the Pope ordered the three bishops to lay the whole of England under interdict. The bishops accordingly published the dreadful sentence on the Monday in Passion Week, March 23, 1208. Having done this, they, together with Jocelyn of Wells, Bishop of Bath, and Giles de Braose, Bishop of Hereford, fled to the Continent. There, Roger of Wendover charges, "they lived on all kinds of delicacies instead of placing themselves as a wall for the House of God; when they saw the wolf coming they left their sheep and fled."

Peter des Roches, Bishop of Winchester, one of John's particular favorites, was soon the only member of the hierarchy left in England.

Archbishop Geoffrey of York was in exile, and the Bishop of Coventry fled to the Continent and died in this year. The Bishops of Rochester and of Salisbury, after enduring much persecution, took refuge at the court of William the Lion in Scotland in 1209. The King in 1208 sent John Grey, Bishop of Norwich, as his justiciar to Ireland, where he remained till 1213. The sees of Lincoln, Chichester, and Exeter were vacant, and John of course made no attempt to fill them, for as long as they were without a bishop the income from the lands attached to the dioceses reverted to the Crown. Philip, Bishop of Durham, died on April 22, 1208. He had paid a thousand pounds in the preceding year "for the King's benevolence," and John collected a further two thousand marks from the Bishop's executors.

The interdict stopped all religious services. Children were baptized privately; confessions were heard at the church door; and sermons were preached only in the churchyard. The dying were shriven and given the Viaticum, but they could not be given Extreme Unction, for no bishop could consecrate the Holy Oils. With these exceptions, all the functions of the Church were suspended. The Mass, the center and heart of Catholic life, could not be celebrated, except for the renewal of the Viaticum, when the priest was permitted to celebrate behind closed doors with no one save a single server present; Holy Communion, the spiritual food of the faithful, could not be distributed; no services of any kind could be held in any church; marriages were contracted at the church door without the usual blessing; bells could not be rung, and the dead were buried like dogs in unconsecrated ground.

This would be a crushing blow to any Catholic community; it was felt with a keenness we can hardly now imagine in the England of that time, where most of the people lived in small villages, almost wholly isolated from the rest of the world. Their lives were hard; they lacked the comforts of life and counted themselves fortunate to

have the bare necessities of food, clothing, and shelter. In those limited lives the Church played a most important part and offered the
people their only means of lifting their thoughts above the daily
round. Frequent Communion was not so widely practiced then as it
is now, but the number of holy days of obligation was greater, so that
the ordinary Catholic probably heard Mass more often then than he
does today. Practically everyone heard Mass every day as a matter
of course.

The village priests, on whom the burden of the care of souls fell,
were in most cases poorly educated. They knew only enough Latin
to be able to read the services; if they had had much more education
they would have had a more lucrative and pleasant post in some nobleman's household, in some bishop's court, or in the employment of
the king himself. Education, in the sense of something more than a
mere ability to read and understand Latin, the universal language
both of the Church and, together with Norman-French, of the
Court, was practically the monopoly of the clergy. Thus almost all
the administrative work of the royal government was in the hands of
men in some stage of Holy Orders.

The village priests, however, were far removed from the intel-
lectual stimulation of such a life and tended to sink to the level of the
peasants among whom they spent their lives and from whose ranks
they had often come. In many cases they were merely vicars for a
monastery or chapter that appropriated the income of the church and
gave the priests a stipend so low that they could barely live on it. So
low were the stipends, in fact, that in 1222 it was found necessary
to fix the minimum at five marks a year. This was equivalent to the
pay of common soldiers and sailors, who of course were fed in addition. This miserable wage might be supplemented by gifts from the
parishioners, but even so it represented a standard of living barely
distinguishable from that of the peasants.

That these men, poorly educated and still more poorly rewarded, held firm to their posts, giving their flocks such consolations as were in their powers, is an impressive tribute to the strength of their faith. Sometimes their lives were far from edifying, particularly with regard to the virtue of celibacy. Gerald of Wales has some sharp things to say of the priest "who prefers a worldly life, to his own ruin and eternal damnation, who keeps a hearth-companion in his house to extinguish all his virtues, and who has his miserable house full of babies and cradles, midwives and nurses." Nevertheless, the village priests and their people kept their faith through these difficult times, and the whole of England was singularly free of heresy.

In any case, there were then, as there always have been, many ordinary men and women who were trying to lead the best lives they could, and to them the stopping of all the services of the Church, the deprivation of the spiritual help and comfort they received from hearing Mass and frequenting the Sacraments, and the breaking of the visible ties that united them in the Church that embraced all Christendom must have filled them with suffering, shame, and horror. To have inflicted such a punishment on several million innocent Christians in order to bring one guilty man to account showed a callous disregard for the welfare of men's souls that ill befitted the Vicar of Christ. One is constantly amazed, throughout this period, at the frequency with which even virtuous and well-meaning prelates launched interdicts and excommunications right and left for what seem to be completely secular offenses.

The interdict was observed throughout England, except by the Cistercian monks. They obeyed it when it was first published, but afterwards the Abbot of Citeaux told them to disregard it, on the grounds that he had not seen an authenticated copy of the papal order. When the Pope learned of this, he ordered the White Monks to observe the interdict in all its strictness.

John's reply to the proclamation of the interdict was swift and violent. He sent his sheriffs and other officers throughout the land to order all priests to leave the kingdom immediately. Let them go to Rome, the King ordered, and force the Pope to treat him justly. He confiscated all property belonging to the Church and diverted the ecclesiastical revenues to the royal exchequer. The clergy had had ample time to plan their course of action in a contingency that all could see was impending, and, with the exception of the bishops who ran away, they refused to leave unless they were expelled by vio- lence. The King's officers may have been unwilling to add to the general troubles by bringing down upon themselves and their master the sentence of excommunication that was incurred *ipso facto* by those that laid violent hands on a cleric, and the King himself may have been moved by a grudging admiration for men who chose to stay and face whatever troubles he might inflict upon them. It would have been well-nigh impossible, in any case, for the whole clergy of England to have gone into exile in a body. At any rate, they were allowed to remain and enjoy the weight of John's displeasure.

Since all their revenues and properties had been confiscated, the clergy subsisted on a small allowance of food and clothing doled out to them by the royal officers, under the supervision of four lawful men of each parish. The Dunstable Annals record that "the King commanded that the goods of the religious should be taken into his hand and that those who refused to sing the services should get out. But afterwards on the fourth day his anger cooled, and the aforesaid goods were put under constables."

John took a wry pleasure in holding the priests' concubines for heavy ransoms, for not all the decrees of Popes, councils, bishops, and synods had yet succeeded in stamping out clerical incontinence. He had the relatives of Archbishop Stephen and of the bishops that had pronounced the sentence seized, stripped of all their possessions, and put in prison. When the King's more irresponsible mercenaries found any clerics traveling on the roads, they dragged them off their horses and mistreated them. Moreover, the victims could not get justice in any court.

Roger of Wendover tells that some of the servants of a certain sheriff brought before the King a robber, with his hands tied behind his back, who had robbed and murdered a priest on the highway. They asked John what punishment they should mete out to the criminal.

"Let him go," ordered the King, "for he has slain one of my enemies."

John made a notable addition to his library while all this was going on. In a letter dated March 29, 1208, to the Abbot of Reading, he acknowledges the receipt at the hand of Gervase, the Sacristan of Reading, of the entire Old Testament in six books, the Treatise on the Sacraments by Master Hugh of St. Victor, the Sentences of Peter Lombard, St. Augustine's *Of the City of God* and his commentary on the third part of the Psalter, and Origen's Treatise on the Old Testament, among others.

Powerful as it was, John knew that the interdict was not the last or the strongest weapon in the Pope's arsenal. There remained the sentence of excommunication by name, which would cut him off from all Christians and force them to avoid any dealings with him, and, as a last resort, the Pope could free his subjects from their oath of fealty. To be prepared for these eventualities, John demanded hostages from his nobles and particularly from those whose loyalty he had reason to doubt. The nobles of whom he made this demand turned over their sons, nephews, or other close relatives to John's keeping, and thus he secured a powerful hold over them.

William de Braose, a member of a family that had come over at the Conquest, was already in John's bad graces on two counts: he was the father of Giles de Braose, Bishop of Hereford, who had pronounced the sentence of interdict and then fled the country, and he owed John money. In 1201 the King had given him the Honour of Limerick on condition that he pay five hundred marks a year for ten years, but over the next six years he paid only seven hundred marks in all. When John's messengers came to William and demanded hostages from him, his wife Maude answered:

"I will not deliver up my sons to your lord, King John, for he foully murdered his nephew Arthur, whom he should have cared for honorably."

This charge, recorded by Roger of Wendover, has especial weight as coming from the wife of a man who was with John in Normandy in April 1203, at the time Arthur is supposed to have been murdered.

William rebuked his wife and told the messengers: "If I have offended the King in any way, I am ready to give satisfaction to him without the need of hostages, according to the decision of his court and of my fellow barons, if he will set a time and place for me to do so."

When this was reported to John, he sent some of his knights to take William and all his family prisoners, but William was forewarned by his friends at court and fled with his family to Ireland, where he took refuge with the Lacy family.

About this time Stephen Langton made an effort to come to England in person and discuss matters with John, for in September the King issued the following safe-conduct:

THE KING, to all ETC. *Be it known that we grant Stephen Langton, a Cardinal of the Roman See, a safe and secure conduct to come to England as far as Dover and to remain there until St. Michael's Day, in the 10th year of our reign, for three weeks. Thus when the three weeks are up, within the eight following days let him return, unless a very strong wind detains him. And in witness of this matter we issue this letter patent to him.* WIT-

NESSED BY G. FitzPeter at Silverstone, the 9th day of September, in the 10th year of our reign.

Nothing came of this, either because Langton did not trust the King or because he was offended by the title by which he was called, which indicated clearly that John did not consider him an archbishop at all, much less Archbishop of Canterbury.

Stern and unyielding though he was in his negotiations with ecclesiastics, John showed a gentler side of his nature to nuns, as the following letter shows:

> BE IT KNOWN *that we have received into our protection and defence Agnes, the Prioress of the Church of Blessed Mary of Clairvaux, and Erenburga, her sister, with her messengers and servants, who have been sent to England with letters from the convent of the same place to beg alms for their house. And we therefore command you to protect them, and we beg you for the love of God to receive them kindly and help them with your alms.* WITNESSED BY JOHN FitzHugh at Woodstock, on the 26th day of November, in the 10th year of our reign.

The Pipe Rolls abound in such entries as: "For eleven thousand herrings bought and given to various nuns, 55s." (From the Pipe Roll of 1211.) During that year alone, John bought 191,000 herrings, at a cost of £37 11s. 1d., and had them distributed among convents in almost every county in England.

In the autumn John received the cheering news of the election of his nephew Otto as Emperor of Germany, and he at once started building up again around the figure of his nephew a coalition of the leading men of the Low Countries, with the eventual aim of uniting them all with him against Philip of France. The fall of Rouen and the loss of Normandy had been followed by no treaty; Philip was simply left in possession of the land, and John never gave up the hope of driving him out. With the accession of Otto to the imperial throne, that hope was now revived.

Otto's election came as the culmination of ten years of civil war. He was the second son of Henry the Lion, Duke of Saxony, and of John's eldest sister, Matilda. During Otto's boyhood, his father was twice driven into exile, and both times he had sought refuge in England. Thus Otto had been at least partly educated there. He had become a great favorite of his uncle Richard, for he was a lad after Richard's own heart. "Roaring like a lion's whelp, driven by the lust for plunder, eager for battle, he fought for victory or death." Richard had made him Count of Poitou.

When the Emperor Henry VI died in September 1197, Richard had set to work to secure his nephew's election. A majority of the electors chose Philip of Swabia in March 1198, but the opponents of the House of Hohenstaufen had not been willing to abide by the results of that election. Under the leadership of the Archbishop of Cologne and influenced both by Richard's bribes and by the dependence of Cologne and the country of the lower Rhine upon their trade with England, the electors of that part of Germany met at Cologne and elected Otto Emperor on June 9, 1198. Otto had immediately bid for the support of the princes of the Low Countries by becoming betrothed to the daughter of the Duke of Brabant. He had further strengthened his position by being crowned at Aix-la-Chapelle by the Archbishop of Cologne, an act which would have been equivalent in England to being crowned in Westminster Abbey by the Archbishop of Canterbury. The fact remained, however, that Otto had been the candidate of only a small party of German princes, and his influence had been confined largely to the area around Cologne.

Civil war of an appalling ferocity broke out. Otto was sustained for a while by English gold, but when Richard died in May 1199 that had come to an abrupt end. John's negotiations with Philip of France tied his hands, and one of the terms of the treaty of Le Goulet, of May 1200, was that John should give no help, either with men or with money, to Otto. Innocent III, however, had supported him with all his strength, and it was in no small part due to his interfer-ence that the civil war continued as long as it did. He had taken over Tuscany, the Duchy of Spoleto, and the March of Ancona, and his attitude throughout the dispute was determined by his resolution to hold on to these territories at any cost. Philip of Swabia was resolved to wrest them from the Pope if he ever got the opportunity, whereas Otto, ever lavish with promises, since he had nothing else to offer, pledged himself to respect those areas as belonging to the Church of Rome.

Otto's position had gone from bad to worse; that he could sustain the struggle as long as he did was a tribute to his military skill and personal bravery, in which he showed himself well worthy of his uncle Richard. Finally Cologne, his last and principal stronghold, capitulated to Philip of Swabia at the end of 1206. Otto escaped to his Duchy of Brunswick and thence to England.

John received him cordially and gave him the sum of six thousand marks. This may have been the beginning of the subsidies which John henceforth poured into the Low Countries, or it may have been part payment of Richard's legacy to Otto, which John had hitherto refused to pay. When Richard died, Otto had sent his two younger brothers to England to collect the legacy Richard had willed him, but John refused to give them anything. John was never one to pay out money unless he could be sure of getting something in return, and Otto's position at the time seemed so hopeless that John may well have decided that he had better uses for the money. Even Queen Berengaria, Richard's widow, had to struggle for years to wrest her dowry from John.

Just when the way was clear for Philip of Swabia to be crowned without any opposition, since even Innocent had at last been forced to accept the inevitable and Philip had agreed to respect the Pope's annexations in central Italy, Philip was murdered in June 1208 by Count Otto of Wittelsbach, in a private quarrel. Germany was sick of civil war, and no one wanted to put forward a candidate to dispute Otto's claim. He was unanimously elected Emperor on November 11, 1208. The long war was over, and once again John's hopes of building up a vast continental coalition against Philip of France revived.

John began to subsidize the leading men of the Low Countries and to carry on a great deal of correspondence with Otto. His brother Henry, the Count Palatine, came to England in the spring of 1209, ostensibly to intercede for Stephen Langton. John gave him a pension of a thousand marks a year, and Henry left his young son to be educated at the English court. Otto was crowned by Innocent in Rome on October 4, 1209, and already he was plotting to seize from the Pope the lands he had promised to respect.

John spent the Christmas of 1208 at Bristol. His second son was born on January 5, 1209 and was christened Richard, after his uncle of immortal fame. Richard's nurse, Eva, was paid fourpence a day, whereas Helen, the young Henry's nurse, received only twopence.

Early in 1209 the Pope, at the request of Archbishop Stephen Langton, who had perforce to remain on the Continent, relaxed the severity of the interdict somewhat by permitting the celebration of Mass once a week in the conventual churches. This privilege was not extended to the Cistercians, however, to punish them for having previously disregarded the interdict, and it did not affect the parish churches, the centers of the religious life of the nation.

England had now been under the interdict for a year, and no very dreadful results had become apparent. The country was prosperous; her foreign trade, based mainly on wool, was increasing steadily; there was no Crusade or expedition against Philip of France to keep

the nobles out of the realm, and they were thus able to turn their attention to the management of their estates. Financially both John and,
indirectly, the whole kingdom benefited greatly from the interdict,
for the confiscation of the ecclesiastical properties brought so much
money into the exchequer that there was no need for any general
taxation. Indeed, when the whole business was over, it was generally
agreed that John took over a hundred thousand pounds from the
Church.

John had insured himself against any overt disaffection on the part
of his nobles by taking hostages from them; he now turned his attention to the northern border. He collected a large force and marched
north, with the intention of making sure that William the Lion, of
Scotland, gave him no trouble. At Norham, in Northumberland, he
drew up his army in battle array, but William, who was now past
sixty-five years of age, was too cautious to accept this challenge. He
sued for peace, and John reproached him with harboring his enemies
and giving assistance to them. A treaty was drawn up between them
on June 28, 1209, according to which William agreed to pay twelve
thousand marks as a fine and to give his two legitimate daughters,
Margaret and Isabella, as hostages for his good conduct in the future.

When he returned from Northumberland John had all the freeholders in England come and swear fealty to him. This order included boys of the age of twelve and upwards, who were obliged to
take their part in the defence of the country. After the King had received their homage he dismissed them with the kiss of peace. So
great was John's power that he succeeded in forcing the Welsh to
come to Woodstock and do homage to him, a thing, remarks Roger
of Wendover, that had never been heard of in the past.

At about this time a certain clerk who was studying the liberal
arts at Oxford accidentally killed a woman and then fled from the
town. The Mayor of Oxford and some of his officials, in their search
for the guilty man, arrested and put in prison three of his fellow clerks

who had rented a house with him. When this case was brought before the King for judgment, he ordered that the three clerks, without benefit of clergy, should be taken outside the town and hanged. In protest, the entire population of the University, masters as well as pupils, numbering some three thousand, left Oxford and migrated, some to Cambridge (which is the first mention we have of that university so renowned for beauty and learning), and some to Reading.

William of Blois, Bishop of Lincoln, had died on Ascension Eve, 1206. As his successor the chapter, at John's suggestion, elected Hugh of Wells, the elder brother of Jocelyn of Wells, Bishop of Bath. John immediately gave him jurisdiction over the temporal possessions of the bishopric as a mark of his great favor. Hugh could not be consecrated in England, however, because of the interdict, and John accordingly sent him to Normandy to be consecrated by the Archbishop of Rouen. When Hugh got out of England he showed his independence by going to Archbishop Stephen Langton, still in exile, and swearing obedience to him. The Archbishop consecrated him on December 20, 1209.

When John learned of this, he declared Hugh a traitor and confiscated all the property he had conferred on the Bishop at his election. Lincoln was a large and wealthy diocese, the largest in England, and its revenues swelled the royal exchequer considerably.

CHAPTER X

EXCOMMUNICATION

1209-1212

AT LAST Pope Innocent III began to realize that the interdict, which had proved effective against Philip of France, would not bring John to submission. Indeed, the publication of the sentence apparently strengthened John's position, for it cut most of the prelates off from any participation in the government and thus gave the King a more nearly absolute hand in the conduct of affairs. It weakened the authority of the clergy from the Archbishop down to the humblest priest and demonstrated that the people could after all dispense with those services of the Church which they had been taught were essential to their welfare in this world and in the next. It diverted to the King's treasury the immense revenues of the Church, and it forced John in self-defense to assure himself of the loyalty of his barons by taking hostages from those of whom he had any doubts.

England during the early years of the interdict was a more nearly united nation than at any other time during John's reign. The King must have presented his case convincingly to his nobles. The endeavors of Innocent III to center the control of the Universal Church, even in its day-to-day administration, in the hands of the Papal Curia naturally aroused the resentment and opposition not only of the bishops but also of the barons. The bishops saw their powers gradually being weakened and their jurisdiction challenged by perpetual appeals over their heads to Rome, but they could make no effective protest against the Supreme Pontiff from whom their powers were derived. The barons could more easily arrive at a working understanding with the bishops, who were members of their own class, whom they met frequently in the Great Council, and with whom they were accustomed to share the administration of the government, than with prelates in far-off Rome. John and his partisans could hardly be expected to realize that this centralization of ecclesiastical administration and strengthening of discipline were greatly to the benefit of the Church.

This was an age when tradition was greatly respected. Customary usages had the force of law, and legal forms (because of the great advances in the formulation of codes of laws and the development of efficient and comprehensive ways of legal procedure under Henry II and his sons) appealed strongly to the powerful class of administrators, a new nobility in themselves, which the increasing complexity of governmental business was calling into existence. John's side of the question of the election of Stephen Langton was clear and convincing to them. Whatever the customary, legal, and valid form for the election of the Archbishop of Canterbury might be; whether the minstermen of Canterbury might elect him, or the bishops of the Southern Province had the right to elect, or the two together had the right; whether the King might licitly suggest the man of his choice or not—regardless of all this, one thing was abundantly clear: neither by custom nor by law could the Pope appoint the Archbishop of Canterbury without the King's consent, and none of Innocent's predecessors had ever claimed such a right. To be sure, they confirmed the choice once made, by whatever means it had been made, and conferred the pallium as a mark of their approval, but they did not appoint the Archbishop.

To say that Stephen Langton had been lawfully and canonically elected by a handful of Canterbury monks in the intimidating presence of the Pope and the College of Cardinals would seem to John and no doubt to most of his nobles mere quibbling. Such an election was much more a violation of the cherished right of free elections for which Innocent had fought so hard than was any of those elections by duly qualified chapters in the presence of the King, to which the Pope, in his ignorance or deliberate flouting of the ancient English custom, had now objected.

And it was to the ancient English custom that John appealed again and again. In a letter to the Pope written at about this time, he expressed his side of the controversy clearly:

> ALL my predecessors conferred archbishoprics, bishoprics, and abbeys in their chamber. As you may read in holy writings, the blessed and glorious King, St. Edward, conferred the bishopric of Worcester in his time on St. Wulfstan. When William the Bastard, the conqueror of England, wanted to deprive him of the bishopric, because he did not know French, St. Wulfstan replied: "You did not give me my staff, and I will not give it to you." He went to the tomb of St. Edward and said in his mother tongue: "Edward, you gave me my staff, and now on account of the King I cannot hold it: so I give it into your keeping, and if you can defend me, do so." He fixed the staff in the tomb of worked stone, and the staff miraculously adhered to the tomb, so that only St. Wulfstan was able to pluck it out again.

John had a final argument that must have seemed of great weight to his council. All the nobles of England had suffered at Philip's hands in one way or another: some had fought against him in the many engagements that had been going on almost without interruption since he came to the throne in 1180; some had lost lands and possessions in the final surrender of Normandy in 1205; and all had contributed to the heavy expense of keeping him at bay. Would they accept as their Archbishop a man who had gained Philip's favor, enjoyed his confidence, and shared in his councils? With such a background, Stephen Langton would seem the last person in whom the King could trust and on whom he could bestow the lands and the temporal powers that the Archbishop of Canterbury, as one of the great tenants-in-chief, enjoyed by virtue of his position.

Against John's obduracy, however, the Pope had a stronger weapon even than the interdict, one that would cut him off from his subjects and from all Christian men and deprive him of the support he had received from his barons. Under the interdict, King and subjects suffered alike, if indeed a man so completely lacking in any religious sense as John seems to have been could be said to suffer. The odium of the interdict fell particularly upon the King, for he was the cause of it, but the tranquil course of events in England since the publication of the sentence showed Innocent that John could bear that odium with ease. The Pope therefore decided, in the autumn of 1209, to excommunicate John by name and thus pronounce a sentence that would cut him off from the Church, make it unlawful for any Christian to associate with him or give him food, drink, or shelter, and damn him in the world to come.

Innocent ordered William, Bishop of London, Eustace, Bishop of Ely, and Mauger, Bishop of Worcester, to publish the sentence of excommunication on every Sunday and feast day in all the conventual churches in England, since these were the only ones in which

Mass could be celebrated. The three bishops, however, had fled to the Continent after publishing the interdict, and they felt no desire to return to England on a mission that would further enrage the King against them. They secured the Pope's permission to delegate the publication of the sentence to the prelates who remained in England, but these clerics, "either through fear of the King or through regard for him," says Roger of Wendover, thus showing that the sympathies of some at least of the English clergy were with John, "became like dumb dogs not daring to bark" and refused to publish the sentence. The decree was promulgated in France, however, and the news soon reached England, where "even in the places of assembly of the people it afforded a subject of secret conversation to all."

His excommunication had no notable effect in alienating John's subjects from him. His Christmas court at Windsor in 1209 was a particularly brilliant one, attended by all the nobles of England. Some no doubt came through fear, for John dealt harshly with all those who showed any signs of disaffection. Others, whose sympathies were with the King in his struggle with Innocent, salved their consciences with the pretext that since the sentence had not been published in England they were not bound to observe it. Yet a third group, the intimate friends and companions of the King, were of the same irreligious temper as their master and paid little heed to the sentence.

The excommunication, however, brought out some of John's worst qualities. He had spent most of his life in an atmosphere of suspicion, distrust, and treachery, and it was natural that he should suspect all about him of treachery. Morbidly suspicious, he began to feel that every man's hand was against him. If, which is doubtful, he had ever had any hope of saving his soul, assuming that John believed that he had a soul and that it could be saved, this hope was dashed to the ground when the Supreme Pontiff cursed him in all his doings, in this world and the next. No man of God could give him good

counsel, for the higher clergy remaining in the realm were his crea-
tures, submissive to his will, and the lower clergy could not reach
his ear. Publicly cut off from the Church, John publicly flouted the
canons of morality. Cruelty and avarice began to appear more openly
in his deeds, but the cruelty put the fear of him into his nobles and
repressed any inclinations they may have felt towards disloyalty and
treachery, and the avarice extorted from his victims sums that would
otherwise have been raised by the regular means of taxation.

Roger of Wendover tells two stories that illustrate the cruelty and
avarice that characterized John's conduct at this time. After the news
of the King's excommunication reached England, a certain Geoffrey,
an official of the Exchequer, began to talk to his fellow clerks at
Westminster about the sentence and expressed the opinion that no
one, and least of all a beneficed cleric, might with impunity remain
in the service of an excommunicated person. Through these scruples
of conscience he left the Exchequer without permission and stayed at
home. When John learned of his absence and the reason for it, he
sent William Talbot, one of his knights, with some soldiers to Geoffrey's house to arrest him and put him in prison. After he had been in
prison for a few days, a heavy sheet of lead in the form of a cope, out
of deference to his clerical character, was put about him. He was
given no food, and at length he died. This was generally felt to be a
cruel punishment, even for a treasury official.

The Jews enjoyed the King's special protection, as he took pains
to point out as early as 1203 in the following letter:

THE KING ETC. to the Mayor and Barons of London ETC.
*We have always loved you greatly, and we have made your laws
and liberties to be well observed, wherefore we believe that you
love us in a special way and freely wish to do those things that affect our honor and the peace and tranquillity of our land. Nevertheless, since you know that the Jews are under our special pro-*

tection, we are amazed that you allow harm to be done to the Jews dwelling in the city of London, for this is manifestly against the peace of the realm and the tranquillity of our land. We are all the more amazed and concerned, because the other Jews throughout England, wherever they dwell, except those in your city, enjoy good peace. Nor are we concerned only for the Jews, but also for our peace, for if we gave our peace to a dog, it ought to be inviolably observed. Henceforth, then, we commit the Jews dwelling in the city of London to your custody, so that if anyone tries to harm them, you may all together help them and defend them, for we shall require their blood of your hands, if perchance any harm befalls them, which God forbid. We well know that these things happen through the foolish people of the town and not through the wise ones, but wise men should restrain the folly of the foolish. MYSELF AS WITNESS, *at Montford, on the 29th day of July.*

In return for this protection, the Jews' financial affairs were under the direct supervision of the Exchequer. Although this status shielded them to some extent from popular persecution, the King's knowledge of their transactions made it easy for him to wring money from them. John embarked on a series of extortions early in 1210, and Roger of Wendover says that he caused all the Jews in England, of both sexes, to be seized, imprisoned, and harshly tortured, in order to squeeze all the money possible from them. The head of the Jewish community at Bristol refused, even after being tortured, to pay anything, whereupon John ordered his agents to knock out one of the Jew's jaw-teeth every day till he paid ten thousand marks. After the Jew had thus lost seven teeth, he capitulated on the eighth day and paid the required sum.

John was strengthened in his opposition to Innocent by the influence of Master Alexander the Mason, a pseudo-theologian, as Roger of Wendover describes him. Master Alexander preached to John the comforting doctrine that the great scourge of the interdict had been brought upon England not through any fault of his own but because of the wickedness of the people, whom God intended to punish by this means. His new spiritual advisor assured John that he had been sent by God to rule his people with a rod of iron, to break them all in pieces like a potter's vessel, and to bind the noble and the powerful with iron shackles.

Venturing next into the fields of theology and canon law, Master Alexander took up the subject of the extent of the papal authority, a matter much discussed then in view of the extravagant claims advanced by Innocent III. Master Alexander declared that the Pope had no power over the lay estates of any ruler or over the government of that ruler's subjects. The Pope's authority, he said, was limited solely to the Church and its property: that was the extent of the power Our Lord had conferred on St. Peter and his successors.

Such doctrine was exactly what John wanted to hear, and the man who preached it stood high in his favor. The King had command of a great many benefices that he had acquired in the general confiscation of 1208, and he bestowed a number of them upon Master Alexander.

The Lacy family, with the two brothers Walter and Hugh Lords of Meath and of Ulster respectively, had become the most powerful in Ireland, and John was by no means certain of their fidelity. His distrust was increased by the fact that Walter de Lacy, the Lord of Meath, had given shelter to his father-in-law, William de Braose, when he fled from England in 1208.

The older generation, with whom John had had dealings during his first visit to Ireland, had pretty well died out and been succeeded by a new one, not quite so lawless but almost equally turbulent. Rory O'Connor, the last High King of Ireland, had died a peaceful death at his abbey of Cong in 1199. The native Irish princes were gradu ally being pushed farther and farther to the west and were being sup-planted by the Norman nobility, who quarreled and fought among themselves with all the enthusiasm the Irish had formerly displayed.

John had sent his cousin Meiler FitzHenry, a bastard son of Henry I by the notorious Nesta, daughter of the King of South Wales, to Ireland as his justiciar in 1200. Meiler's term of office was a difficult and troubled one. John de Courci, the conqueror of Ulster, defied Meiler's authority and was engaged in almost constant war with Hugh de Lacy. Hugh eventually drove John out, and the King made him Earl of Ulster in 1205. Hugh then turned against Meiler, and he and his brother waged open war against the justiciar. William de Burgh, who was engaged in the conquest of Connaught, was an-other trouble-maker, but Meiler succeeded in depriving him of his estates.

In 1208 the Lacy brothers finally drove Meiler FitzHenry out of the country. John replaced him with John Grey, Bishop of Nor-wich, but his talents were administrative rather than military, and the power of the Lacys was unchecked. With the object of asserting his supremacy in Ireland, curtailing the power of the Lacy's, assuring himself of the fealty of the Anglo-Norman nobles and the Irish princes, and placing the country under the supervision of a man he could trust, John determined on an expedition to the island.

He sailed from Pembroke with a large army in seven hundred vessels and landed in Ireland on June 6, 1210. When he reached Dublin, more than twenty of the Irish chieftains hastened to do hom-age and swear fealty to him. He reduced a number of the Irish cas-tles and led his army into the County of Meath. William de Braose had already escaped to Wales when he learned of John's expedition, leaving his wife and eldest son in Meath. Walter and Hugh de Lacy fled to Scotland and thence to France. The King besieged the castle in which Maude de Braose and her son had taken refuge, captured the castle, and confiscated the Lacy lands. Maude and her son William, who was a grown man, fled to Scotland. Duncan of Carrick captured them in Galloway and turned them over to John. He sent them back to England, loaded with chains, and had them confined in Windsor Castle. Maude, by accusing John of the murder of Arthur, had aroused his implacable wrath, and he had her and her son starved to death at Windsor.

William Marshal had married Isabella de Clare, the daughter and heiress of Strongbow, and thus succeeded to his enormous estates in Ireland, chief among which was the lordship of Leinster. He went over to see his Irish lands for the first time in 1207, but before he would let him go, John forced him to surrender all his castles in England and to leave his son Richard as a hostage for his fidelity, which only a mind like John's could ever dream of suspecting. William, too, had a great deal of trouble with Meiler FitzHenry, who tried to deprive him of some of his lands.

When William de Braose and his family fled to Ireland, William Marshal sheltered them for twenty days when they first landed, before they went on to the Lacys. John reproached William for having given refuge to his mortal enemy.

"Sire," William replied, "I sheltered my lord when he came to my castle in great trouble. If I took care of him when he was in distress, you should not take it in bad part. I did not think that I was doing anything wrong, for he was my friend and my lord (Marshal held land of Braose in England), and I did not know that you had anything against him. You were good friends when I left England to come here. Now if anyone except you wants to say that there is anything more to the matter than this, I am ready to defend myself according to the judgment of your court."

John grudgingly accepted William's explanation, but he took a number of his knights as hostages.

With the able assistance of John Grey, the King set about reorganizing the administration of Ireland and bringing it into conformity with the efficient English model. He promulgated English laws and customs and appointed sheriffs and other officials to govern according to those laws. He established a coinage uniform with that of England and had pennies, halfpennies, and round farthings minted, stamped with the image of a harp. In England the only coin minted was still the silver penny, which was halved and quartered to make halfpennies and farthings.

John left the Bishop of Norwich as his justiciar in Ireland and, after arranging affairs there to his satisfaction, returned to England on August 29. This had been a brilliant expedition, capably managed, which accomplished all that John intended it should and ensured the tranquillity and good government of Ireland for a number of years.

Whilst John was in Ireland, his first legitimate daughter, Joan, was born, on July 22.

Immediately after his return, John ordered all the prelates remaining in England to meet him in London. When they had assembled, he wrung money from them unmercifully. The White Monks alone were forced to pay forty thousand marks. By the rules of their Order, they could possess no money, and John took delight in forcing this observance upon them.

John's ally, Otto, meanwhile, was openly breaking his promises to Innocent with regard to the lands the Pope had annexed in central Italy. In August 1210, he attacked Tuscany, and in November he embarked on the conquest of Apulia. He made no secret of his determination to conquer Sicily and unite it to the Empire, a policy which Innocent had steadfastly opposed. Otto paid no attention to the Pope's warnings, and in November 1210, Innocent excommunicated him, released his subjects from their oaths of allegiance, and began working with Philip of France in trying to stir up a revolt against Otto in Germany.

The King spent the Christmas of 1210 at York, where the earls

and barons gathered for his court. The properties of the archbishopric had been in the King's hands since Geoffrey had fled from
England.

During the spring of 1211 John busied himself with preparations
for an expedition into North Wales. Llywelyn ap Iorwerth, who
had married John's bastard daughter, also named Joan, in 1206, had
been extending his influence over most of Wales, and John was unwilling that any one Welsh chieftain should have such power as his
son-in-law was assuming. If Wales could not be brought directly
under English control, it was better that the country, whose moun-
tainous terrain made conquest and peaceful administration particularly difficult, should be ruled by a number of smaller chieftains
whose wranglings among themselves might divert their energies from
attacks on the English borders.

John assembled his army at Whitchurch and marched into Wales
on July 8, 1211. He penetrated as far as the Snowdon district and
routed the Welsh forces. He captured the city of Bangor and burned
it, and he seized the Bishop of Bangor, who had defied him on account of his excommunication. Llywelyn was forced to sue for
peace, and he sent his wife to her father to try to secure honorable
terms for him. Then Llywelyn came to John and made his submission. The King deprived him of most of his lands, asserted the English supremacy over North Wales, and took twenty-eight young men
of noble birth as hostages, to secure the good behavior of the Welsh
in the future.

John's position was now strong indeed. He had in three successive
campaigns forced Scotland, Ireland, and Wales into submission,
which not even his father had been able to do, and he had nothing
to fear from any of those countries. "There was no one who did not
obey his nod," says the Barnwell annalist. Consequently, when messengers from the Pope came to discuss the possibility of making peace,

John could take a high stand. From Wales he had returned to Whit-church, and from there he went to Northampton, where he met the Pope's emissaries on the Feast of the Assumption, August 15, 1211.

Innocent had sent Pandulf, a sub-deacon of the Papal Curia, and Durand, a Templar, to see if they could effect a reconciliation, for it was now obvious that none of the measures Innocent had yet devised was sufficient to bring John to submission. Indeed, he had waxed more powerful under the interdict and excommunication than he had ever been before, and the deadlock promised to continue indefinitely. After discussing the matter with the messengers and with the Great Council, which he had summoned to Northampton, John declared his willingness to allow Stephen Langton and all the bishops who had sought refuge on the Continent to return to England, with the implication that it did not much matter whether they stayed abroad or came back. England had got along very well without them and could probably get along just as well with them.

John was adamant on one point, however: he refused to make any compensation to them for the financial losses they had incurred or to return to them any of the past revenues from the sees and benefices that had fallen to the Crown. He was willing to restore their tem-poral fiefs to the clergy, but he would not deliver to them the income that had accrued from those fiefs since the interdict had been pro-nounced. That money had already been collected and spent, a great deal of it in the form of subsidies to his allies on the Continent. With this message the envoys returned to the Pope.

At this council at Northampton the King levied a scutage of two marks on each knight's fee, to be paid by those who had not done military service in the campaign in Wales.

John welcomed to England at about this time a powerful ally, Reginald of Dammartin, Count of Boulogne. Reginald was one of the greatest vassals of Philip of France. Through his wife, Ida, the heiress of Boulogne, he had received that county, with its ports of

Calais and Boulogne. In addition, Philip had given him John's former county of Mortain and that of Aumâle, and Reginald's daughter and heiress, Maude, was betrothed to Philip's son by Agnes of
Meran, Philip Hurepel. It is eloquent testimony to the strength of
John's position at this time that so wise and experienced a statesman
as Reginald should have decided that his chances were better as an
ally of John than as a vassal of Philip and that he should have sided
openly with the English King. When Philip learned of Reginald's
connection with John, he marched against his vassal and drove him
out of France. Reginald took refuge in England and set about helping John build up his alliances on the Continent with all those who
feared or distrusted Philip's growing power. John gave the Count of
Boulogne three hundred pounds a year, and Reginald did homage
and swore fealty to him.

William de Braose, who had contrived to escape to France in the
preceding year, died at Corbeuil on August 9, 1211 and was buried
in Paris. Stephen Langton officiated at the funeral, a gesture that
could hardly have endeared him to John.

Innocent's envoys, Pandulf and Durand, had in the meantime returned to Rome and reported the results of their interview with the
King. The Pope would be satisfied with nothing less than complete
submission on John's part, and a mere granting of permission for the
exiled prelates to return to England, without any recompense for their
confiscated revenues, was not enough. It was obvious that no one
was paying much attention to the sentence of excommunication laid
on John. The Pope therefore sought to ensure its observance by extending it to all who associated with the King "at the table, in council, or in conversation." Finally, he absolved John's subjects from
their oaths of fealty and allegiance to the King, so that they were no
longer bound in conscience to obey him. This sentence, again, could
not be published in England, but news of it traveled across the Channel and soon reached the ears of John's subjects.

The King spent the Christmas of 1211 at Windsor. The Pipe Roll records the purchase, for the Christmas feast, of 60 pounds of pepper, 18 pounds of cumin, half a pound of galingale (the aromatic root of a variety of sedge), three pounds of cinnamon, one pound of cloves, half a pound of nutmeg, two pounds of ginger, 10,000 herrings, 1,800 whitings, 900 haddocks, and 3,000 lampreys, as well as 1,500 cups, 1,200 pitchers, and 4,000 plates. The breakage at one of these royals feasts must have been considerable.

The gallant Constable of Chester, Roger de Lacy, died in January 1212. When Château-Gaillard fell on March 8, 1204, Philip of France held Roger for a heavy ransom. John contributed a thousand pounds for his release. When Roger returned to England, John made him Sheriff of Yorkshire and of Cheshire to reward him for his heroic defense of Richard's stronghold. He served as a justiciar and was one of John's intimate friends.

On Easter Sunday, March 4, 1212, John gave a great feast at St. Bridget's Clerkenwell, and whilst he was at table he knighted the young Alexander, the son of William the Lion of Scotland.

During this summer John had the first dockyard built at Portsmouth, as the following letter shows:

THE KING to the Sheriff of Southampton, ETC. *We order you without delay to have our dock at Portsmouth closed with a good strong wall, by the view of lawful men, as our beloved and faithful servant, William, Archdeacon of Taunton, tells you, to safeguard our galleys and ships; and have additions made to the same wall, as the same Archdeacon tells you, in which all the appurtenances of our ships may be safely kept. And make haste to do these things this summer, lest through your fault in the coming winter we suffer any damage to our ships and galleys and their appurtenances. And when we learn the cost, we will have it ac-*

counted to you. MYSELF AS WITNESS, at the Tower of London, on the 20th day of May.

Mauger, the exiled Bishop of Worcester, died at Pontigny in France on July 1.

On the night of July 10 the Church of St. Mary in Southwark caught fire, and the conflagration quickly spread over the south side of the river. The new stone bridge across the Thames, which had been begun in 1176 and which was to stand for over six hundred years, had been finished in 1209, and wooden houses, as well as a chapel dedicated to St. Thomas of Canterbury, had been built on it. The fire spread to them and thus crossed to the north side of the river. Houses at this time were almost all built of wood, and even the few stone houses were thatched with straw or reeds. Consequently there was nothing to stop the blaze, and it swept over the greater part of London. Many lives were lost; Matthew Paris estimates that a thousand people perished in the fire.

London had already acquired a reputation as a wicked metropolis. This is how Richard of Devizes describes it:

EVERY sort of man from every country under the heavens crowds together there; each race brings its own vices and its own customs to the city. No one lives there free from crime; every quarter of the city abounds in grave scandals; that man is counted greatest who most excels in rascality. . . . Whatever is evil or malicious in any part of the world, you will find it in this one city. Do not approach the chorus of pimps; do not mingle with the crowds in eating houses; avoid dice and gambling, the theater and the tavern. You will meet with more braggarts there than in all France; the number of parasites is infinite. Actors, jesters, smooth-skinned lads, Moors, flatterers, pretty boys, effeminates.

pederasts, singing girls, quacks, belly-dancers, sorceresses, extortioners, night wanderers, magicians, mimes, beggars, buffoons: all this tribe fill all the houses."

Although Llywelyn ap Iorwerth had in the previous year bound himself to keep the peace, during the summer of 1212 he broke forth again from his hiding places in North Wales. The Welsh captured and destroyed the castles John had built to guard the border, killed the garrisons, and burned several towns. The King hastily called together an army to subdue them. When he reached Nottingham, without stopping to eat or drink, he ordered the twenty-eight young hostages that he had taken the year before to be hanged on the gibbet forthwith.

With the hanging of the hostages out of the way, John sat down to dinner. Whilst he was at table two messengers came, bearing letters from William the Lion and from Joan, the wife of Llywelyn. The purport of the letters was identical; both warned him that his nobles were plotting against him and that if he persisted in his expedition to Wales some of his disaffected barons would either kill him or deliver him over to the Welsh for destruction.

John was so alarmed by these letters that he immediately abandoned the campaign against the Welsh and dismissed his army with the following letter:

THE KING to all his earls and barons who see this letter, ETC. *We thank you because you have come in such force to Chester in our service, but we cannot go there at present, because certain affairs of ours call us back. And therefore we command you to return to your own parts with the knights and people you brought with you, and we will multiply our thanks to you.* MYSELF AS WITNESS, *at Nottingham, on the* 16th *day of August, in the* 14th *year of our reign.*

He again sent messengers to all the nobles he distrusted to demand
hostages of them, and he did not attempt to disguise his distrust, as
the following letter to the Earl of Huntingdon shows:

THE KING to Earl David: WHATEVER GREETING IS DUE TO
YOU. *You have delivered your son to us as a hostage for your
faithful service. And now we command you, as soon as you see
this letter, to deliver up our castle of Fotheringhay to our faithful
servants, Simon of Pattishull and Walter of Preston, for our use.*

Although he had just given a demonstration of how he might treat
the hostages of those who were unfaithful to him, none of his nobles
dared to refuse him, and they sent their sons, brothers, nephews, or
other relatives to him as pledges of their loyalty.

Two men, however, fled the kingdom and thus tacitly announced
their treasonable designs. Eustace de Vesci, who had married Margaret, the bastard daughter of William the Lion, took refuge in Scotland, and Robert FitzWalter fled to France.

For the first time since the imposition of the interdict we hear of
widespread discontent and disaffection among the barons. They had
sided, for the most part, with John in his struggle with the Pope, and
the confiscation of the ecclesiastical revenues had lifted the burden of
taxation from them. The scutage of 1211 to pay for the Welsh campaign was the first general tax John had levied since he seized the
Church lands. With the enforced absence from John's councils of
the bishops and abbots, who may on the whole be presumed to have
exercised a moderating influence, the King became increasingly stern
and repressive. He distrusted everyone except his most intimate
friends, and his major concern was so to increase his power that he
could hold his barons in check in any eventuality. Stern repression,
the taking of hostages, the punishment of individual malcontents by
crushing fines or the confiscation of their lands, and other measures

to enforce the support of a sullen and disaffected baronage were effective only as long as the barons remained divided and found no common cause to unite them. That they were beginning to attempt concerted action is indicated by the events of this summer. Although John could find no evidence of the existence of the plot against which he had been warned, it is probable that, at the least, the idea of some form of united action was being discussed by the more discontented among his barons.

Roger of Wendover gives three principal reasons for the rising feeling against John. In the first place, he charges, the King had violated the wives and daughters of many of his nobles. Matthew Paris and later writers repeat this accusation. John's private life was undoubtedly bad, and he seems to have been quite lacking in any sense of morality.

The second charge is that John had reduced many of his nobles to poverty by his unjust exactions. His need of money was great. The cost of the normal administrative operations of the government, to which was added the heavy burden of accounting for the Church lands, was constantly increasing, and, furthermore, John had waged three military campaigns in three successive summers. He was, moreover, sending large subsidies to his nephew Otto and to his other allies on the Continent. Against these extraordinary expenditures and in addition to the normal revenues, John had received the income from the Church properties, the levies upon the Jews and the clergy in 1210, and the confiscated estates of those who, like William de Braose, Eustace de Vesci, and Robert FitzWalter, had fled the country. In his need for money, John was no doubt driven to laying heavy fines, abusing his rights of wardship, and exacting disproportionately large reliefs when the heirs of tenants-in-chief entered upon their holdings. The Pipe Rolls for this period abound in entries of quite large sums of money paid "to have the King's good will" by various individuals who had aroused John's wrath by one means or another. In many cases these payments probably represent purely arbitrary sums demanded by the King. Robert de Vaux, for instance, got himself involved with another man's wife, and John found out about it. Robert had to give him five of the best palfreys "that the King may keep silent regarding Henry Pinel's wife," and he had to pay 750 marks "to have the King's good will."

The third charge against John arises from the second. Roger of Wendover states that many nobles were opposed to the King because he had exiled their parents or kindred and confiscated their estates. This seems to have been especially true at the beginning of the interdict, when the King expelled from the country not only the clergy whose loyalty he doubted but also their relatives, and confiscated their estates.

In short, says Roger of Wendover, the King had as many enemies as he had nobles. When they learned that the Pope had released them from their oaths of allegiance to John, it was reported that they sent a letter to Philip of France and invited him to invade England, seize the kingdom, and be crowned "with all honor and dignity." On the other hand, however, at this same time twenty-seven of the leading Anglo-Norman noblemen in Ireland, headed by the ever-faithful William Marshal, sent a signed declaration to John, assuring him that they were "ready to live or die with the King and that they would faithfully and inseparably cleave to him until the very end."

All these discontents were fanned by the preachings of Peter of Pontefract, a Yorkshire hermit, who was popularly believed to have the gift of prophecy. He declared that John would not be King on the next Ascension Day or afterwards, for on that day the crown would pass to another. This prophecy was circulated throughout the kingdom and excited a great deal of interest. When John heard of it he had Peter brought before him and asked the hermit whether he meant that the King would die on that day or whether he would be deposed.

"Rest assured that on Ascension Day you will not be King," Peter replied. "If I am proved to have told a lie, do what you will with me then."

"Be it as you say," said John, and he had Peter put into prison in Corfe Castle to await the outcome of his prophecy.

At about this time, and certainly before the summer of 1212, John sent an embassy to Muhammad al-Nasir, Sultan of Morocco, to endeavor to enlist his help. John had been working unceasingly to build up a coalition against Philip of France sufficiently strong to counterbalance his growing power and, if possible, destroy it. The allies were headed by the Emperor Otto and included many of the strongest nobles whose territories lay to the northeast and east of Philip's. Their plans were now sufficiently advanced for them to have agreed upon the strategy of their attack. That plan was for their forces, when they felt that they were strong enough, to attack Philip on the northeast whilst John at the same time struck from the south, through Poitou. The weakness of the plan was that John could not be sure of assembling an army large enough to offer a serious threat to Philip from the south. He could not depend on his English barons to follow him to the Continent, and the Poitevin nobles were treacherous and unreliable. Ever since the battle of Alarcos in 1196 the Muslims had been the dominant military power in Northern Spain, and it occurred to John to see if he could induce them to help him.

Matthew Paris says that John sent three messengers, the knights Thomas Hardington and Ralph FitzNicholas and the monk Robert of London, to "Murmelius, the great king of Africa, Morocco, and Spain." Murmelius is a corruption of Amir-al-Muminim, Prince of the Faithful, a title of the Emir of Cordova, later assumed by the Sultan of Morocco. The Sultan at this time was Muhammad al-Nasir, who had succeeded his father, the victor of Alarcos, in 1199. John offered, in exchange for his help, to give up himself and his kingdom to the Sultan, to hold as a tributary from him, to renounce Christianity, and to embrace Islam.

The weak point of the embassy was that John had little to offer the Sultan in exchange for his help. His financial difficulties, already aggravated by the drain of payments to the members of the coalition, would not permit him to purchase Muslim aid. John hit then on the only offer in which he thought the Sultan would be interested. Promises came easily to him, and it was easy to promise to do homage to the Sultan and to become a Muslim. After all, John had little reason to call himself a Christian and still less to value the name. It may have appealed to his wry sense of humor to offer to put his kingdom, in which the Pope had forbidden all religious services for the last four years, under the protection of an infidel.

The Sultan questioned the messengers about their master. They described him as gray-headed, strong in body, stoutly built, and not tall. (As a matter of fact, when John's tomb was opened in 1797, his skeleton was found to measure five feet, five inches.) The Sultan dismissed John's offer, probably on the grounds that he could see no advantage in accepting it and that he needed all his strength for the approaching conflict with Alfonso VIII of Castile. The fact that Muhammad al-Nasir was crushingly defeated by Alfonso at the battle of Las Navas on July 16, 1212 makes it unlikely that this embassy was sent after that time.

After the Sultan had dismissed the ambassadors, he called Robert of London back to him and questioned him more closely. Robert told him, reports Matthew Paris, that John was a tyrant rather than a king, a destroyer rather than a governor, an oppressor of his people and a friend to foreigners, a lion to his subjects and a lamb to foreigners and to his enemies. He was an insatiable extorter of money and an invader and destroyer of his subjects' possessions. He hated his wife and was hated by her. The Queen, Robert informed the Sultan, was an incestuous, evil-disposed, and adulterous woman. She had often been unfaithful to the King, and he had had some of her lovers strangled with a rope on her very bed. He was envious of many of his nobles and had violated their daughters and sisters, and he was wavering and lax in the observance of his religion.

Matthew Paris got all of this from Robert of London himself. The King made him Abbot of St. Albans, where Matthew Paris later was a monk. It should be remembered, however, that the chronicler did not begin writing till twenty years after John's death.

John's distrust of his Queen shows up curiously in an order providing her with pages:

> THE KING, to Ralph Raleigh and Geoffrey de Martigny. *We are sending the two sons of Richard of Umframville, Odinell and Robert, to you. We command you to have them serve before the Lady Queen at her dinner every day, but their tutor is not to come before the Lady Queen. And have them sleep at night in the hall, and have them taken care of honorably.* WITNESSED BY THE KING, *at Durham, on the 3rd day of September.*

The two lads named in this letter were among the four sons that Richard had to deliver to the King as hostages "for his faithful service," as well as his castle of Prudhoe.

SUBMISSION

R 1212-1214 ℜ

IN THE autumn of 1212 Archbishop Stephen Langton and the Bishops of London and Ely went to Rome to discuss the situation in England with the Pope. England had now been under the interdict for four and a half years, and the public religious life of the country was virtually extinct. Neither the interdict of the country nor the personal excommunication of the King had brought John to terms; the absolution of his subjects from their vows of fealty had provided some encouragement to the more discontented of the barons, but it had failed to shake John's strong grasp on the kingdom. One measure remained, and that the Pope, after consulting with his cardinals and bishops, decided to use. He decreed that John should be deposed from his throne and that "another, more worthy than he, to be chosen by the Pope, should succeed him," as Roger of Wendover reports.

Innocent entrusted the congenial task of deposing John to Philip of France and promised him that he and his successors should have perpetual possession of the kingdom of England. The Pope gave the projected expedition against John the character of a crusade by writing to various prominent men who were known to be John's enemies and urging them to assume the Cross and follow Philip in this holy war.

Pandulf was present when the Pope and his counsellors reached this decision. Innocent ordered him to return to France with the English ecclesiastics and see that the papal commands were obeyed. Pandulf privately asked Innocent what should be done in case John repented and showed his willingness to come to terms. The Pope then dictated a set of conditions and promised that if John would agree to them the whole matter might be settled without resorting to the drastic measure of invading England.

Whilst these affairs were being arranged at the papal court, Geoffrey, the exiled Archbishop of York, died in Normandy on December 18, 1212. His life as Archbishop had been marred by unceasing squabbles, quarrels, and lawsuits with the clergy and magnates of his diocese, the canons of his cathedral, who seem to have been a particularly stubborn and intractable group, the bishops of his province, the Archbishop of Canterbury, and the King. One prefers to remember him as the only faithful one among Henry's sons, gentle, loyal, and loving to his father on the King's deathbed, staying with him when all the rest had deserted and betrayed him.

John kept his Christmas at Westminster, attended by only a few of his nobles. His open confession at Nottingham during the preceding summer that he feared and distrusted his barons seems to have weakened his hold over them, for this was the first time that many of them dared to absent themselves from his court.

The three English bishops came to Philip in January 1213, with the welcome tidings that the Pope had authorized him to invade

England and deprive John of his crown, and Philip started laying his plans.

John heard of the contemplated invasion of his realm, and he began to prepare to defend the country against attack. On March 3, from the New Temple, he sent letters to the bailiffs of the seaport towns, beginning: "We command you that immediately on receiving these our letters you go in person, together with the bailiffs of the ports, to each of the harbors in your bailiwick and make a careful list of all the ships there found capable of carrying six horses or more; and that, in our name, you order the masters as well as the owners of those ships, as they regard themselves, their ships, and all their property, to have them at Portsmouth at mid-Lent, well equipped with stores, tried seamen, and good soldiers, to enter into our service for our deliverance."

To his sheriffs John ordered: "Give warning by good agents to the earls, barons, knights, and all free and serving men, whoever they may be, that they be at Dover at the end of the coming Lent, equipped with horses and arms and all they can provide, to defend our person and themselves and the land of England, and let no one who can carry arms remain behind under penalty of being branded with cowardice and of being condemned to perpetual slavery; and let each man follow his lord."

This was the true voice of an English king, calling his Englishmen to defend their land, lest they be called "nithing" by their fellows. His barons, standing on the letter of the law, might refuse to follow their King across the Narrow Seas in an attempt to recapture his continental dominions, but at the threat of invasion the host assembled as it had in the days of Alfred. When the appointed time came, an enormous army met at Barham Down, near Canterbury. Men poured in from every part of England. Bishop John Grey and William Marshal arrived from Ireland with five hundred knights and a body of horse soldiers, practically the whole knight-service due from Ireland. These forces, says Roger of Wendover, were made up of "men of divers conditions and ages, who dreaded nothing more than the name of coward."

The King dispatched forces to Ipswich, Dover, Feversham, and other threatened ports. The remainder was so great that provisions failed, and John had to send some of the more inexperienced men back home. The main body, estimated at sixty thousand, he kept in readiness at Barham Down. "Had they been of one heart and one disposition towards the King of England and in defense of their country," remarks Roger of Wendover in a fine burst of patriotism, "there was not a prince under heaven against whom they could not have defended the Kingdom of England." The fleet assembled at Portsmouth was relatively even stronger than the land forces.

Philip meanwhile assembled his council at Soissons on April 8. The English bishops read the papal mandate deposing John and inviting Philip to be the instrument of that deposition. The council accepted the invitation, and Philip ordered his fleet to assemble at Boulogne and his army to gather at Rouen on April 21. To put the final touch to his novel position as the champion of Holy Church, Philip had Ingeborg released from her long imprisonment and effected a reconciliation with her.

While the two forces were thus poised, Philip ready to strike at England and John in full strength awaiting the threatened invasion, the sub-deacon Pandulf made one last attempt to persuade John to submit. He sent two Brothers of the Temple across the Channel to Dover. They came to John and told him that they had been sent by Pandulf to ask for an interview in which he might propose a form of peace whereby the King could be reconciled to God and the Church.

John, who would rather negotiate than fight, ordered the Templars to return to France and bring Pandulf to him. The Pope's familiar landed at Dover on May 13 and went at once to John. He

warned the King that Philip had assembled an enormous army and
fleet, which the exiled clerics and fugitive Englishmen had joined, to
expel him from England by force. John was well aware, through his
spies, of the size of Philip's forces and knew that his navy, at any
rate, was far superior to the French fleet. The words that struck terror to his heart were Pandulf's warning, which John had some reason
to believe true, that Philip had had letters from almost all the nobles
of England offering their fealty and support. Pandulf exhorted John
to be as penitent as if he were on his deathbed, submit himself to
the Church, and make his peace with God.

John capitulated; the long struggle was over.

Roger of Wendover gives four principal reasons for the King's
"repentance and atonement." First, he says, John had been under
excommunication for over three years and had so offended God and
the Church that he had given up all hope of saving his soul. This
probably had little weight with the King; there is nothing to indicate
that John could not have borne up quite cheerfully under the sentence
of excommunication for the rest of his life.

The second reason was his fear of Philip, who, with a great army,
was planning his downfall.

The third, and this is probably the heart of the matter, was that
John was afraid to meet Philip in battle for fear that his own nobles
would either abandon him in the field or deliver him up to Philip.
They were rotten with treachery, as later events were to prove, and
John knew it.

The last reason illustrates the strong superstition that took the
place of religion in John's hardened heart; more alarming than all the
rest, says the chronicler, was the fact that Ascension Day was drawing near, when the prophecy of the hermit Peter foretold that he
would lose his crown. Peter was in prison, awaiting the outcome of
his prediction, and it was widely believed that events would prove
him to be right.

John made his submission at Dover on this same day, May 13, 1213, in the presence of his earls and barons and a great gathering of people. He swore to abide by the commands of the Pope in all the matters for which he had been excommunicated; to give peace and full safety to Archbishop Stephen Langton, the exiled Bishops of London, Ely, Hereford, Bath, and Lincoln, the prior and monks of Canterbury, Robert FitzWalter and Eustace de Vesci, and all the rest of the clergy and laity connected with the affair; not to hurt them in person or in property; to receive them into his favor, and not to hinder them in the performance of their duties and the exercise of their full authority.

In return, the Archbishop and bishops were to give security on oath and in writing that they would not make any attempt against John's person or crown as long as he afforded them safety and kept the peace.

John promised furthermore to make full restitution for their confiscated property to both clergy and laity that were concerned in this matter, to release and restore to their full rights all men he had imprisoned in this affair, to remove the sentence of outlawry against the ecclesiastics and laymen involved, never again to pronounce the sentence of outlawry against the clergy, and to restore all that he had received from ecclesiastics since the beginning of the interdict, except the customary and lawful dues.

As a pledge of his good intentions, John promised that as soon as someone empowered to absolve him arrived he would deliver to the messengers of the exiled clerics the sum of eight thousand pounds to defray their immediate expenses. If any question arose as to the amount of the compensation due, John agreed that it was to be settled by the Pope's legate; matters that could not be so settled were to be referred to the Pope, by whose decision John promised to abide. When all these matters were settled, the interdict was to be lifted.

The charter setting forth these provisions was witnessed by Earl William of Salisbury, Count Reginald of Boulogne, Earl William of Warenne, and Earl William of Ferrars, who swore on the King's soul that he would keep the terms of the agreement.

Reginald was one of the greatest of John's foreign allies; the remaining three witnesses belonged to the small group of the King's most trusted and loyal friends. William "Longsword," Earl of Salisbury, was a bastard of Henry II by an unknown mother and hence was John's half-brother. He has not hitherto figured in this narrative because he had the gifts, rare indeed among Henry's sons, of prudence and of keeping out of trouble. He was unswerving in his loyalty to John, who had employed him on a number of important missions. King Richard had given him, in 1198, the hand of Ela, the daughter and heiress of William, the second Earl of Salisbury, who had died in 1196, and through her Longsword acquired the large estates and title of Salisbury.

Earl William of Warenne was the son of Hamelin, a bastard son of Geoffrey of Anjou. Hamelin and Henry II were half-brothers, and thus William and John were cousins. William came into possession of his father's estates in 1202. When John lost Normandy, William relinquished his Norman holdings and remained faithful to John.

Earl William of Ferrars was a member of the old Norman nobility. His mother was a sister of William de Braose, and he had married Agnes, a sister of Ranulf de Blundevill, Earl of Chester.

John had now made his peace with the Church, but he had no assurance that his submission to the Pope would cause Philip to abandon his plans for invading England. John conceived a scheme for placing himself under the direct protection of the Pope, an act that would change the nature of Philip's intended invasion from a holy war called by the Pope into an unlawful and sacrilegious attack on the Pope's own domain.

On May 15, the Eve of the Ascension, at Dover, in the presence of his barons and in the sight of a great crowd, John resigned his crown into the hands of Pandulf, the Pope's representative, and performed the act of feudal homage and allegiance, swearing: "I, John, by the grace of God King of England and Lord of Ireland, will from this time forth be faithful to God, to St. Peter, to the Church of Rome, and to my liege lord Pope Innocent and his Catholic successors."

This act gave Innocent that suzerainty over England that William the Conqueror had stoutly denied to Gregory VII. John confirmed it by a charter declaring: "Not by force or from fear of the interdict, but of our own free will and consent and by the general consent of our barons, we assign and grant to God, to His holy Apostles Peter and Paul, to the Holy Church of Rome, our mother, and to our lord Pope Innocent and his Catholic successors the whole Kingdom of England and the whole Kingdom of Ireland; and henceforth we retain and hold those countries from him and the Church of Rome as vicegerent. And we have made our homage and sworn allegiance to our lord the Pope and his Catholic successors; and we bind our successors and heirs in like manner to do homage and render allegiance."

The charter was witnessed by the Archbishop of Dublin; John Grey, Bishop of Norwich; Geoffrey FitzPeter, the Chief Justiciar; the Earls of Salisbury, Pembroke, Warenne, Winchester, Arundel, and Ferrars; Count Reginald of Boulogne; and William Bruyere, Peter FitzHerbert, and Warin FitzGerald. As a token of his vassalage to the Supreme Pontiff, John bound himself and his successors to pay a thousand marks yearly to the Pope.

This act was without precedent in English history. It had never occurred to even the most pious and saintly of John's predecessors, every one of whom, with the possible exception of William Rufus, exceeded John in his love and reverence for the Church, to surrender the kingdom to the Pope and to hold it of him as a feudal fief. It was a brilliant stratagem, designed to free John from his present dangers; it had little practical effect on the government of England, and John's son later repudiated it.

The next day, the Feast of the Ascension, came and went, and John was still safe and sound and still King of England. Taking the hermit Peter at his word, therefore, John had him brought from Corfe Castle, where he had been kept prisoner, to Wareham. There, together with his son, he was tied to a horse's tail, dragged through the streets of the town, and hanged. Roger of Wendover remarks that many people thought that Peter did not deserve to be punished so cruelly, for John's resignation of his crown on Ascension Eve into the hands of the Pope's representative was thought to lend some truth to Peter's prophecy.

Pandulf returned to France on May 22, taking with him John's charters of submission and of fealty and the sum of eight thousand pounds, as a part of the restitution due to the exiled clerics. He strongly advised the bishops, who were fully satisfied with the terms of John's submission, to return to England and receive the rest of the indemnity.

John also wrote to the Archbishop's brother:

THE KING, to his beloved Master Simon Langton: GREET-INGS. *Since we have accepted the terms of peace sent to us by the Lord Pope, we have commanded our venerable father, the Lord Stephen, Archbishop of Canterbury, and his fellow bishops to come to England safely and without delay. And since we wish henceforth to number you all among our friends, we command you to come safely to England, and we counsel the aforesaid Lord Archbishop and bishops to put aside all hesitation and hindrance and hasten to England.* WITNESSED BY THE LORD PE-TER OF WINCHESTER, at Wingham, on the 27th day of May.

There remained the more difficult task of dissuading Philip, the erstwhile champion of Holy Church, who was smugly awaiting the signal to snatch John's crown from his head as a glorious climax to a lifetime of enmity. Pandulf advised him to call off his plans for invading England, dismiss his troops and ships, and go home in peace. Things were now in quite a different posture: England was, through John's act of fealty, a papal fief. Instead of winning that remission of his sins that the Pope had promised him as a reward for the congenial task of deposing John, Philip would now be excommunicated if he proceeded to any hostile act against John, the Pope's faithful vassal and liege man, or against England, the Pope's fief. John could well chuckle as he sat safe across the Channel and thought of his rival's discomfiture.

Philip's rage knew no bounds. He declared that he had already spent sixty thousand pounds on his preparations for the invasion, which he had undertaken at the Pope's command, and that he was not to be dissuaded from carrying through a project on which he had spent so much time and money. Philip might even yet have gone ahead and defied Pandulf's orders if trouble had not arisen with Count Ferrand of Flanders.

Ferrand had for some time been secretly committed to John's cause. He now tried to dissuade Philip from the invasion, telling him that he had no claim whatever to the English crown, now that the Pope's orders had been annulled, and that such a war would be an unjust one. At last Ferrand flatly refused to help Philip. Philip declared him his enemy, and Ferrand fled from the court. Philip promptly invaded Flanders and ordered his fleet, which had assembled at Boulogne, to the Swine, the port of the rich commercial town of Damme.

Ferrand sent word of these new developments to John and begged for help. John sent a fleet of five hundred ships, under the command of his brother, William Longsword, with the Count of Holland and

Reginald of Boulogne, and a force of seven hundred knights and many foot and horse soldiers. With a fair wind, on May 30 they soon sighted the Swine, where they found the whole of Philip's fleet collected. The English scouts learned that the ships were guarded only by a few sailors, for the soldiers that should have been on guard had gone out to collect booty and were busy ravaging the rich Flemish towns.

Salisbury immediately attacked the French fleet and met with little resistance. The English forces captured three hundred French ships loaded with corn, wine, flour, meat, arms, and other stores and sailed them off to England. Another hundred or more ships were drawn up on the shore, and these, after removing their stores, they burned. "One would have said the sea was on fire," says the biographer of William Marshal. Some of the English disembarked and set off in pursuit of the fleeing French, but when they met up with Philip's main forces they were obliged to turn back to their ships.

This complete destruction of Philip's fleet forced him to abandon the intention, if he still entertained it, of invading England, and he turned his attention to Flanders, where he was faced by the armies of a powerful coalition headed by the Emperor Otto.

When John learned of Philip's reverses, he was filled with joy at this practical assurance that no amount of treachery or trickery could now bring Philip to England, and he dismissed the great army at Barham Down.

Whilst Philip was thus beset in the north by the coalition of his enemies that John had long been fostering, John saw his best opportunity to regain his lands on the Continent. He accordingly assembled an army at Portsmouth to invade the western coast of France, but when his barons learned what his purpose was they refused to follow him. Roger of Wendover says that they refused on the grounds that John was still excommunicated. This may have been their pretext, but it is likely that their real reason was that they did not con-

sider themselves bound, by the laws of military tenure, to serve overseas. It is quite likely, too, that they remembered John's failure to
make the least exertion to save his continental territories whilst he
still had possession of them and that they refused to help him regain
that which he had refused to exert himself to save.

In any event, John seems to have accepted their excuse that he
was still excommunicated, for he took immediate steps to alter that
situation. He sent warrants, signed by twenty-four of his earls and
barons, to the Archbishop of Canterbury and the exiled bishops, who
were still in France, urging them to lay aside all fears, return to England, and receive their rights and the indemnities he had promised
them.

He had already revoked the sentence of outlawry that he had laid
on the clergy in the first heat of his anger:

> BE IT KNOWN *that we have publicly revoked and do now revoke*
> *the sentence commonly called outlawry that we caused to be laid*
> *on ecclesiastical persons, and we declare by this our letter patent*
> *that the affairs of ecclesiastical persons do not concern us and*
> *henceforth we will not pronounce that sentence against ecclesi-*
> *astical persons.* MYSELF AS WITNESS, *at Battle, on the* 13th *day*
> *of June, in the* 15th *year of our reign.*

He also recalled Robert FitzWalter and Eustace de Vesci and restored all their lands to them.

On the advice of Pandulf, the clergy accepted John's invitation
and landed at Dover on July 16, 1213. The King was at Winchester, and there the bishops met him on July 20. When he learned of
their approach, he went out to meet them, fell prostrate at their feet,
and with tears begged them to have pity on him and on England.
Stephen Langton, seeing thus for the first time his King, raised him
from the ground and led him to the door of Winchester Cathedral.

There the clergy chanted the 50th Psalm, "*Miserere mei, Deus, se-cundum magnam misericordiam tuam,*" and "in the presence of all the nobles, who wept with joy," says Roger of Wendover, "they absolved him according to the custom of the Church." John then renewed his coronation oath, swearing that he would "love Holy Church and her ordained members and would to the utmost of his power defend and uphold them against all their enemies; and that he would renew all the good laws of his ancestors, especially those of King Edward, and destroy bad laws, judge his subjects according to the just decrees of his court, and restore his rights to each man."

The King also swore again to make restitution for all the property he had confiscated in connection with the interdict and set the following Easter as the day by which all restitution would be made. If he failed to make restitution by that time, he agreed that the sentence of excommunication might be renewed against him. The King then renewed his oath of fealty and allegiance to the Holy See.

Stephen Langton took John by the hand and led him into the Cathedral, where the Archbishop celebrated Mass in the presence of the King and his barons. Afterwards there was a great feast, at which the Archbishop, the bishops, and the barons all sat at the same table with the King, amid general rejoicing.

John issued a summons on the following day, July 21, for a council to meet at St. Albans on August 4. This was to be more than the customary Great Council, for in addition to those who were ordinarily summoned John ordered the sheriffs to send four faithful men and the bailiff from each township, for the purpose of finding out how much damage had been done by the confiscation, what the losses had been, how much was due as compensation, and to whom it should be paid. As an earnest of his reconciliation with Stephen Langton, he ordered the two justiciars to consult with the Archbishop in their governing of the kingdom during his intended absence.

John was eager to start on his projected expedition to Poitou. He gave charge of the kingdom to Geoffrey FitzPeter, his Chief Justiciar, and Peter des Roches, Bishop of Winchester, who, with John Grey, Bishop of Norwich, alone of the bishops had remained faithful to him during his long struggle with the Pope. He returned to Portsmouth, freed from the excommunication that his barons had advanced as a pretext for not following him to Poitou, and found that in the interval they had hit upon a fresh excuse. This time a great number of knights came to him and complained that their long stay under arms had exhausted all their money. Unless he paid them from his treasury, they refused again to follow him. John was enraged at this effort to extort payment for the service that he insisted was due him under the terms of feudal tenure, and he refused to pay them. The King embarked with his attendants and set sail, in an effort to shame his barons into following him, but they went home. John landed at Guernsey and then returned, burning with rage and intent upon punishing his disobedient barons.

In the meantime the two justiciars met the Council at St. Albans. In the presence of Archbishop Langton, the King's reconciliation with the Church was announced. The Chief Justiciar, acting for the King, ordered that the laws of Henry I should be kept by all and that all unjust laws should be abolished. Sheriffs, foresters, and other agents of the King were ordered to stop extorting money, inflicting injuries, and levying illegal taxes, as had been their practice. This council, which Bishop Stubbs calls "the first representative assembly on record," was of great importance, not only because it included for the first time the representatives of each township, but also because it was there that "the laws of King Henry" were first mentioned as the ideal to which men wanted to return. In view of Stephen Langton's actions at the next meeting of the Council, it is likely that he, rather than Geoffrey FitzPeter, was the one who conceived the idea of using the charter that Henry I had issued at his crowning in 1100 as the standard of good government. It is hardly probable that many people at the Council had any idea of what the laws of King Henry were, but the phrase would summon up pictures of the good old days when barons had their rights.

John meanwhile had collected an army and started out to punish his barons. Stephen Langton came to him at Northampton and warned him that such an arbitrary act as the punishment of the barons without due process of law would violate the oath he had taken on the occasion of his absolution "to judge his subjects according to the just decrees of his courts." John angrily replied that the Archbishop had no business to meddle in lay affairs and that he, the King, would not cease to exercise his authority on the Archbishop's account.

In a rage, John set out for Nottingham on the next day. Stephen followed him and boldly declared that if the King persisted, he would excommunicate every member of his army. The Archbishop held firm till he induced John to abandon his design and to name a day when his barons might be tried in court in a lawful way.

The next meeting of the Council was held at St. Paul's in London on August 25, 1213. Stephen Langton opened the proceedings with a sermon on the text, "My heart hath trusted in God, and I am helped; therefore my flesh hath rejoiced." When the Archbishop announced his text, someone in the assembly cried out: "You lie; your heart never trusted in God, and your flesh never rejoiced." The crowd beat the man till he was rescued by the officers of the peace, whereupon Stephen continued his sermon.

During the Council, Cardinal Langton called some of the barons aside and asked them: "Did you hear how, when I absolved the King at Winchester, I made him swear that he would do away with unjust laws and renew good laws, such as those of King Edward, and cause them to be observed by everyone in the kingdom? A charter

of the first Henry, King of England, has just now been found, by
which you may, if you like, recall your long-lost rights and your former condition."

This would indicate that the Cardinal had not wasted his time
whilst he was cooling his heels in France; he seems to have landed in
England with a well-defined plan for curbing John's absolute power.

The Archbishop then caused the charter to be read aloud to the
assembly. The charter that Henry I issued on the day of his crowning, August 5, 1100, was an attempt to secure the loyalty of all
classes and particularly that of the barons, and a pledge to do away
with the abuses and evil practices introduced by William Rufus.
Since it served to some extent as a model for the Great Charter, it
may be interesting to note some of its provisions.

Henry, after declaring that he had been crowned by the common
consent of the barons, announced that the Church was free and promised not to sell it, farm it out, or take anything from its domains whilst
any see or abbey was vacant. Next he promised to do away with all
evil practices, which he proceeded to mention in part. He promised
not to force the heir of any tenant-in-chief to redeem his inheritance
by what amounted to an act of purchase, but to collect from him only
the just and lawful relief, and he ordered that his tenants should do
the same with their vassals. He promised not to take any property
from a subject in return for the royal permission for the marriage of
his daughter or sister; not to retain any of her property when he gave
an heiress in marriage in exercise of the right of wardship; to allow
widows their dowry as a marriage portion and not to give them in
marriage again without their consent, and to appoint the widow or
some other near relation as a guardian of the children's land, rather
than to entrust it to some favorite for his enrichment, as Rufus had
done. Again Henry enjoined that his barons should act in the same
way towards their tenants.

Henry ratified the wills of his subjects and provided that if a man died intestate his wife, children, or parents should distribute his money for the good of his soul, as seemed best to them; Rufus would probably have confiscated it. The King promised not to exact excessive bail in case of forfeiture and to punish offenders not arbitrarily but according to their offences. Lastly, he promised that all knights who held their land by military tenure should be exempt from all amercements and contributions, so that they might provide themselves with horses and arms and thus be fit and ready for the King's service and for the defense of the country.

The enthusiasm with which the barons heard these provisions is an indication of the extent to which John had acted contrary to them. In the presence of the Archbishop they swore that when the opportunity arose they would stand up for their rights and, if necessary, die for them, and Cardinal Langton promised them his assistance.

John of course soon learned that the Archbishop and the barons were plotting against him, and Matthew Paris states that the King sent messengers to Innocent with a large sum of money and the promise of more, to urge the Pope to curb the Archbishop and excommunicate the barons.

The Papal Legate, Cardinal Nicholas, Bishop of Tusculum, arrived in England at Michaelmas. Innocent had given him the mission of settling the disagreement between the King and the bishops over the amounts of the compensation the King was to give them. Although England was still under the interdict, the people, dressed in their holiday clothes, received the Legate everywhere with music and processions, imagining in their simplicity that he would immediately erase their shame by lifting the interdict. As soon as Cardinal Nicholas reached Westminster he degraded the Abbot, who was accused by his monks of incontinency and of wasting the Abbey's funds.

The citizens of Oxford, who had been under a special interdict for the hanging of the three clerks in 1209, came to the Cardinal and begged for absolution. Among other things, the Legate enjoined on them as penance to go barefoot and clad only in their drawers, carrying scourges and chanting the *Miserere*, to each of the churches in Oxford, at the rate of one church each day, and to receive absolution from the priests of each parish.

John gave permission, during this summer, to some monks in Oxfordshire to try out a novel idea they had conceived, and the clerk who wrote the letter seems to have had some difficulty in phrasing it:

> THE KING, to the Sheriff of Oxford, ETC. *Be it known to you that for the love of God we have granted the Abbot and canons of Osney permission to have made a leaden canal under the ground, whose round concavity will have cross-wise four thumbs-breadth within the circumferences, so that they may have a flow of water from the Thames to the offices of their Abbey, wherever it may most conveniently be made, and we grant that they may have the flow of this water by means of that canal forever.*

Geoffrey FitzPeter, the Chief Justiciar, died on October 2, 1213. Matthew Paris says of him: "He was a most firm pillar of the kingdom, a noble-minded man, learned in the law, expert in the treasury, revenues, and all good offices, and related by blood or marriage to all the magnates of England, for which reason the King feared him above all other mortals without any liking for him, for he held the reins of the government. At his death England was like a ship at sea without a pilot."

When John was told of the Justiciar's death, he laughed heartily and said: "When he arrives in hell, let him greet Hubert Walter, whom he will no doubt find there. Now, by God's feet, I am for the first time King and Lord of England!"

As Geoffrey's successor in the office of Chief Justiciar John appointed the faithful Peter des Roches, Bishop of Winchester. This

did not sit well with the barons, for they were jealous of Peter, a native of Poitou, as a foreigner, and they resented the energy with
which he set about collecting men, money, and supplies for John's
expedition to France.

A meeting of the Council was held at St. Paul's in London at the
beginning of October, in the presence of the King and the Papal
Legate, for the purpose of fixing the compensation due to the clergy.
The discussion continued for three days. John offered to pay a hundred thousand marks immediately and to give his oath and pledge
that if the Legate and the bishops found that the damage inflicted was
in excess of that sum he would make full restitution before the following Easter. The Legate considered this a fair offer and advised the
bishops to accept it. They, on the other hand, wanted to make an exact investigation of the property confiscated and the damage done,
consider these findings at a council, and then arrive at the sum due
them. The Legate Nicholas was indignant that the bishops would not
accept the King's offer at once, and they in turn accused him of favor-
ing John unduly. The King, however, was quite willing to delay the
payment as long as the bishops liked and did not press them to accept
his offer.

At the conclusion of the Council, before the high altar and in the
presence of the clergy and the people, John renewed his allegiance to
the Pope. He resigned his crown and his kingdom into the hands of
the Papal Legate and received them back from him as a papal fief.
He gave Nicholas a copy of the charter of submission that he had
given Pandulf in the preceding May at Dover, stamped with golden
seals, for the use of the Pope.

The Council assembled again at Reading a month later, but the
King did not make his appearance. On the third day they met again
at Wallingford, and there John repeated his offer of restitution. The
clergy, however, were much exercised over the problem of how to
calculate the value of the castles and houses that had been demolished

and of the orchards and woods that had been cut down. At that time, if the King suspected anyone of disloyal tendencies, his first act had been to order the man's castle demolished so that he could not use it as a stronghold and a base for rebellion. John probably began his operations against the bishops when the interdict was pronounced by demolishing such castles as were under their control. England was in a fever of building at the beginning of the thirteenth century. Extensive work was being done on most of the cathedrals, churches were building all over the land, and, as a result of the long period of peace, general prosperity, and settled conditions in the country, private dwellings in great number were being erected. All this building created a demand for timber, and it is likely that John had turned some of the confiscated estates to further profit by felling the trees on them. At last the King and the bishops agreed to the appointment of four barons as arbitrators, to whose decisions they promised to agree.

The Council met again at Reading at the beginning of December, and at this meeting each one, layman as well as cleric, who was concerned in the matter of the interdict produced a list of his confiscated property and of the amount of money he had lost. The sum was staggering, and the Legate sided with the King in declaring that it was beyond all reason and far beyond his ability to pay. The claimants remained obstinate, and John postponed making restitution till a compromise could be reached. The arbitration of the four barons apparently was not resorted to. In the case of Stephen Langton and the bishops who had fled to France, John made a further payment of fifteen thousand marks, to be divided among them.

Matthew Paris tells that at this time John began to entertain evil thoughts about the resurrection of the dead, by which the chronicler probably means that John spoke and acted as though he did not believe in a life beyond the grave. In this connection he tells of a jest the King made, when a fat stag was killed in the hunt and was being skinned in his presence. "See how fat this animal has grown," observed the King, "and yet he has never heard a Mass!"

Innocent III, on November 1, 1213, wrote to his Legate, ordering him "to cause suitable persons, according to your own judgment, to be ordained to the bishoprics and abbacies in England now vacant, either by appointment or by canonical election, who shall be remarkable not only for their manner of life but also for their learning, and at the same time faithful to the King and of use to the kingdom and also helpful in giving assistance and advice, the King's consent being previously obtained."

When Cardinal Nicholas received this letter, he consulted with John and set about filling the vacancies with men whom the King suggested. Innocent had apparently forgotten all about the prized right of free election by the canonical chapters. John had a free hand to appoint bishops and abbots, in many cases without even the formality of an election by chapter or monks in his presence, and he used the opportunity to reward the clerics who had been faithful to him during the interdict.

The Legate's appointments aroused many complaints and protests from those who thought that they had a right to participate in the elections or that their claims to various vacancies were being overlooked. Stephen Langton, who would never have been Archbishop but for the active intervention of the Pope, was the loudest in his protests against the appointment of bishops in the Southern Province by the Papal Legate under the authority of the Pope's command. Some clerics appealed to the Pope over his Legate's head, and these men Nicholas suspended and sent to the Roman Curia. The Legate was so destitute of humanity, Roger of Wendover records, that he refused to allow these malcontents one penny from the revenues of the appointments they were protesting to pay their expenses to Rome to appeal against his actions. Nicholas furthermore bestowed vacant benefices and parish churches without consulting the patrons of these livings.

John kept the Christmas of 1213 at Windsor and distributed festive cloaks to a number of his barons.

Stephen Langton held a council of his clergy at Dunstable in January 1214, to discuss the affairs of the Church in England. The clergy were united in their indignation against the Papal Legate, who was filling vacancies in the Church with the King's nominees, so that it appeared to them that Nicholas was more concerned with pleasing the King than with promoting the welfare of the Church. After a lengthy discussion, the Archbishop sent messengers to the Legate, who was then at Burton-on-Trent, to inform him that the Archbishop had appealed to Rome and to forbid him to make any further appointments to vacancies till the appeal should have been heard. At the same time Stephen asserted that he alone had the right to appoint priests to the vacant churches in his diocese.

Cardinal Nicholas paid no attention to this message and continued to fill vacancies with men pleasing to John. He conferred with the King about the Archbishop's appeal to Rome, and with John's consent he sent Pandulf to the papal court with the mission of denying the Archbishop's accusations and overriding his appeal. When Pandulf had audience with the Pope, he vilified the character of Stephen Langton and greatly praised the King. John, he declared, was the most humble and moderate king he had ever seen. Innocent had great confidence in Pandulf, and he accepted the sub-deacon's estimate of John's character.

Pandulf was vigorously opposed by Master Simon Langton, the Primate's younger brother, who argued strongly for the Archbishop's side of the case. Pandulf had brought with him the charter of submission and fealty to the Holy See, sealed with gold, which John had given the Legate in the preceding September, and this may have influenced Innocent in the King's favor. Pandulf declared that the

Archbishop and the other clergy were showing themselves too grasping and covetous in the matter of the restitution that was due them, that they were oppressing the King and treating him unjustly, and that they were attempting to claim rights and authority that did not belong to them. The sub-deacon's advocacy of the case prevailed, and Innocent declined to admonish his Legate or to restrict his powers, as Stephen Langton had requested.

John began to fear that the controversy over the amount of the restitution would go on indefinitely. The haggling and the delay were not of themselves unpleasing to him, but as long as they continued England remained under the interdict. John was preparing for another expedition against Philip, and he did not want to afford his barons the excuse of refusing to accompany him because of the interdict. He therefore sent two knights, Thomas and Adam Hardington, the former of whom had been one of his ambassadors to the Sultan of Morocco, and a clerk, to Rome, to join Bishop John Grey, who had gone there in the previous October to be absolved by the Pope from the excommunication that had been laid on him by name as one of the King's evil counsellors during the interdict. John instructed these four to lay his case before the Pope and to appeal to him to set the terms for the restitution, so that the interdict might be lifted.

The great system of alliances that John, at the expense of untold treasure, had been building up against Philip was now at the height of its power. The coalition was headed by the Emperor Otto and included the Counts of Holland, Boulogne, and Flanders, who had all sworn allegiance to John, and the Dukes of Lorraine and of Brabant. A strong English contingent, headed by William Longsword, joined the other forces, and throughout 1213 they harassed Philip's army, ravaged Flanders, and fought a series of inconclusive engagements with the French.

John and his allies felt that the time had now come for a concerted effort against Philip. The strategy agreed upon was a simultaneous attack on France through Flanders and the northeast by the allies and on the south through Poitou by John.

In pursuance of this design, John, with a large army, embarked at Portsmouth on Candlemas Day, 1214. Before he left England he placed the country "in the custody and protection of God and the Holy Roman Church and the Lord Pope and the Lord Nicholas, Bishop of Tusculum and Legate of the Holy See," and he appointed as "our Justiciar of England the venerable father, our Lord Peter, Bishop of Winchester, for as long as pleases us, to have custody in our place of our land of England and the peace of our realm."

He also ordered Thomas Sanford to "deliver to our beloved and faithful servants, Peter de Maulay and Reginald de Pontibus, 40,-000 marks, fifteen golden cups, one silver cup, one golden saltcellar, one golden crown, and one casket with gold and one red casket with jewels."

John landed at La Rochelle on February 15. Many of the Poite-vin nobles came to swear fealty to him and to join his forces. He cap-tured a number of castles belonging to the disaffected nobles and tightened his hold on Aquitaine. Before he could proceed to any ef-fective operations against Philip, however, he had to subdue the re-bellious members of the Lusignan family, who had been his bitter enemies ever since he took Isabella away from Hugh. Hugh was now Hugh IX, Count of La Marche, and the three brothers, Hugh, Count Ralph of Eu, and Geoffrey of Lusignan, were the strongest nobles in Poitou and the leaders of the opposition to John.

In a letter sent back to England, John described the steps in his victory over the three brothers. On May 16, the Friday before Whit-sunday, he marched to Miervant, a castle belonging to Geoffrey, and began the assault early the next morning, "although many people would not believe that it could be taken by assault," as John com-placently reported. At one o'clock the garrison surrendered. On

Whitsunday John laid siege to Novent, in which were Geoffrey and his two sons. After three days, when the walls were almost breached by the stone-throwers, Hugh of La Marche came and, realizing the hopelessness of his brother's situation, persuaded him to surrender and throw himself on John's mercy.

At Parthenai, on May 25, the three brothers did homage and swore fealty to John, and the King promised his legitimate daughter Joan to Hugh's son, also named Hugh. (This marriage did not take place. In the end, after John's death, it was his widow, Queen Isabella, who married the young Hugh, the son of the man to whom she was betrothed when she married John.) The letter reporting all this was written at Parthenai, and John closed optimistically: "Now, by the grace of God, an opportunity is afforded us of attacking our mortal enemy, the King of France, beyond Poitou."

John made good progress at first. He captured Nantes, where he took prisoner Robert, the son of the Count of Dreux, and then, on June 19, he laid seige to the castle of La Roche-au-Moine, which commanded the road between Nantes and Angers. He evidently intended to settle down for a protracted stay, as the following letter indicates:

THE KING, to his beloved and faithful subjects, the Abbot of Beaulieu, Brother Alan Martell, and Master Arnulf: GREET-INGS. *We send to you our beloved and faithful Reginald de Pontibus the elder and command you to believe and to do whatever he tells you about bringing the Lady Queen to us and about bringing to us as much of our treasure as we told you, and our horses and Richard our son and Joan our daughter, together with Andrew and Elias de Beauchamp. And in testimony of this,* ETC. MYSELF AS WITNESS, at La Roche-au-Moine, on the 19th day of June, in the 16th year of our reign.

Philip sent his son Louis to the relief of the besieged castle, and when John learned that the French army was approaching he sent spies to find out its strength. They returned and told him that his forces were much larger than the French and urged him to go forth and meet the enemy in battle, for they were certain that he would win the victory. The King ordered his army to prepare for battle, but the Poitevin nobles, of whose treachery he had had ample proof in the past, refused to fight. This desertion forced him to retreat to the south on July 2. Louis was now approaching from Chinon. When he heard that John had lifted the siege of La Roche-au-Moine he thought that the English were advancing to attack him. Knowing that John's forces were superior to his, Louis turned back to Chinon.

John's ambassadors at Rome, in the meantime, had prevailed on Innocent to put an end to the haggling over the restitution, settle the terms, and order the interdict to be lifted. The Pope directed that John pay the Archbishop and the Bishops of London and Ely the sum of forty thousand marks, less what he had already given in the two previous payments before the exiled clergy returned and at the council at Reading. The remainder of the restitution, the sum of which had not yet been fixed, was to be paid at the rate of twelve thousand marks a year in two equal payments on All Saints' Day and on Ascension Day. Innocent then ordered his Legate, Cardinal Nicholas, to lift the interdict as soon as the first payment had been made and security given for the remainder.

When this letter reached Nicholas, John was still abroad, but before he left the country he had given the Legate and William Marshal full authority to act in this matter. They called a council at St. Paul's of all the persons who claimed to have been injured financially because of the King's actions when the interdict was imposed, and the Legate explained the provisions of the restitution directed by the Pope. Accounts were rendered of the amounts already paid, and the remainder was put under the suretyship of Bishops Peter des Roches and John Grey.

With the matter thus settled, on June 29, 1214 the Legate, at St. Paul's, amid the chanting of the *Te Deum* and the ringing of the bells, lifted the interdict, which had lain on England for six years, three months, and six days.

As soon as the fact became generally known that the King had undertaken to make restitution for the properties he had confiscated because of the interdict, the Legate was besieged by a vast throng of "abbots, priors, Templars, Hospitallers, abbesses, nuns, clerks, and laymen," all clamoring for a share. They claimed that although they had not been driven out of England, they had nevertheless been so persecuted for the Faith by the King and his agents that they had been stripped of everything and knew not where to turn. Nicholas told them that he had no authority to go beyond the provisions of the Pope's letters and advised them to lay their complaints before the Pope and ask for justice from him. When they heard this advice, the whole throng went sadly home.

Whilst John was forced, by the refusal of the Poitevin nobles to fight against the French, to retreat to La Rochelle and remain inactive there, his allies to the north proceeded to put their part of the plan into effect. Philip had headed for Lille when the allies overtook him at Bouvines, a village between Tournai and Lille. He had halted there for the night, on Saturday, July 26. It was a hot July, and Philip made his camp on the banks of the River Marcq so that the men and their horses might refresh themselves.

The allied commanders held a conference on the following morning and discussed the advisability of attacking Philip. As it was Sunday, Reginald of Boulogne said that it would be wrong to fight on that day and thus profane the Sabbath with slaughter and bloodshed. The Emperor Otto agreed and said that he had never won a victory on a Sunday. Hugh of Boves, however, called Reginald a traitor to

John, from whom he had received much land and money, and declared that if the battle were postponed it would be a great loss for King John. He quoted the proverb: "Delay is dangerous when things are ready," and so taunted the others with cowardice that they agreed to fight at once.

The allied forces were divided into the usual three armies of mediaeval warfare. The first, on the right, was commanded by Ferrand of Flanders, Reginald of Boulogne, and William Longsword; the center by William of Holland and Hugh of Boves, and the third, the left, by the Emperor Otto. Philip in the meantime had had the bridge across the Marcq destroyed so that his army, fighting with the river at its back, could not retreat. This was to be no ordinary engagement, with the main emphasis on capturing prisoners of high rank to be held for ransom and on the plundering of the countryside, but a fight to the finish.

It is impossible to form any idea of the number of men involved. Estimates vary widely, depending upon the nationality of the one doing the estimating. Some French writers place the allied troops at 80,000 and the French at 25,000. On the other hand, the English all say that they were greatly outnumbered, some by as much as four to one.

The right wing charged first, with such fury that they broke through the French ranks and forced their way to Philip. Reginald of Boulogne unhorsed the French king, forced him to the ground, and raised his sword to kill him. One of Philip's bodyguard, Pierre Tristan, threw himself upon his King and received the blow intended for Philip. This gave the French an opportunity to drive Reginald off and assist the King to remount. The right wing of the allies, after their first charge had failed to rout the French, were forced to fall back. They found themselves hemmed in between the French in front and their own center army to the rear of them.

In the confusion, Reginald encountered Hugh of Boves. "Here is the battle you advised us to fight," he said, "and which I thought we should not. Now you are going to flee, seized with panic like all the rest; but I am going to fight, and I shall be either captured or killed."

The three leaders of the first army, Ferrand, Reginald, and William Longsword, were captured. The French episcopate made a good showing in this battle. King Richard's old enemy, the stout-hearted Bishop of Beauvais, went into the conflict armed only with a club. With it he succeeded in beating William Longsword from his horse and thus captured him. The Bishop-elect of Senlis captured Reginald of Boulogne.

The second army, led by William of Holland and Hugh of Boves, retreated before the French, and the whole brunt of the French attack then fell upon the forces commanded by Otto. He fought with such lion-like courage that he had three horses killed under him. Neither side could prevail; the scorching July afternoon was drawing to a close, and both armies were utterly exhausted. Otto was allowed to retreat unconquered, and he and his followers fled to Valenciennes and thence to Cologne. Of all the vast forces of the coalition, only seven hundred Brabantines remained on the field, and they refused either to flee or to surrender. Philip had them all massacred.

Philip made a glorious triumphal procession to Paris, with Ferrand, Reginald, and William Longsword in his train. The students of the University of Paris led the celebrations. "Indefatigably, for seven successive nights," says William the Breton, "they did not stop feasting, leaping and dancing, and singing."

John entered into negotiations to effect the release of his brother and his allies, but Philip attempted to drive a hard bargain and to impose a difficult choice on John, as the following letter shows:

To THE venerable fathers in Christ the Lord Nicholas, by the grace of God Bishop of Tusculum and Legate of the Apostolic See; the Lord Stephen, Archbishop of Canterbury, Primate of

All England, and Cardinal of the Holy Roman Church; the Lord Peter, Bishop of Winchester and Justiciar of England; the other Bishops of England, and his earls and barons: JOHN, by the same grace King of England, ETC.

Our beloved brother William, Earl of Salisbury, kept in chains by the King of France, has let us know that he will be entirely released from prison and set free, if we will allow Robert, the son of Robert, Count of Dreux, whom we hold captive, to go free in exchange for him. And since this same Robert is related to the aforesaid King of France, we by no means would or will set him free without your advice, especially since we have been given to understand that if this same Robert is set free from his chains and returns to his country, the Count of Boulogne will be put to death and the Count of Flanders will never come out of prison, which would by no means be to our convenience or honor. We command you therefore faithfully to give us counsel in these matters. Be it known to you that it has been proposed to us to release the aforesaid Earl of Salisbury and Robert of Dreux, under hostages, for a suitable period, within which they will return to the prisons where they formerly were, but we will do nothing concerning their final liberation until we have had your advice thereupon, which you will be pleased speedily to signify to us by your letters patent, by the bearer of this present, our son Oliver. MYSELF AS WITNESS, at St. Maixent, on the 6th day of September.

In the end, William Longsword was exchanged for Robert of Dreux. The Counts of Boulogne and Flanders, however, Philip regarded as rebellious vassals and traitors, and he kept them in prison. Reginald died, chained to a huge log, after thirteen years of close imprisonment, and Ferrand was released after thirteen years.

When the news of this crushing defeat was brought to John, he knew that the labor of years and the expenditure of a vast treasure had come to nothing. He had spent forty thousand marks that he had taken from the Cistercians during the interdict and untold sums be-sides in arming and paying the members of the coalition. Philip's victory was so complete that John could hope to salvage nothing from the defeat of his allies; there was nothing left on which to rebuild his hope of overcoming Philip. Otto struggled on from his last strong-hold in northeastern Germany against his rival Frederick, but it was a losing fight from the beginning. Nevertheless Otto kept up the contest, futile though it was, till his death of an overdose of medicine on May 19, 1218.

John contrasted the strength of his position when he was last in Poitou with the defeat that he had now met, and he exclaimed: "Since I became reconciled to God and submitted myself and my kingdom to the Church, nothing has gone well with me, and every-thing unlucky has happened to me."

After Philip had celebrated his triumph, he turned to the south to meet John. In spite of his victory over John's allies, Philip made no attempt to repeat that success in Poitou. His most important task was to consolidate his gains in the north, and the conquest of Aquitaine, whether John were there or not, would be an extremely difficult mat-ter. The two kings accordingly, on September 14, 1214, agreed on a truce to last till the Easter of 1220, with each side retaining what it had at the time of the treaty.

Walter Grey, the nephew of John Grey, Bishop of Norwich, had been the King's Chancellor since 1205. He was elected Bishop of Worcester to succeed Mauger, who had died in 1212, and was con-secrated at Canterbury on October 5, 1214.

His uncle, John's intimate friend, had meanwhile been chosen Bishop of Durham, albeit unwillingly, by the minster-men of Dur-ham in obedience to a letter from the Pope brought to them by the Legate. Durham was a much richer and more influential see than was

Norwich, which John Grey had held since 1200. After they had made the election as the Pope had ordered, the minster-men appealed to Innocent in favor of their own candidate, Richard Poore, Dean of Salisbury. Innocent decided in favor of his own nominee, as might have been expected, but he consoled Richard by having him elected Bishop of Chichester, which see had been vacant since the death of Simon FitzRobert in 1207. Richard was accordingly consecrated by Stephen Langton at the same time that he conferred the episcopate on Walter Grey.

John Grey, however, did not live to become Bishop of Durham. He was in Poitou during the summer of 1214 and died near Poitiers on October 18. Although he was called one of the King's evil counsellors, he seems to have had an unexceptionable character and to have been of blameless private life.

"THE FIELD CALLED
RUNNYMEDE"

ᴀR 1214–1215 Sᴅ

JOHN returned to England on October 15, 1214 and set about collecting the scutage that had been levied by his Justiciar, Peter des Roches, in the previous May, in an effort to raise money for his hard-pressed master. The scutage had been levied only on those tenants-in-chief who had not accompanied the King to Poitou, but many of them, and particularly those living north of the Humber, refused to pay it. The Exchequer succeeded in collecting only about a quarter of the amount due.

When he pressed for payment, John met with stiff resistance. The barons based their refusal to pay on the assertion that they were not bound to military service in a foreign war and hence were not liable to scutage in place of that service. Deeper than that, however, lay their objection to the regularity with which John had levied scutages as a means of financing his administration and his subsidies to his allies on the Continent as well as his military expeditions. Funda-

mentally, the barons were trying, by attempting to force him to respect and confirm their ancient rights and privileges, to keep and
extend the benefits they derived from the feudal system of military
tenure whilst at the same time evading the responsibilities that it entailed.

None of John's barons was the absolute owner of his lands and
estates; he was a tenant only. The tenure of the land had been bestowed on him or his ancestors by the king, and most of the lay barons
held land by knight-service; that is, in return for the use of the estate
they were bound to serve in person and to furnish the king with a
specified number of knights in time of war. This obligation to military service was in addition to the regular feudal dues and aids that
accompanied other forms of tenure as well.

The barons' claim that they were not bound to serve in a foreign
war rested on no sound precedent, and John could assert in rebuttal
that both his father and his brother had exacted knight-service in wars
outside England. If John were right, he would have been justified in
demanding, not a scutage from those barons who had refused to follow him to Poitou, but the forfeiture of their estates. The tenants by
knight-service did not have the privilege of deciding whether they
would serve the king in war by personal attendance or whether they
would pay scutage in commutation of that service; that was a matter
for the king to decide. By refusing to serve in time of war they had
violated the feudal contract by which they held their lands, and hence
they were liable to forfeit those lands to the Crown.

From John's point of view, then, he was being moderate in his
demands when he attempted to collect scutage from those tenants
who had refused to accompany him to Poitou, even though that
scutage was at the rate of three marks on each knight's fee instead of
the customary two marks. The refusal of those barons to render military service and to pay scutage seemed to him an obvious attempt to
strike at his royal authority, to undermine the whole involved struc-

ture of land tenure, and to betray on the part of those barons a desire to assert that they were the absolute lords of their estates and not tenants only.

The nobles, on the other hand, had many individual causes for complaint in John's abuses of his rights of wardship, of reliefs, of primer seisins, and the like. The complicated scheme of rights, dues, and customs had never been exactly defined and set down in writing; the only standard was the traditional one of what was just or customary. If John demanded, for example, a crushing relief before he would give an heir seisin of his estates, there was little that the heir, individually, could do about it. Since these acts of injustice were individual acts, coming at different times and affecting victims in different parts of the country, there was never any one occasion when all who felt themselves injured could unite to demand justice or to defend their rights.

The imposition of the scutage of 1214, however, did present such an occasion. If John had returned victorious to England, it is not likely that any effective protest would have been made against the scutage or against anything else within reason that he might choose to do. As it was, he came back utterly defeated, with the mighty coalition in Flanders broken up and its leaders defeated or in prison. He was no longer the most powerful ruler in Europe; now he was a vanquished king with no allies to strengthen him and with his treasure squandered on a dream of conquest that came to nothing.

The disaffected barons met at Bury St. Edmunds, the site of the greatest abbey in England, at the tomb of the martyred King, a shrine that equaled in riches, importance, and popularity that of St. Thomas at Canterbury. They met "as if for religious duties," according to Roger of Wendover, which would indicate that the meeting probably took place on or near the feast of St. Edmund, November 20. The charter of Henry I, which Stephen Langton had shown them at the council at St. Albans in August of the previous year, was pro-

duced and discussed. Again they received it with approval and enthusiasm because, although in the most vague and general terms, it
limited the power of the king in the exercise of his feudal authority.

The barons then gathered in the abbey church of St. Edmund
and, beginning with the greatest, swore before the high altar that if
John refused to grant the liberties and laws of the charter of Henry I
they would renounce their allegiance to him and make war on him
till he should grant and seal a charter embodying their demands. In
memory of this event, the Borough of Bury St. Edmunds counts
among its proud titles that of "Cunabulum Legis," as well as that of
"Sacrarium Regis." Finally, the barons agreed that they would all go
together to the King immediately after Christmas and present their
demands to him and that in the interval they would arm and provision
themselves, so that if John refused their requests they would be able
to proceed at once to seize his castles and compel him to accede.

There is no record that Stephen Langton was present at this meeting, in spite of the leading part he had played in calling the barons'
attention to the charter of Henry I. Having once indicated to them
the objectives they should seek, he seems henceforth to have concentrated his efforts on inducing the King to arrive at an understanding with his barons. Certainly he could hardly have united with them
in agreeing to make war on the King if he refused their demands.

John realized, as soon as he returned to England, that he was faced
by a potential opposition stronger and more widespread than any he
had encountered before. He did not know how many of his barons
he could depend upon; suspicious and distrustful as he was, he felt
that they were few. Among the bishops he could count on the support only of his own nominees; from the rest he could expect no
help. In order to placate the bishops and win them over to his side,
on November 21 he granted a charter conceding the right of free
election of their bishops to the cathedral chapters. This was merely
the confirmation of a customary right that the chapters, in theory at

least, had always enjoyed, but at any rate it promised an end to the highhanded appointment of bishops that John and the Papal Legate had been making, in violation of that right. He had previously, on All Saints' Day, in accordance with his agreement, paid the Arch-bishop and the bishops the semi-annual payment of six thousand marks in compensation for their losses during the interdict.

The Queen during this year gave birth to her second daughter, who was named Isabella after her mother. John's relations with his Queen seem to have become strained after the royal couple returned to England, for on December 3 he issued the following letter:

> THE KING, to Theodoric the German. *We command you to go without delay to Gloucester with the Lady Queen and there to confine her in the chamber in which Joan our daughter was nursed, until we give other orders in this matter. We have com-manded the Sheriff of Gloucester by our letter directed to him, which we send to you, to receive her and to provide whatever is necessary for her and for you.* MYSELF AS WITNESS, at Corfe.

William the Lion, King of the Scots, died at Stirling on Decem-ber 14 and was succeeded by his son Alexander, a lad then sixteen years old.

John kept his Christmas court at Worcester, but he remained there only one day. He then hurried up to London and stayed at the New Temple.

The barons, as they had agreed, presented themselves before John on the Feast of the Epiphany, January 6, 1215. They were in mili-tary array, and their bold tones in speaking to the King showed their determination. They demanded that he restore the good laws of King Edward and the provisions of the charter of Henry I, as he had sworn to do when he was absolved at Winchester in 1213.

John replied that so serious a matter required due deliberation, and he proposed that they agree to a truce till Low Sunday, April 26, to give him time to consult with his advisors. The barons were familiar with his delaying tactics and were unwilling to be put off with promises they knew would prove vain. After much discussion, John suggested that three of the most respected men of the kingdom stand surety for his good faith, and the barons agreed. Stephen Langton, Archbishop of Canterbury, Eustace, Bishop of Ely, and William Marshal, Earl of Pembroke, accordingly took oath that the King would on the appointed day satisfy all their reasonable demands.

In order to make sure of the support of the clerical party, John renewed his charter to the Church in more explicit terms on January 15. He promised that, no matter what customs might hitherto have been observed and what rights he and his ancestors might have claimed, in all the cathedrals and abbeys of England the election of prelates should be free forever henceforth. He reserved to himself and his heirs, however, the custody and revenues of vacant sees, but he promised not to hinder or delay elections, provided the permission to elect had first been asked. That permission he promised not to refuse or delay, and he agreed that if he should refuse or delay to give his consent the electors were authorized to proceed with the election as though the permission had been given. He stipulated that after the election had been made his assent should be asked, and he promised not to refuse his assent unless he could give a legitimate reason for doing so. He sent a copy of this charter to the Pope and asked him to confirm it.

Having thus, as he hoped, got the Pope and the bishops on his side, John had all the nobles of the kingdom to swear fealty to him alone against all men and to renew their homage to him. As a final precaution, on Candlemas, February 2, he assumed the Cross of the Crusader, which in theory protected his person and his lands from all attacks of his enemies. As Roger of Wendover points out, he did this through fear rather than through devotion, for it is most unlikely that he had any intention of emulating his brother Richard's heroic example.

Eustace, Bishop of Ely, died at Reading Abbey on February 3 and was buried in his cathedral. He was a man of great knowledge and discretion, and he added a Galilee porch to his cathedral, the glory of the Fenlands.

Innocent III on March 30 confirmed the charter granted by "Our well-beloved John, the illustrious King of the English," to the cathedral churches of England, and John could feel that he had strengthened his hand at the Papal Curia.

Master Alexander, John's favorite theologian during the interdict, had been richly rewarded with various benefices, but when the Archbishop and the rest of the clergy returned to England, he was stripped of all his livings. He determined to appeal to the Pope, and John gave him a letter of recommendation:

> To his lord and most holy father, Innocent, by the grace of God Supreme Pontiff, JOHN, by the same grace, ETC. *Be it known to Your Holiness that those lies that were put upon Master Alexander of St. Albans, our clerk, were spread by the breath of malice, wherefore it may fittingly be said without a shadow of falsehood that what was put upon Isaias by the Jewish people, upon Moses for the Ethiopian woman, upon Paul for the Seven Churches, that also was put upon Master Alexander by the slanderous mob. Therefore it is that we most devoutly beseech Your Paternity, if it should happen that the same Master Alexander presents himself at the feet of Your Holiness, to deign to show him all humanity, according to the multitude of your mercy, for the love of God and of us.* WITNESSED *at the New Temple in London, on the 23rd day of April.*

From the muddled Scriptural allusions, from the effrontery of comparing Master Alexander to Moses, Isaias, and St. Paul, and from the sudden descent from the pompous Latin to the vernacular "sevnchurches," one is led to suspect that Master Alexander himself composed this letter and brought it to John for his seal.

John entrusted his younger son Richard to his faithful friend Peter de Maulay on April 29:

> WE SEND *to you our beloved son Richard, commanding you to take good and diligent care of him and to provide him and his tutor, Roger, and two trumpeters and his washerwoman with all things necessary for them.*

The disaffected barons assembled at Stamford during Easter Week, April 19–26, with a great show of strength, armed and accompanied by their retainers. The army numbered two thousand knights, in addition to the horse and foot soldiers and the attendants.

Roger of Wendover gives a list of the "chief promoters of this pestilence," and an examination of some of the names involved indicates how widespread the disaffection was and what prominent nobles were concerned in it.

The principal leader of the baronial party was Robert FitzWalter, one of the richest men in England. He engaged in trade, and the King gave him special privileges for his wine ships. He was Lord of Dunmow in Essex and of Baynard's Castle in the southwest of London. His wife, Gunnor, the daughter and heiress of Robert of Valognes, brought him some thirty knights' fees in the North. With Saer de Quincy he had been governor of Vaudreuil in Normandy and had ignominiously surrendered it without resistance to Philip in 1203. By this act of cowardice they became the laughingstock of England and France. Philip put them in prison and held them for a ransom of five thousand marks. When John demanded hostages from the nobles whom he suspected of plotting against him in 1212, Robert confessed his guilt by fleeing to France. He contrived to convince the exiled bishops that he was being persecuted in their cause, and John was forced to grant him peace and forgiveness as one of the terms of his reconciliation with the Church. Robert returned to England with the exiled clergy, and John restored his estates to him. Later legends say that he had a daughter, Matilda, whom John tried to seduce. When she refused his advances, John had her poisoned. Since these legends confuse "The Chaste Matilda" with Robin Hood's Maid Marian, not much credence is to be given them.

Eustace de Vesci, who had married Margaret, a bastard daughter of William the Lion, was a close associate of Robert FitzWalter. He took a prominent part in the negotiations that led to William's act of homage to John at Lincoln in 1200. When Robert FitzWalter fled to France, Eustace at the same time escaped to Scotland. He too was named in John's charter of submission, and the King likewise restored his lands to him.

Another of the disaffected barons was Richard Percy, one of the Northern magnates. He was a grandson of Godfrey, Duke of Brabant. His father, Joscelin of Louvain, married Agnes, the heiress of the great Percy family, and took her name. Richard accumulated vast estates in the North. He took over the administration of the lands belonging to his older brother's son, a minor; he seized his mother's lands when she died in 1196, and he inherited the lands of his aunt, the Countess of Warwick.

Robert de Ros had married Isabella, another bastard daughter of William the Lion, and had also been one of the envoys to Scotland in 1200. John made him Sheriff of Cumberland in 1213 and gave him a license to send a ship laden with wool and hides across the seas and to bring back a cargo of wine. In spite of these favors, his connection with Eustace de Vesci and his properties in the North outweighed his allegiance to the King.

Saer de Quincy, the first Earl of Winchester, had an early start in the practice of rebellion, for in his youth he had joined the young Henry in his war against the King in 1173. He shared with Robert FitzWalter the ignominy of the surrender of Vaudreuil. He had little property and was often in debt to the Jews. In 1204, however, he came into extensive lands. He had married Margaret, the daughter of Robert of Beaumont, Earl of Leicester. Robert died in 1190, and his son and heir, Robert "FitzParnell," died childless in 1204. The vast Leicester estates were then divided between Amicia, who had married Simon de Montfort, and Margaret. Saer de Quincy, as the husband of the younger heiress, was created Earl of Winchester by John in 1207. He was one of the King's justiciars from 1211 to 1214, and it is not clear why he should have joined the conspiracy.

Richard, Earl of Clare, and his son Gilbert were among the few surviving members of the old Norman nobility, most of whom had disappeared or been disposed of by the time of Henry II. Richard, the sixth Earl, was a second cousin of Isabel of Clare, the heiress of the younger branch of the family, who married William Marshal. Richard had married Amicia, one of the three heiresses of William, Earl of Gloucester, and he and his son Gilbert were among the greatest nobles in the land.

Roger Bigod, the second Earl of Norfolk, was likewise a member of a Norman family. His father had distinguished himself by his treachery and turbulence during the reigns of Stephen and Henry II; his mother was Juliana, a sister of Aubrey de Vere, Earl of Oxford. Roger was a justiciar under Richard and John, but he lost the King's favor and was imprisoned in 1213. During the next year, however, he accompanied John to Poitou. By 1215 he was out of favor again and in rebellion against the King.

William Mowbray was the nephew of Richard, Earl of Clare; his mother Mabel was Richard's sister. Mowbray was one of the barons who fortified their castles and prepared for civil war when

John succeeded to the throne. He was pacified, however, by the promises made by the King's representatives at Northampton and took the oath of fealty to him.

Robert de Vere, the third Earl of Oxford and hereditary Great Chamberlain of England, was the younger brother of Aubrey de Vere, who had been one of the King's "evil counsellors" during the interdict. Aubrey died without issue in 1214, and Robert, upon succeeding to the title and estates, joined the party of the Northern barons.

William Mallett, a descendant of a companion of the Conqueror, was appointed Sheriff of Dorset and Somerset, in which latter county his lands lay, in 1211, and in 1214 he accompanied John to Poitou with ten knights and twenty soldiers. Thus he could not have been among the barons from whom John attempted to collected scutage in 1214, and his presence among the leaders of the confederation indicates a discontent more deep-seated than a mere protest against the payment of the scutage. Associated with him was William of Montacute, likewise descended from a companion of the Conqueror and the possessor of estates in Somerset. William de Beauchamp, Lord of Bedford, had also taken part in John's last expedition to Poitou.

The name whose inclusion in this list seems the most surprising is that of William Marshal the younger, the eldest son of that model of fidelity and chivalry, William Marshal, Earl of Pembroke, who had served Henry II and his sons with scrupulous honesty, faithfulness, and loyalty, and who even at this time was one of John's most trusted advisors. The younger William was married in 1214 and seems to have come of age at about that time. It is not evident that he had any specific grievances against the King, and his defection was perhaps caused by his friendship with his mother's relatives, the Clares.

Two sons of Geoffrey FitzPeter, John's former Chief Justiciar, also took a prominent part in the rebellion. The elder son, Geoffrey, resumed the name "de Mandeville," the old family name of the Earls of Essex. In 1214 he married Hadwisa, John's divorced first wife, and paid an enormous fine for the privilege. His younger brother, William, married Christina, the daughter of Robert FitzWalter. These marriages are probably sufficient explanation for the presence of these two names in the list of rebellious barons.

John de Lacy, Constable of Chester, was the son of Roger, famed for his fidelity and valor in the defense of Château-Gaillard in 1203. He had apparently reached his majority only two years before he adhered to the cause of the rebels, and no reason for his doing so is clear.

It is to be observed that not one of these man took any noteworthy part in the government of the country, either before or after the rebellion.

This list of names indicates that the disaffection was not limited to any one part of the country or to any particular group of barons, but that it was a general protest against John's increasingly despotic government. It began, to be sure, among the Northern barons, most of whom refused to accompany John on his expedition to Poitou, and for this reason the rebel party is usually referred to as the "Northerners." The movement spread, however, chiefly to Lincolnshire and to Essex, a county dominated by Robert FitzWalter. Roger of Wendover says that the barons were led by Stephen Langton, who was at their head. When they assembled, however, Langton was with the King at Oxford, where he was awaiting their arrival, and there is no evidence that the Archbishop took an active part in their deliberations.

The barons went to Brackley, in Northamptonshire, on April 27. When John learned that they were there, he sent Stephen Langton and William Marshal, with other prudent men, to find out their demands. The barons gave the messengers a list of the laws and established customs of the kingdom that they said the King had been violating, and they threatened that unless he immediately promised to observe those laws and confirm his promise under his seal they would seize his castles and force him to comply.

Stephen Langton and the other envoys returned to John with the list and the messages of the barons. When their demands were read to him, John exclaimed indignantly: "Why, among these unjust demands, did the barons not ask for my kingdom as well? Their demands are vain, foolish, and utterly unreasonable." He declared with an oath that he would never grant his barons such liberties as would make him their slave.

Neither Stephen Langton nor William Marshal could induce him even to consider the demands. He sent them back to the barons with the defiant message that he would grant none of them. This was equivalent to a declaration of war. When the barons received John's message they solemnly renounced their oaths of allegiance and fealty to him, and a canon of Durham Cathedral released them from their vows. They could now take up arms against the King with a clear conscience.

They elected Robert FitzWalter their leader, with the resounding title of "Marshal of the Army of God and of Holy Church," and proceeded to Northampton, where they laid siege to John's castle. They had no stone-throwers or other engines of war and consequently spent a fortnight in fruitless efforts to reduce it. They suffered numerous casualties, and Robert FitzWalter's standard-bearer was pierced through the head by an arrow from a crossbow.

John realized the seriousness of the situation and made an effort to recall the more moderate barons to their allegiance. He wrote an open letter on May 10, declaring, in terms identical with those used later in the Great Charter, that he conceded "to our barons who are against us, that we will not seize or dispossess them or their men, nor will we proceed against them, except by the law of our realm or by the judgment of their peers in our court, until such time as consideration may be given by four men whom we will choose on our part and four men whom they will elect on their part, and by the Lord Pope, who will be superior to them."

He had alerted his knights in Poitou for possible service in England during the preceding February, and he now summoned them to his service, as the following letter shows:

THE KING, to his venerable father in Christ, Peter, by the same grace Bishop of Winchester: GREETINGS. *We command you to send some discreet servant of yours in whom you have confidence, together with your letters, to deliver our castle of Winchester to our faithful Savaric de Mauléon to have custody of and in which to receive our Poitevins.* MYSELF AS WITNESS, at Reading, on the 11th day of May, in the 16th year of our reign.

He also summoned all the knights of Devonshire to his service and promised to pay the expenses of all except those that owed him knight-service for their lands.

The barons, meanwhile, abandoned their attempt on Northampton and went to Bedford. There they were welcomed by William de Beauchamp, the lord of the castle. Messengers came to them from the citizens of London, inviting them to come there immediately. The barons at once set out. They camped at Ware and then, by marching all night, arrived in London early in the morning of May 24. The gates were open, and most of the citizens were at Mass. The barons entered by Aldgate without meeting any resistance, for the rich citizens favored their cause and the poor ones were both unable and afraid to put up any protest.

The barons stationed guards at the gates and took over the city. They sent letters to all the principal nobles who remained faithful to the King, inviting them to join their cause and stand firm and fight for their rights and warning them that unless they did so the barons would make war on them, destroy their castles, burn their houses, and lay waste their lands. William of Albini, Lord of Belvoir, was one of those who now deserted the King and joined the baronial party.

John, on the other hand, issued a general warning concerning the treachery of the Londoners:

THE KING, to all his bailiffs and faithful subjects. *Be it known that the citizens of London in common have fraudulently and seditiously withdrawn from us and our service and our allegiance. And therefore we command you, whenever they or their servants or their chattels pass through your territory, to inflict upon them, as our enemies, all the evil and shame that you can.*

At this point Roger of Wendover gives a list of the barons who were faithful to John and who were singled out by the rebels for special attention. Among them were William Marshal, Earl of Pembroke, and his nephew, John Marshal, to whom the King had given charge of Lincolnshire in the preceding January; Ranulf of Blundevill, Earl of Chester, who had accompanied John to Poitou in 1214 and to whom the King had entrusted the castle of Newcastle-under-Tyne on May 20; William Longsword, Earl of Salisbury; William, Earl of Warenne, John's cousin; William de Fors, Earl of Aumale and Lord of Holderness; Henry, Earl of Cornwall, a bastard son of Reginald of Cornwall and hence John's cousin; William of Albini, Earl of Arundel, a grandson of Adeliza, Henry I's widow, and also John's cousin; Henry of Braybroc, a justiciar and under-sheriff of Rutland, Buckingham, and Northampton; and Henry of Cornhill and his son-in-law, Hugh de Neville. Most of these men either were related to John in some degree or were his trusted friends and servants. Even some of these, when they received the barons' letters, deserted their master and went over to the rebels.

The country was thrown into disorder, and the administrative and judicial systems were paralyzed. The pleas of the Exchequer and of the sheriffs' courts came to a stop throughout the land, because many of the Barons of the Exchequer, the itinerant justices, the sheriffs, and other officers of the King deserted him.

John realized that he was so deserted by his barons and their followers that his castles were at their mercy and that he had no effective forces left with which to defend himself. Roger of Wendover, with great exaggeration, says that of his host of followers scarcely seven knights remained faithful to him. He decided to pretend at least to submit to his barons. He sent the faithful William Marshal with other messengers to treat with them. He declared his willingness, for the sake of peace and for the good of the kingdom, to grant the barons the laws and liberties they demanded, and he asked them to appoint a day and a place for a meeting at which these matters might be discussed.

The messengers went to London and reported to the baronial leaders. They were filled with joy at having brought the King to submission without the necessity of waging civil war, and they sent back word to John to meet them in a meadow lying between Staines and Windsor, on the Thames, on Monday, June 15.

On the appointed day John, with the small group of his advisors and friends, met the army of the barons. The two parties stationed themselves at opposite ends of the field, and the parley began. It was a long discussion, probably lasting all day, but John was defeated and knew it, and he could not effectively resist the demands made of him. The barons had, in the preceding April, sent the King a list of their demands, and they would of course have formulated by this time a rough draft at least of the charter they intended to wrest from the King. The Great Charter is dated June 15, 1215, and it is probable that by the end of that day John had capitulated to the substance of the barons' demands and perhaps had set his seal to a document embodying them, although the discussion of precise wording and of minor points continued for several days longer.

The Great Charter was wrested from John by a group composed of his barons or tenants-in-chief, supported by their tenants and by the richer citizens of London, with Stephen Langton, the Legate Pandulf, and the bishops as more or less impartial witnesses and referees. The majority of its provisions are directed towards clarifying the nature of the feudal contract between John and his barons, correcting the abuses which had crept into that contract, and defining the limits of the King's power not over the realm as a whole but only over his barons. A second important group of provisions accepts almost completely the legal reforms and innovations instituted by Henry II and forces John to renounce those specific abuses of the legal administration of which he had been guilty. A few short and vague provisions are thrown in as sops to the under-tenants and to the citizens of London, whose support was essential to the barons.

The document in those provisions relating to feudal tenure, dues, and services is reactionary in principle; it looks back to the time of Henry I and makes no provision for the changes in the structure of society which had occurred since then. The chapters dealing with legal procedure, however, are less reactionary in spirit. They express a deep and merited distrust of John and his personal followers and a profound respect for the integrity and competence of the royal justices. These chapters would seem to have been formulated by men brought up in the tradition of the great school of lawyers trained under Henry II by Ranulf Glanville, Hubert Walter, and other members of the Curia Regis. There is no attempt to re-establish the legal jurisdictions of the barons that Henry had taken away from them; the competence of the royal courts is not challenged. Most impressive of all is the fact that in the long list of grievances and complaints of extortion, venality, violation of due custom, rapacity, and abuses of the royal power, no word is said in disparagement of the royal courts and the judicial system. John was an evil tyrant, as almost every chapter of the Charter implicitly asserts, but it is evident that he did not carry his tyranny to its logical end. The King's Court and the justices appointed by him and responsible only to him are above reproach; men have no confidence in the King but all confidence in his courts. Not even in his most evil moments did it occur to him to attempt to corrupt the fountain of justice, appoint venal and subservient justiciars, and use the courts as an instrument of his tyranny. No more impressive monument to the memory of Henry II could be found than the fact that even John still respected the judicial system that he had devised and made no attempt to undermine it.

In the preamble John states his motives for granting the Charter: "Out of respect for God, and for the health of our soul and of those of all our ancestors and heirs, to the honor of God and the exaltation of Holy Church, and for the amending of our reign." Then follows a list of those by whose counsel he has acted: Stephen Langton, the Archbishop of Dublin, the Bishops of London, Winchester, Bath, Lincoln, Worcester, Coventry, and Rochester; Master Pandulf, "the sub-deacon and familiar of our lord the Pope"; the Master of the Knights of the Temple; the Earls of Pembroke, Salisbury, Warenne, and Arundel; the Constable of Scotland; Warren FitzGerald, Peter FitzHerbert, Hubert de Burgh, Seneschcal of Poitou, Hugh de Neville, Matthew FitzHerbert, Thomas and Alan Basset, Philip of Albini, Robert of Roppesley, John Marshal, and John FitzHugh. Most of these laymen were mentioned by Roger of Wendover in his list of men faithful to John.

The first chapter of the Charter declares that the English Church shall be free and have her rights entire and her liberties inviolate and confirms the freedom of elections that John had already granted in his charters of November 1214, and January 1215. This is the extent of John's concessions to the Church, and the fact that it carries only an assertion that the Church shall be free, a statement so vague as to be almost meaningless, and a repetition of a right already granted twice over would seem to indicate that Stephen Langton had little active part in the framing of the barons' demands. If he were indeed one of the men primarily responsible for the formulation of the document, it seems strange that he did not see fit to include a number of the disputed points that had long been a source of friction between the Crown and the Church. Now, if ever, when John was at the mercy of his barons and faced by an array of force that could have intimidated him into accepting almost anything they chose to put before him, was the time to induce him to renounce the wardship of ecclesiastical lands during a vacancy, to extend the jurisdiction of the courts christian, to exempt the clergy from aids, scutages, and levies, and to extend the sphere of clerical influence. That none of these is mentioned would make it seem that Stephen Langton's part in the proceedings, no matter how much encouragement he may have given to the barons in private, was limited, in his official capacity, to that of an impartial witness and referee between the King and his barons.

This chapter concludes with the statement that "we concede to all free men of our kingdom . . . all the underwritten liberties." The words "free men" deprive the document of that universal application to all Englishmen of whatever degree that is sometimes claimed for it. Villeins were not free men, and perhaps three men out of four at this time were villeins. Neither John nor his barons were concerned with them; such rights as they had depended on the custom of the manor and the will of their lords.

The barons then proceeded to a separate listing of their grievances and the remedies they proposed for them. These are examined in some detail in the Appendix to this book, both because they furnish valuable light on the structure of the society of the time and because they indicate the sort of conduct of which John had been guilty. Seen in this light, the Great Charter is a summing up of all of John's abuses of his power and position, of his flagrant disregard for the established customary rights of his barons, and of the rapacity with which he seized upon every pretext to extort money from his subjects.

The greater share of the blame for the abuses of John's reign should of course be laid on the King's personal viciousness, his lack of principle, honor, and decency, his indifference to the claims of religion, his contempt for those standards of chivalry and manly courage that made Richard the idol of his age, and his determination to extort every possible penny from his subjects. None of these can be in any way extenuated or condoned. It should be borne in mind, however, that John's troubles were primarily financial; that the ordinary revenues of the Crown were by no means sufficient to meet the vast expenses that his attempts first to hold and later to regain his continental possessions entailed; and that the worst of his excesses arose directly from his pressing need for money. As King of England, Lord of Ireland, Duke of Normandy, Duke of Aquitaine, Count of Anjou, and the rest, John felt it his duty to hold on to those lands at any cost, once he had recovered from the pathological fit of languor that caused him to let Normandy slip from his grasp without a struggle; if the ordinary revenues of the Crown were not enough for his needs, he supplemented them by any means that occurred to him.

Although the Exchequer was an office of ever-increasing importance and complexity, it does not seem to have occurred to its officials to draw up anything resembling a budget. The King lived from hand to mouth; no attempt was made to estimate future expenditure or anticipated income, and when the King needed money he cast about for the quickest and easiest way of raising it. The individual chapters of the Great Charter are clear evidence of what some of those ways were.

After the long list of specific abuses and the steps to be taken to right them that make up the body of the Charter, the document concludes with a number of general provisions relating to the scope of the Charter and the means whereby it is to be enforced.

Chapter Sixty-one, the longest and most complicated one of the Charter, contains the "form of security for the observance of the peace and liberties" and sets up the involved machinery for securing the observance of the provisions of the Charter. The assembled barons are to elect twenty-five of their number, who are with all their might to observe, hold, and cause to be observed the peace and liberties that John has conceded to them. If the King or any of his officers wrongs anyone or transgresses any of the provisions of the Charter, the offense is to be reported to four of the members of the committee of twenty-five, and the four barons are then to come before the King or his Chief Justiciar, if the King is out of the country, and petition for redress of the wrong. If the wrong is not righted within forty days, the four barons shall so report to the whole committee of twenty-five, and they, together with the "community of the whole land," shall be authorized to force the King to comply by seizing his castles, lands, and possessions and by any other measures short of harming the King's person and the persons of his wife and children.

Everyone throughout the country is to swear to obey the twenty-five barons and to help them, if need be, in forcing the King to obey the Charter. The committee of twenty-five is to be a self-perpetuating body; if any member dies or leaves the country, the remainder are to elect another in his place. Furthermore, in case there is disagreement among the twenty-five or in case not all of them are able to be present, matters shall be decided by a majority of those present.

Finally, John promised not to seek anything from anyone by which any of these concessions and liberties might be revoked or diminished. This was put in to prevent him from appealing to the Pope, whom he had recognized as his feudal overlord, to cancel or annul any of the provisions of the Charter.

This device for securing John's compliance with the Charter seems vague in many respects and awkward and unworkable in

others. It must be remembered, however, that this was an unprece-
dented experiment in trying to force a king to keep the law. The
barons knew John well enough to realize that they would have accomplished little indeed in forcing him to seal a charter and swear a
solemn oath with many witnesses to keep it. Outright deposition, although there were precedents for it in the time before the Conquest,
no doubt seemed to them too extreme a course to be followed at the
present juncture because the sentiment of the country probably would
not have supported it. There was no claimant to the throne whom
the country would accept as king, and of course any form of government other than a monarchy was so far removed from their experience
and the political theory of the day as to be quite unthinkable. Moreover, John was under the direct protection of the Pope, his overlord,
and of the Cross he had taken as a crusader, and the moderate party,
headed no doubt by Stephen Langton and still powerful in the councils of the barons, would not have accepted such an extreme measure.

Hence it is a credit to their ingenuity, their resourcefulness in the
field of government and administration, and their moderation that
they should have devised a scheme so novel for its day. The threat
of proceeding to open violence as a last resort was probably intended
by them not as an actual eventuality but as a means of convincing
John that they meant business and that the whole country would help
them in forcing him to right their wrongs. The composition of the
committee would further impress John with the conviction that they
would not lightly acquiesce in further misgovernment or condone any
infraction of his oath. Of the list of the twenty-five barons as given
by Matthew Paris, only two, William de Fors, Earl of Aumale, and
William of Albini, Earl of Arundel, were among the small number
of John's supporters, whilst fourteen, Robert FitzWalter, Eustace
de Vesci, Richard Percy, Robert de Ros, Saer de Quincy, Gilbert
of Clare, Roger and Hugh Bigod, William of Mowbray, Robert
de Vere, William Mallett, William Marshal the younger, William

Huntingfield, and John de Lacy, were named by Roger of Wendover among the leaders of the baronial party.

Chapter Sixty-two pardons all transgressions occasioned by the discord between the King and his barons and committed since the last Easter.

The concluding chapter declares that it is the King's will that the English Church be free and that the men in his kingdom may have and hold all the aforesaid liberties, rights, and concessions, for themselves and their heirs, in all things and places. It concludes: "Given by our hand in the field called Runnymede, between Windsor and Staines, on the 15th day of June, in the 17th year of our reign."

"TO GOD
AND ST. WULFSTAN"

❦ 1215–1216 ❧

THE NEGOTIATIONS concerning the Char-
ter were carried on from Monday, June 15, till Friday,
June 19. When they were concluded, each side remained
in wary watchfulness, the King at Windsor and the barons in London. On the 19th John sent letters to all his sheriffs, forest officers,
bailiffs, and other officials, announcing that by God's grace a firm
peace had been restored between him and his barons and free men,
as they might see by the copies of the Charter that he was sending
to each of them. He ordered that the Charter be publicly read in
each bailiwick and firmly observed. Sheriffs were ordered to cause
every one to swear to obey the twenty-five barons in the contingen-
cies mentioned in the Charter and to take an oath to that effect at a
time and place to be appointed by the barons. At the next county
court twelve knights were to be elected to inquire into all abuses by
the King's officers.

John was immediately besieged by a host of claimants to lands and castles of which they said he had illegally disseized them, but he refused to be rushed into a wholesale relinquishment. He replied that they had to support their claims by the testimony of trustworthy men, and he appointed August 16 as the day when he would hear their claims at Westminster. He did, however, restore the Tower of London and Rochester Castle to the Archbishop of Canterbury, who was entitled to them by ancient custom.

He also released some of his hostages and returned castles to their owners, as the following letters of June 21 show:

THE KING, to the Constable of Northampton: GREETINGS. *We command you without delay to deliver to Henry, the son of Earl David, the bearer of this letter, all hostages of the same Earl David who are in your custody.*

THE KING, to Saer, Earl of Winchester: GREETINGS. *We command you that, inasmuch as Earl David had done his homage to us, you return to him his castle of Fotheringhay, which we had committed to your care; and if perchance he should die before he has made his homage to us, then do you deliver up the castle to us.*

On June 23 he wrote to Hugh of Boves, the leader of his mercenary troops, who was waiting at Dover for further orders. John directed him not to keep any of the soldiers, but to send them back to their homes across the Channel without delay. He also wrote on the same date to Stephen Harengod, informing him that peace had been made and that the barons had tendered their homage. He ordered Stephen to collect no more fines on account of the barons' revolt, to return any money that he might have collected since the final ratification of the peace on the 19th, and to release all captives and hostages taken during the troubles.

Whether or not John acted in good faith in these matters is impossible to tell, but the available evidence would seem to indicate that he did. During the period immediately following the sealing of the Charter, at any rate, he took steps to put into effect those provisions that might be accomplished by his command alone. His letter dismissing the foreign mercenaries is perhaps the best indication that he thought that the crisis had passed and the immediate danger was over.

Another sign that he was convinced that peace had been attained was the fact that he began collecting the jewels that he had put in various religious houses for safekeeping. The items mentioned in the following receipt, although they are not so costly as some of the jewels that he entrusted to other houses, show how John loved to adorn his person:

THE KING, to all ETC. *Be it known that on the Friday next after the nativity of St. John the Baptist we received at Winchester from the hands of Nicholas, Canon of Waltham, 13 silver cups weighing 50 marks and 3 ounces and a half, and one brooch with 6 sapphires and 6 garnets, and another brooch with 3 sapphires and 3 garnets and various other stones, and a third brooch with 2 sapphires and 4 garnets and 2 pearls and small turquoises, and a fourth brooch with 2 sapphires and 4 garnets and 2 pearls and other small stones, and a fifth brooch with small sapphires and small garnets, and a sixth brooch with 8 green jaspers. Also one belt of smooth black leather with which the King is wont to gird himself, and another belt of red leather with sections with small lions, and a third belt of chased red leather, and a fourth belt of red leather with stones in the buckle and tongue and with raised sections, and a fifth belt of red leather with 11 green jaspers, and a sixth belt of black leather with sections with various stones in the buckle and the sections. These were all entrusted to the Abbot, the Prior, and the convent of Waltham for safekeeping by our orders, and in testimony of this matter we have had this our letter patent made for them. My-self as witness, at Winchester, on the 27th day of June, in the 17th year of our reign.*

The barons, however, took no such view of matters. They re-mained in London with their forces and showed no inclination to disperse. They watched the King with distrustful eyes, and to John it must have seemed that they were preparing to use force again and heap further indignities upon them. To keep themselves in martial spirits, to make a show of their strength for the benefit of the King, and no doubt to provide a spectacle for their friends and allies, the citizens of London, they staged a tournament at Hounslow on July 6.

Robert FitzWalter, "Marshal of the Army of God and of Holy Church," and the other great men of that army sent a letter of invi-tation to William of Albini. After he had deserted the King in May, William had supported the barons at Runnymede and then retired to his castle of Belvoir. They pointed out the strategic importance of London and warned that certain people were only waiting for them to leave the city so that they might occupy it. They had therefore agreed to have a tournament, for their security and the safety of London, and they invited William to come provided with horses and arms, so that he might win honor there. As a final inducement, Robert FitzWalter added: "Whoever does best there will have a bear, which a certain lady will send to the tournament."

Perhaps on the grounds that he already had a bear, William did not accept the invitation but remained at Belvoir.

Even if he had once intended to adhere to the provisions of the Charter and submit his actions to the hostile scrutiny of the commit-tee of barons, John now realized, from the fact that they remained under arms in London, that they were plotting further mischief. He

accordingly set to work to free himself from that humiliating agreement and to revenge himself on the men who had brought him so
low. Roger of Wendover says that he determined to strike at his
enemies with two swords, the one spiritual and the other material. To
sharpen the spiritual sword, he sent Pandulf to Rome to show the
Pope a copy of the Charter, and, despite his promise not to do so,
to induce Innocent to absolve him from his oath to observe it.

The fulsome language of the letter that Pandulf carried from
John to the Pope is in marked contrast to the intemperate terms in
which he had formerly addressed Innocent:

> To his reverend lord and most holy father, Innocent, by the
> grace of God Supreme Pontiff; JOHN, by the same grace King
> of England ETC.: GREETINGS and the reverence due to such a
> lord and father.

> *We bow down before the presence of Your Paternity and
> offer, as best we know how to and can, many thanks for the care
> and solicitude which your paternal benevolence unceasingly de-
> votes to our defence and that of our realm of England, although
> the hardness of heart of the prelates of England and their dis-
> obedience maliciously impede the effect of your pious foresight.*

> *We, however, devotedly acknowledge the sincere affection
> which Your Clemency bears to us and which, although at pres-
> ent it is thought useless by the proud and the malevolent, to their
> folly, will yet be, God willing, to our safety and peace and will
> bring confusion and terror to our enemies.*

> *And although the Lord Pandulf, your faithful sub-deacon
> and the Bishop-elect of Norwich, is most necessary to us in Eng-
> land, inasmuch as he faithfully and devotedly upholds the honor
> of the Roman Church and ours and that of our whole realm, yet
> in no other way can Your Paternity be better informed of our
> condition and that of our realm than by him.*

We therefore reluctantly send him to your feet, devoutly beg-ging that when you have learned from him especially and from our other faithful messengers of the injuries which have been in-flicted upon you in our person, you will apply the hand of your paternal sollicitude to the governing of our realm and the keeping of our dignity, accordingly as your excellent discretion deems expedient what by God's grace you have done and are doing.

Holding for certain that we have, after God, your person and the authority of the Apostolic See as a friend and singular defence, we breathe in the confidence of your protection.

The "other faithful messengers" were the members of an impos-ing delegation that included the Archbishops of Bordeaux and Dub-lin, Richard de Mariscis, the King's Chancellor, the Abbot of John's monastery at Beaulieu, and John Marshal and Geoffrey Lutterel. The letter they bore was intended further to incite the Pope against the barons. "Although the earls and barons of England were devoted to us before we submitted ourself and our land to your rule," John plaintively observed, "since that time and because of that, as they publicly say, they violently rise up against us."

To prepare the material sword, at some time during the summer John sent his trusted servants Walter Grey, Bishop of Worcester, Richard de Marisco, William Gernon, and Hugh of Boves to the Continent in an effort to raise an army there. His agents were em-powered to offer lands and money to all who would join his forces and to give warrants to the soldiers for their pay. These forces were ordered to assemble at Dover at Michaelmas. Throughout England he directed the constables of the royal castles to lay in stocks of pro-visions and arms and to increase their garrisons so as to be ready to defend the castles at a day's notice.

When Pandulf and the other messengers arrived in Rome, they reported all that had taken place between John and his barons to the

Pope and showed him a copy of the Charter. When he read it, Innocent exclaimed: "Are the barons of England trying to depose a King signed with the Crusader's Cross and placed under the protection of the Apostolic See and to transfer to another the dominion of the Roman Church? By St. Peter, we cannot let this injury go unpunished!"

After he had consulted with his Cardinals, on August 24 he issued a bull reciting the injuries "our dearest son in Christ, John, the illustrious King of the English," had suffered at the hands of his barons, forbidding, as overlord of England, under pain of excommunication, either the King to observe or the barons and their accomplices to force him to observe the provisions of the Charter, and declaring that document utterly null and void.

At the same time he sent a letter to "the noble men of England," ordering them to renounce the Charter they had obtained by force and threats, by which they constituted themselves both judges and executioners. Innocent directed them to send proctors to the forthcoming Council of the Lateran to appear before him. He would then, he said optimistically, so arrange matters that the King would be content with his rights and honors and the people would rejoice in peace and liberty.

With this annulment of the Charter by the Pope, the only authority the barons would recognize as superior to both themselves and the King, John had been eminently successful in his use of the spiritual sword. The controversy over the election of the Archbishop of York gave him an opportunity to humiliate Stephen Langton, whom he had never trusted and who, he was now convinced, was one of the prime movers of the barons' rebellion, encouraging them in every way and putting his learning and ingenuity at their service.

The archepiscopal see of York had been vacant since the death of Geoffrey, the King's half-brother, in exile in 1212. During the troubled June of 1215, hardly a propitious time, the canons met to elect an archbishop, and John sent them a letter from Runnymede recommending Walter Grey, newly consecrated Bishop of Worcester, formerly Chancellor of the kingdom, and the brother of John Grey, Bishop of Norwich. Walter had been educated at Oxford, and the canons of York, who may all have been Cambridge men, rejected him because he was, they said, illiterate. Instead they chose, on account of his learning, one of their fellow canons, Simon Langton, the younger brother of the Archbishop of Canterbury.

John viewed this attempt to elevate Stephen Langton's brother as instigated by the baronial party, and he knew that if they succeeded it would be a great triumph for them and for Stephen Langton. He at once sent ambassadors to protest to the Pope against this election. Stephen Langton, they declared, had aided and abetted the barons in their rebellion against the King, and if Stephen's brother were made Archbishop of York the two Primates between them would succeed in destroying the peace of the kingdom. They intimated to the Pope that Walter Grey would be most pleasing to the King as the new Archbishop.

Giving ear to John's objections, on September 13 Innocent refused to approve the election of Simon Langton, declared it null and void, and ordered the canons of York to send proctors to Rome to conduct the election before him and with his advice. If the Archbishop of Canterbury could properly be elected in such a manner, so also could the Archbishop of York.

There was yet a sharper and more powerful spiritual sword to be used against John's enemies, and the Pope obligingly placed it in his hands. In a letter addressed to Peter des Roches, Bishop of Winchester, the Abbot of Reading, and Pandulf, Innocent accused the Archbishop of Canterbury and some of his bishops of ignoring the business of the Crusade, the mandates of the Apostolic See, and their own oaths of fealty by giving no help or favor to the King against the disturbers of the kingdom but, on the contrary, of being in the councils of these disturbers, if not actual participants in their wicked conspiracy.

These men, declared the Pope, were worse than Saracens, since they were trying to drive from his throne the very man who was planning to come to the help of the Holy Land. Therefore Innocent laid the bonds of excommunication on all these disturbers of the King and the realm of England, together with their accomplices and helpers, and laid their lands under interdict. He most strictly ordered the Archbishop and his bishops to proclaim this sentence throughout all England on every Sunday and feast day with bells ringing and candles lighted, till such time as the said disturbers made satisfaction to the King for their misdeeds and faithfully returned to his service. If any bishop neglected to obey this order, he was to be suspended from his office and his subjects released from their obedience to him.

None of the bishops paid much attention to this bull of excommunication, and Stephen Langton did not publish it in his province. Peter des Roches and Pandulf, therefore, who had been charged by the Pope to see that his orders were carried out, went to the Archbishop to discover why he had not obeyed the instructions. They found Stephen Langton already aboard a ship, ready to start on his way to Rome to the General Council, the Fourth Lateran, that had been summoned to meet on November 1. Armed with the papal commands, they ordered him to direct his suffragan bishops to publish the sentence of excommunication in the manner specified.

The Cardinal replied that a tacit sentence had indeed been pronounced against the barons, but he refused to publish it or to order his suffragans to do so till he had appealed with his own voice to the Supreme Pontiff. The Pope had provided Peter des Roches and Pandulf with powers to meet just such a contingency, and they therefore pronounced the sentence of suspension upon him, forbidding him to enter a church or to celebrate Mass.

Stephen Langton humbly observed this sentence and went to Rome as a suspended prelate, forbidden to exercise his priestly office, out of favor with the Pope, to whom he owed his elevation to the episcopacy, hated by his King, who had procured his humiliation, discredited in the eyes of his fellow bishops, and with nothing to show for his efforts as the successor of St. Augustine except a land torn by a civil war that he was accused of having fomented. Hot on his heels followed the King's proctors, the Abbot of Beaulieu and two knights, Thomas Hardington and Geoffrey of Crawcombe, to present their master's complaints against the Primate.

John had had the spiritual weapons of interdict and excommunication used against him, and he knew how little impression they made on a thick skin. Some of his barons had skins as thick as his, and against them he prepared to use the material sword. He spent July and August in going from one royal castle to another, making sure that they were in a state of readiness. On September 1 he arrived at Dover, and he spent that month there and in Canterbury, preparing for the arrival at Michaelmas of the foreign mercenaries being recruited by Hugh of Boves and his other agents abroad.

Meanwhile all sorts of wild stories about him were circulating through the country, spread, perhaps, by agents of the barons to add to the general confusion. Some said that he had become a fisherman; others, a merchant or a roving pirate; some said that he had turned apostate; others, that he had drowned. Even the usually well-informed Roger of Wendover says that he hid in the Isle of Wight for three months, living in the open with sailors.

Around Michaelmas his mercenaries began pouring in. "From Poitou and Gascony came Savaric de Mauléon and Geoffrey and Oliver de Buteville with many knights and soldiers and promised faithful service to the King; from Louvain and Brabant came Walter Buck and Gerard and Godeschal de Soceinne wth three battalions of soldiers and crossbowmen who thirsted for nothing so much as for human blood; and from Flanders and other provinces came many who wanted the goods of others and who gave the King great hopes," says Roger of Wendover.

These mercenary soldiers, or Brabantines, as they were commonly called, were the scum and the scourge of Europe. Recruited from the dregs of society, they plundered, ravaged, and pillaged wherever they went, spreading terror and destruction in their wake. They brought an element of cold-blooded ferocity into mediaeval warfare that appalled their contemporaries, most of whom observed the code of chivalry and fought as though a battle were merely a glorified tournament. Their conduct was so inhuman that the Third Lateran Council forbade any Christian ruler to employ them.

Hugh of Boves collected a large army and set sail from Calais. A great storm arose, and they were shipwrecked in the Channel. Hugh's body was washed ashore at Yarmouth, and thus he came to claim Suffolk, which, together with Norfolk, John had promised him as a reward for his help. The beaches around Yarmouth were littered with the bodies of drowned soldiers and their wives and children, and the story spread that John had promised to drive out or exterminate the English and give the land to these foreigners. Roger of Wendover says that they numbered more than forty thousand, and they were all devoured by the beasts of the sea and the birds of the air. When news of this disaster was brought to John, he was almost mad with rage and disappointment and took no food that day.

The barons meanwhile had not been idle. They remained in strength in London and wrote many letters to William of Albini, the Lord of Belvoir, reproaching him for not joining them and urging him to come to London. At Michaelmas he yielded to their en-treaties. After stocking his castle of Belvoir with provisions and arms and entrusting it to faithful men, he joined the barons. They told him of a plan they had conceived. The King with his large host of mercenaries was at Dover, and the barons proposed to block the roads and bottle him up in Kent, so that he could not besiege them in London.

Stephen Langton, to whom the King had entrusted Rochester Castle, had turned it over to the barons. They picked a strong body of troops, amounting to a hundred and forty knights and their retinues, placed them under the command of William of Albini, whom they knew to be of stout heart and well versed in the arts of war, and sent them to occupy the city of Rochester. Thus they would command the road between Dover and London. To bolster the courage of this detachment, the barons swore on the Gospels that if John were to besiege Rochester they would come at once to drive him off.

When William of Albini arrived there he found the castle stripped bare of all provisions, arms, and furniture, and his troops had nothing with which to defend it except what they had brought with them. There was a general movement to abandon the enterprise and return to London, but their commander so exhorted and taunted the knights with the name of deserters that they set to work with a will, stripped the city of all its provisions and carried them into the castle, and settled down to defend it.

John of course learned of all this at once. He immediately moved his mercenaries to Rochester and laid siege to the castle on October 11. His troops occupied the city and stabled their horses in the Cathedral. His stone-throwers kept up an incessant rain of missiles on the besieged garrison, and John himself took command of the operations.

When the barons in London learned of the siege, in accordance with their oath they set out to succor William of Albini. They marched as far as Dartford, about fifteen miles, with a gentle south wind blowing in their faces, and then they turned round and marched back to London. They fortified the city well and settled back to observe the outcome of the siege of Rochester, passing their time, says Roger of Wendover, in playing with dice, drinking the best of wines, and practicing various vices.

William of Albini meanwhile was left to bear the full brunt of John's attacks. When the King saw that the barons were not going to do anything to help William, he knew that it was only a matter of time till the garrison would be forced to surrender. He accordingly laid in a stock of wine:

> THE KING, to Brother Roger the Templar: GREETINGS. *Be it known to you that we need wine. Wherefore we command you, if you can find any wine for sale at Sandwich, to buy it for our use and send it to Rochester at our expense without delay.* MYSELF AS WITNESS, *at Rochester, on the 22nd day of No-vember.*

He also sent to Dover for the nine casks of wine that remained out of his stock there.

His stone-throwers and crossbowmen worked day and night. The besieged garrison fought back with grim desperation and inflicted many losses on the royal army. They had not many provisions to be-gin with, and they were soon reduced to eating their horses.

One day John and Savaric de Mauléon, his Poitevin captain of mercenaries, were riding round the walls of the castle and looking for weak spots where the stone-throwers might be aimed. A cross-bowman on the walls saw them and pointed them out to William of Albini.

"My lord, would you like me to kill our bloody enemy the King with this arrow that I have ready?" he asked the Lord of Belvoir.

"No, man," he replied; "far be it from us to cause the death of the Lord's anointed."

"But he would not spare you in a like case," the soldier argued, but William persisted in his chivalric regard for the person of his King.

The stone-throwers could do little damage to the sturdy outer walls of the castle. At last John had the walls mined. He fired the supporting timbers with forty fat sides of bacon, and most of the outer walls collapsed. The starving garrison then took refuge in the tower and inflicted such damage on the King's soldiers that they drove them off time after time. Miners next set to work under the walls of the tower. The garrison, meanwhile, had eaten the last of their horses and were faced with starvation.

On St. Andrew's Day, November 30, 1215, defeated by hunger but not by their enemies, William of Albini and his garrison surrendered. They had lost only one knight, who was killed by an arrow, and suffered few wounds, whilst they had inflicted great damage on their besiegers. The siege had cost John sixty thousand marks, according to Ralph of Coggeshall.

John at once ordered all the captured knights to be hanged. Savaric de Mauléon, who was a gentleman, as well as a poet of some repute, protested against such barbaric behavior.

"My lord king," he remonstrated, "our war is not yet finished, and you should remember how the fortunes of war change. If you have us hang these men, our enemies the barons might capture me or some other nobles of your army and hang us, after your example. Do not let this happen, for then no one would fight in your army."

John unwillingly followed his advice. William of Albini and most of the other knights he sent to Corfe Castle to be kept in close confinement; some were sent to Nottingham Castle, and the remainder were distributed among various royal dungeons. He turned the soldiers, except the crossbowmen, over to his own soldiers as prizes to be ransomed, but the crossbowmen, who were responsible for killing many of his own men, he ordered hanged.

Shortly after the fall of Rochester, John's ambassadors, Thomas Hardington and Geoffrey of Crawcombe, returned from Rome and reported on their success at the Holy See. John had obtained every-thing he wanted from the Pope. They told him that when Stephen Langton presented himself before Innocent, he did not attempt to defend himself against their accusations of having favored and helped the barons against the King, of having refused to pronounce the eccle-siastical censures against the barons, and of rebelling against the Pope's orders. Stephen's only reply to their charges was to beg the Pope to free him from the sentence of suspension that lay on him.

"Brother, by St. Peter," Innocent replied, "you will not thus eas-ily be absolved for having inflicted so many and such injuries not only on the King of the English but also on the Roman Church. We will decide with the full deliberation of our brothers how we shall punish such rash excesses."

Innocent's verdict was that the sentence of suspension should stand, and he wrote to all the suffragan bishops of the Province of Canterbury, announcing that he had ratified the suspension of Stephen Langton and ordering them to show no obedience to their Archbishop.

The canons of York then presented Simon Langton to the Pope as Archbishop-elect of York and begged him to confirm the election. Innocent reminded them that he had already refused to accept Simon. He once more declared the election null and Simon Langton hence-forth ineligible for episcopal orders without a special dispensation from the Holy See. He ordered the canons to proceed at once with another election and threatened to provide them himself with a pastor if they did not do so. The canons, who had been given authority to do so by their chapter, then elected Walter Grey, whom they had pre-viously rejected as illiterate. This defect, they now said, was out-weighed by his purity of life, which he had maintained from his birth to the present day.

When they informed the Pope of their new choice and their reasons for it, Innocent said: "By St. Peter, virginity is a great virtue,
and we give him to you," and bestowed the pallium on Walter Grey.
The new Archbishop returned to England owing the Papal Curia
ten thousand pounds for his election.

John now divided his forces, so that he might keep the barons bot-
tled up in London and at the same time defend the North against the
incursions of the Scots. He appointed William Longsword, Falkes
de Breauté, Savaric de Mauléon, William Brewer, and Walter Buck
commanders of the southern detachments, whilst he himself proposed
to lead the expedition into the North.

The southern forces at once set to work, spreading terror wherever they went. The constables of Windsor, Hertford, and Berkhamstead were given the assignment of watching London and cutting off the barons' supplies. The Thames was still open, however,
and the city was amply provisioned by water. William Longsword
and Falkes de Breauté overran Essex, Hertfordshire, Middlesex,
Cambridgeshire, and Huntingdonshire. They ravaged those counties
thoroughly, taking tribute from the towns, making the inhabitants
prisoners, burning the buildings of the barons, cutting down orchards,
spreading fire, and taking great booty as far as the suburbs of London
itself. Falkes captured Bedford Castle on December 2, while its lord,
William de Beauchamp, was in London.

John arrived at St. Albans on December 18 and ordered the
chapter to send copies to all the churches in England of the Pope's
letter suspending Stephen Langton. Then he set out for the North,
taking with him William de Fors, Earl of Aumale; John Marshal,
nephew of the Earl of Pembroke; Philip of Albini, and some of his
mercenary captains, as well as an army of foreigners, crossbowmen,
and lawless men. On his way to Northampton he laid the country
waste, burning houses and barns, driving off cattle, and robbing and
plundering. The keepers of the barons' castles fled when they heard

of his approach, and John put his own men in these fortresses. He reached Northampton on December 21 and Nottingham on Christ-mas Eve. He spent Christmas at Nottingham and then went to Langer, where William of Albini had a castle that he had entrusted to his son Nicholas, who was a clerk, and a body of knights.

John sent a messenger to tell Nicholas that if he did not surrender the castle at once his father, who was then confined in Corfe Castle, would never eat again. Nicholas knew that this was no idle threat, and he immediately surrendered. John turned the castle over to two of his Poitevin mercenaries and continued northward.

He reached York on January 5, Durham on the 8th, and Berwick on the 14th. He stayed in Berwick, the northernmost point of his expedition, a week, reducing the castle there. He set fire to the town with his own hands when he withdrew, exclaiming: "We will drive the little red fox (Alexander) from his lair."

John's forces spread terrible devastation wherever they went. Part of their ravages were no doubt committed through wanton cruelty, but much of their plundering was due to the fact that John's treasury was low, and instead of paying his mercenaries he allowed them to take whatever spoils they could find. The soldiers plundered houses and churches alike and tortured their victims to extract money from them. The campaign into the North was so successful that only two castles remained in the hands of the barons. John put his own men in command of all the castles, with garrisons of foreign soldiers to keep the countryside subdued, and he ordered them to complete the work that he had begun of destroying all the property of the rebel barons. He spent February in Yorkshire and Lincolnshire, capturing the castles of the barons, placing them and his own castles in the custody of loyal men, and making sure that they were in a good state of defence, so that "the little red fox" might not be able to come South and join the rebels.

Whilst John was thus occupied in the North, part of his Southern forces kept up the blockade of London by land and others invaded the Isle of Ely. Falkes de Breauté, to whom John had entrusted the castles of Oxford, Northampton, Bedford, and Cambridge; William Longsword, and Savaric de Mauléon, with their armies, laid waste the whole district. They plundered the Cathedral and threatened to burn it, but the Prior paid them nine marks and saved it. They captured fifteen knights and held them for ransom.

In January 1216, letters arrived from the Pope, excommunicating by name the leading barons of the rebellion and laying the city of London, their stronghold, under interdict. The sentence was published and observed throughout the kingdom, except in London. The barons and the citizens of London persuaded themselves that the letters had been obtained from the Pope by misrepresentation, and they advanced the theory, once favored by the King, that the Pope had no jurisdiction over lay affairs. They did not consider themselves bound to observe either the sentence of excommunication or that of interdict but celebrated the divine services throughout the city, ringing the bells in defiance and singing with loud belligerent voices.

While John was reducing the North and his captains were keeping London under observation and harrying all the region around it, the barons stayed in the city "like pregnant women," as Roger of Wendover remarks, thinking only of food and drink. Thus they slept, but the King did not sleep; he made himself master of all their lands and possessions and of every castle and town in the country, save only London. Part of the barons' inactivity may have been due to sheer funk, which increased from day to day as they learned the calibre of the forces John was employing. No doubt the barons and their retainers were not sufficient in number to defeat John and his large foreign armies. Principally, however, their indecisiveness through this winter arose from their lack of leadership. William of Albini seems to have been their most capable leader, and he, through their cowardice and incompetence, was now a prisoner in Corfe Cas-

tle. Although he was no military genius, John had had far more experience in war than any of the barons who were attempting to oppose him. William Marshal and William Longsword were the most
experienced and capable military leaders in England, and they were
both on the King's side. In addition to these men, John had the services of a group of mercenary captains, men like Savaric de Mauléon
and Falkes de Breauté, who had spent most of their lives fighting and
who lived only for the pleasure of war. The English baronage had
grown soft, while John had grown harder and more experienced with
every year.

The barons, unwilling and unable to fight for their own cause, descended to the depths of treachery. They sent Saer de Quincy, Earl
of Winchester, and Robert FitzWalter, two men who had previously
distinguished themselves for treachery and cowardice, to France to
offer the crown of England to Louis, Philip's son, a young prig of
twenty-eight. His pretensions to the English throne were given a
shadow of legality by his having married, in 1200, Blanche of Castile, a granddaughter of Henry II. The shadow was but a faint one,
for even if one set aside John, as the barons were trying to do, there
still remained the two living sons of Matilda, Henry's eldest daughter,
and Blanche's brother Henry, all of whom had a better claim to the
throne, assuming it to be vacant, than did the husband of one of the
granddaughters of Henry II.

The barons, however, were not interested in the finer points of
hereditary succession. They were determined to get rid of John, and
they knew that Philip was the only foreign prince able and willing
to help them and that without his help they could not succeed. They
therefore seized on Louis's being married to Blanche as a lucky acci-
dent that might give some justification to their doings. If they got rid
of John they would have to find another king to take his place, for a
monarchy was the only form of government they could imagine.
Louis would do as well as anyone else, although he was not a figure to

arouse popular enthusiasm, being cold-blooded, studious, cautious, and colorless.

The proposition that these two messengers laid before Philip sounded immensely attractive to him and represented the culmination of his life's ambition; to see his son seated on the throne of England would be a fitting climax to a lifetime of enmity towards the King of England. Philip, however, had had dealings with English traitors, and with these two in particular, before, and he declined to commit himself till he had some guarantee that the barons would not betray him in turn. He accordingly demanded that they send over twenty-four of their most eminent men as hostages of their good faith. The barons had no choice but to comply, and their hostages were kept at Compiègne while Louis began his preparations for invading England.

To assemble and equip the forces necessary for such an expedition was a big undertaking and would require a long time. To keep up the spirits of the barons and also to report on their trustworthiness, Louis sent an advance party to London. Although John controlled all the land approaches to the city, the Thames was still open, and the Frenchmen sailed up it and landed in London on February 27, 1216. The barons gave them an enthusiastic welcome and, shortly after their arrival, organized a tournament in their honor. The participants wore armor of padded cloth and carried only their lances, as was usual in a tournament. Towards the end of the day's sport a Frenchman accidentally inflicted a mortal wound on Geoffrey de Mandeville, Earl of Essex, who died within a few days.

While Louis was making his preparations in France, John returned from the North at the beginning of March and joined Falkes de Breauté in Bedford. They marched through Cambridge, Bury St. Edmunds, and Framlingham with their forces and arrived before Colchester Castle, which was still held by the rebel barons, on March 14. After a short siege the garrison surrendered on the 25th, and three days later John captured the castle of Robert de Vere, Earl of Oxford, at Hedingham.

John's control of the Eastern Counties was now complete. He spent April in making a wide swing around London, visiting the castles that formed a ring about the city and making sure that they were well stocked with troops and provisions and ready to withstand attack. He visited Hertford, Enfield, Berkhamstead, Windsor, Reading, Franham, Guildford, and Rochester and arrived at Dover on April 26.

Louis meanwhile wrote to the barons in London, thanking them for having conducted themselves in a strenuous and manly way, urging them to be equally strong and strenuous in the future, and promising that by Easter Sunday he would have his forces assembled at Calais and ready to cross over to England.

On Easter Sunday, April 10, the Abbot of Abingdon, to whom the Pope had entrusted the task of pronouncing the sentence of excommunication upon the rebellious barons, renewed the sentence, including in it the French troops which had arrived in London, and caused it to be read in all the conventual churches in England. The barons and the citizens of London ignored this sentence, as they had the previous ones.

News of Louis's designs on England reached Innocent quickly, and he sent the Legate Gualo to France to forbid him to invade England or to harm John in any way, since England was a fief of the Holy See and John was under the Pope's especial protection, both as his vassal and as a crusader. Gualo appeared before Philip at Lyons a fortnight after Easter and delivered his message. Philip replied that John had never been the true King of England in the first place, because he had been convicted of treachery by his brother Richard, and therefore he could not give his kingdom to the Pope. Even if he had been the true King, however, he had forfeited his kingdom by the murder of his nephew Arthur, for which he had been condemned in Philip's court. Finally, argued the wily Philip, even if John had been the true King up to the moment of his surrendering his crown to the Pope's legate, he had no right to give away the kingdom without the consent of his barons. To this point the nobles of Philip's court gave noisy assent.

Therefore, Philip concluded triumphantly, no matter how one looked at it, the Pope had no claims to dominion over England. This affair did not concern the Pope, and it likewise did not concern him, Philip added, since he had no designs on the country.

The conference was continued on the following day, and Louis appeared, at his father's request. Gualo begged Louis not to invade or occupy England, the patrimony of the Roman Church, and he begged Philip not to permit his son to go on such an expedition.

Philip asserted that he had always been devoted and faithful to the Pope and the Roman Church, but that Louis should be allowed to state his reasons for his claims to England. Louis then advanced the arguments that John had been convicted in Philip's court of the murder of Arthur, that he had been deposed by his own barons, and that he had given his kingdom to the Pope without the consent of the barons. Furthermore, although John could not resign his crown to the Pope, he could resign it without specifying to whom it should go after it had passed out of his hands, and that he did when he surrendered it to Pandulf at Dover on Ascension Eve, 1213. The throne being thus vacant, the barons had offered it to Louis by reason of his wife Blanche, whose mother was the only one of John's brothers and sisters then living.

This was all legalistic nonsense, with little or no basis in fact, and Gualo paid scant attention to it. He forbade Louis under pain of excommunication to enter England and his father to allow him to go. Louis appealed to Philip not to hinder him in securing his rights and declared that if necessary he would fight to the death to defend his wife's inheritance. With this act of defiance, Louis withdrew from the conference, and Gualo asked for a safe-conduct to the coast.

On the next day, the Feast of St. Mark, April 25, Louis came to his father at Melun and begged him not to obstruct his proposed expedition. He said that he had sworn to help the English barons and that he would rather be excommunicated by the Pope for a time than to break his oath to his English friends. This decision no doubt warmed Philip's heart, and he gave his permission and his blessing. Louis sent messengers to Rome to lay his side of the case before the Pope and went on with his preparations.

Louis's messengers appeared in Rome around the middle of May. Innocent was one of the greatest lawyers of the time, and he made short work of the arguments they advanced. To their charge that John had murdered Arthur, he replied: "When Arthur was captured at Mirebeau, not as an innocent man but as a guilty man and as a traitor to his lord and uncle, to whom he had done homage and sworn allegiance, he could by law be condemned to even the vilest death without a trial."

While Louis was assembling and fitting his forces at Calais, John was on his guard at the Cinque Ports. He deployed his army along the coast and spent the first three weeks of May in watchful waiting. Most of his naval preparations came to naught, however, when a storm arose and wrecked the greater part of his fleet. In the face of a strong wind from the northeast, Louis and his forces embarked aboard six hundred and eighty vessels and landed near Sandwich on May 21. Simon Langton sailed in the same ship with Louis and served as his chaplain.

The French were in such numbers that John was forced to withdraw. He had posted garrisons in the North, in East Anglia, and in the ring of castles about London, and with his forces thus dispersed and his fleet destroyed he did not have enough men to oppose Louis's army. He left Hubert de Burgh in command of Dover Castle and retreated to Winchester. He arrived there on May 28 and at once raised the Dragon Standard.

Louis occupied the whole of Kent, except Dover Castle, and went on to London. There the barons and citizens welcomed him and did homage and swore fealty to him as their King. The monks of Westminster, however, refused to receive him, and he sent his soldiers to break open the doors of the King's treasury and carry off everything in it. Louis swore that he would establish good laws and restore their rightful inheritances to the barons. He appointed Simon Langton as his Chancellor and wrote to all the barons who had remained faithful to John, demanding that they come and do homage to him or else leave the kingdom.

With his forces augmented by some of the barons and their followers, Louis set out in pursuit of John. When Louis laid siege to Winchester, John set fire to the city in four places and retreated to Ludgershall and Devizes and then south to Wilton. Louis seemed to have gained the upper hand, and some of the barons who had hitherto remained faithful to John deserted to the French. William Longsword, the Earls of Warenne and of Arundel, and the younger William Marshal joined with Louis. Hugh Neville came to him, surrendered the castle of Marlborough, and did homage to him.

On June 8, at Devizes, John found time to write to Berengaria, Richard's widow, concerning the semi-annual payment that was due her on Ascension Day. Berengaria had had a most difficult task in getting a settlement of her widow's dower from John. As was his custom, he was lavish with promises but laggard with payments. In 1201 he agreed to pay her a thousand marks a year, but he failed to live up to the agreement. In March 1206 he issued a safe-conduct for her to come to England and return, no doubt for the purpose of discussing the settlement.

Berengaria at last lost patience with him, and in September 1207 she appealed to the Pope. Innocent, as the protector of widows and orphans, wrote a sharp letter to John. John, he said, would give Berengaria no satisfaction for her lawful claims, and none of her people dared even to cross over to England to discuss the dower with him. He ordered John to send proctors to him to arrive at a settlement of her claims.

John of course paid no attention to Innocent's letter, and the Pope wrote him again, in February 1209. He listed Berengaria's grievances and complained of John's failure to answer them. Then he enumerated the lands in England that belonged to Berengaria by the terms of her marriage settlement and ordered John to settle with her concerning the income from those lands. This letter, too, John ignored.

John was induced at least to treat with her after his reconciliation with the Church, for in November 1214 he wrote her that her messengers, who were returning to her, would tell her what terms had been agreed upon. Whatever these terms were, he evidently did not keep them.

In September 1215, over sixteen years after Richard's death, John wrote to the Pope to inform him that he had reached an agreement with his sister-in-law. Berengaria, styling herself "once the humble Queen of England," at the same time wrote an open letter to interested parties to inform them that she and John had renewed their agreement. The King had paid her two thousand marks in settlement of the arrears, and he agreed to pay her a thousand pounds a year, in two installments, at All Saints' and on Ascension Day.

John probably made the payment on All Saints' Day, but when the next payment was due, on Ascension Day, 1216, he was in considerable difficulty, as he explained to her.

THE KING, to his beloved sister Berengaria, once Queen of England, GREETINGS and the sympathy of sincere love.

Since, at the instigation of the enemy of the human race and by the efforts of our Barons, whom that same enemy has stirred up against us, our Kingdom of England has been and is disturbed, and now more than ever, with the coming of Louis, the eldest son of the King of France (who, fearing to offend neither God nor the Church, is trying to take our kingdom away from us), we have already spent the greatest part of the money which we had ordered to be spent in wresting the Holy Land from the hands of the enemy, and every day we are obliged to spend more and more.

We earnestly beg your affection, in which we have full faith, requesting you, at this time when we are undergoing such adversities, patiently to accept the delay at present of the payment of the money which we owe to you, until such time as, through Him Who moves the soul as He wills, the dark cloud is cleared away from us and our kingdom rejoices in full tranquillity, and we, with the greatest thanks, will make you full account of the money we owe you.

Louis, meanwhile, turned northeast from Winchester to Odiham and laid siege to the castle there, which was occupied by three knights and ten soldiers. This gallant little band kept the French at bay, and on the third day of the siege they sallied forth, captured thirteen of their enemies, and regained their tower unscathed. They surrendered after a week, and the French were greatly amazed when they discovered that the garrison that had put up so heroic a defence consisted of only thirteen men.

On St. John's Day, June 24, Louis laid siege to Dover Castle. It was held by Hubert de Burgh with a force of a hundred and forty knights and a strong contingent of soldiers, and it was provisioned for a long siege. Louis sent over to France for an especially effective stone-throwing machine known as "La Malvoisine" and set to work battering the walls of the fortress. Hubert de Burgh and his men replied with such vigor that the French retired to a respectful distance from the walls. Louis was enraged by this stouthearted resistance and swore that he would stay there till he had captured the castle and hanged its defenders. The French settled down for a protracted siege in the hope of starving the garrison into surrender, as John had done at Rochester.

Whilst John remained in the Southwest, around Corfe Castle, the baronial forces at last emerged from London and invaded East Anglia. Under Louis's leadership they recaptured Colchester, occupied Norwich, and reduced King's Lynn. The Northern barons picked up courage and occupied York and Lincoln, and Alexander crossed the border and invaded Northumberland.

The barons made frequent raids out of London into East Anglia. They captured the castle at Cambridge and ravaged Yarmouth, Dunwich, and Ipswich. Then they laid siege to Windsor Castle, where John had placed Ingelard d'Athie in command of a force of sixty knights and their retainers. Windsor promised to be as tough a nut to crack as Dover was turning out to be.

Meanwhile John spent a month, from mid-July to mid-August, in subduing the Welsh border, where trouble was brewing. He marched from Bristol through Gloucester, Tewkesbury, and Hereford to Shrewsbury. He left Shrewsbury on August 14 and proceeded by way of Bridgenorth to Worcester, where he subdued the city and laid a heavy fine on it.

His next objective appears to have been the reconquest of East Anglia. He went through Burford and Oxford to Wallingford and Reading and thence to Bedford, where Falkes de Breauté had made his headquarters. On his way, he addressed a letter to some of his barons who had sickened of their bargain with Louis and had agreed to return to their fealty to the King.

THE KING, to all those of the Counties of Sussex, Kent, Surrey, and Southampton, who have sworn together and united in
his fealty and service, GREETINGS.

*We are very grateful to you because you have come together
in our fealty and service and have turned away from your former
doings; and we beseech you steadfastly to persevere in our service and fealty and faithfully to stay with us, paying no heed to the
oath which you, albeit unwilling, swore to Louis, the son of the
King of France: for, on the occasion of that oath, we conceived
no bitterness of soul or anger against you, and, if we did conceive
such a feeling, we dismiss it entirely.*

*Since the time has not come when you can give us any help,
we order you to be ready and prepared to come to us at our command when we shall order you to do so, being certain that we
shall receive you with such benefits and such rewards, and that
we shall so observe your former liberties and, having observed
them, increase them, that you will be forever grateful to us, and
that, seeing the rewards we shall give you and the increase of
your liberties, the rest will the more strongly and gladly return
to our service.*

MYSELF AS WITNESS, at Oxford, September 3.

*Those, moreover, who enjoy no liberty, we shall so enrich
with liberties and honors that they will be forever grateful to us.*

John recaptured Cambridge from the barons on September 17
and proceeded to the important castles of Hedingham and Clare. The
baronial forces remained in London, contenting themselves with occasional forays to the north of the city, while the main effort of their
party was directed against the castles of Dover and of Windsor,
which stood firm against their attacks.

John then turned his attention to Lincolnshire, where a few individual barons and their retainers had succeeded in occupying some of his castles. Gilbert de Gant and his forces, who were laying siege to Lincoln Castle, fled when they learned that John was approaching. The King went to Grimsby and then south through Boston and Spalding to King's Lynn, where he arrived on October 9. He was greeted with great enthusiasm by the citizens, who had felt the heavy hands of the barons and welcomed their deliverance by their King.

The barons in the meantime were beginning to realize the hopelessness of the predicament into which they had got themselves. John was far from being defeated. Since the surrender of Winchester, the last really serious blow that Louis had been able to inflict on him, John's position had grown stronger instead of weaker. He had subdued the Welsh border in a sweeping campaign of a month; he had marched across the Midlands unopposed and joined forces with his most capable captain, Falkes de Breauté; his recapture of Cambridge and his descent upon Hedingham and Clare showed that he could regain the whole of East Anglia any time he wanted to; and his lightning raid through Lincolnshire gave proof that the barons' gains in the North would probably melt away like the besiegers of Lincoln when the King moved against them. Meanwhile, his castles of Windsor and Dover were resisting the efforts of Louis's best fighters and gave no signs of surrendering.

In addition to these discouraging military reverses, the barons had to put up with the insolence of Louis. He taunted them with their treachery and clearly showed them that he did not trust them; he took their lands and honors away from them and gave them to his Frenchmen, and he surrounded himself with French counsellors and made it clear that no Englishman had any influence with him. The barons had asked for a French king, and now they were getting a whole set of French rulers who took over all the affairs of the government. The barons repented heartily of their bargain; there was a great deal of friction between them and the French nobles; and at last a number of them in disgust deserted Louis and went back to John. They were greatly encouraged by the warm welcome he gave them, laying aside, as he had promised, all vindictiveness.

The King left Wisbech on October 12, and in his haste to cross the River Welland he refused to wait till the tide had completely subsided. He forced his followers to cross the treacherous sands, and the sands closed in on them and swallowed all his carts and baggage horses. With them all his treasure, jewels, and personal belongings sank out of sight beneath the mud, and he and his army narrowly escape the fate of the baggage trains.

John went on to the Cistercian abbey at Swineshead, sick with rage. Roger of Wendover says that he gorged himself that night with peaches and new cider; at any rate, he was seized with dysentery and a high fever. In great pain he left Swineshead on October 13 and spent the 14th and 15th at Sleaford, where he was bled. Barely able to hold himself in the saddle, he rode on to Newark on the 16th.

There he became so ill that he realized he could not recover. According to the biographer of William Marshal, he said to those gathered about his bed:

"My lords, I must die; I cannot overcome this sickness. For the love of God, beg the Marshal to forgive me the wrongs I have done him and which I heartily repent. He has always served me loyally; he has never done anything against me, no matter what I have done or said to him. For the love of God, my lords, beg him to forgive me! And since I am more sure of his loyalty than of any other's, I beg you to entrust him with the charge of my son, who will never succeed in holding this land, except through him."

He confessed his sins to the Abbot of Croxton and received the Last Sacraments at his hands. He made his will and designated his eldest son, Henry, then nine years old, as his heir. He had all those with him to swear allegiance to Henry, and he sent letters under his seal to all the sheriffs and constables who were faithful to him, ordering them to receive Henry as their King. Messengers came to him with letters from about forty of his nobles who had deserted him and then sickened of their treachery, begging to be allowed to make their peace with him and return to his allegiance, but he was too ill to attend to them.

The Abbot of Croxton asked him where he wanted to be buried in case his illness proved mortal, and John replied: "To God and St. Wulfstan I commend my body and soul." He died in the night of Wednesday, October 19, 1216, at the age of forty-eight.

John's body was dressed in royal robes, with a tunic of cloth-of-gold, a dalmatic of red samite bordered with jewels, and a mantle of cloth-of-gold thrown over his right arm. In his gloved hands he held a sceptre in his right and a naked sword in his left. He wore buskins and sandals, with golden spurs. Over his head was drawn a monk's cowl.

The body was borne to Worcester, where the Bishop, Sylvester of Evesham, celebrated the Requiem Mass. John was buried before the high altar, between the shrines of St. Oswald and St. Wulfstan, who are shown censing him on his tomb.

There is a wealth of information about Henry II and Richard, compared with the little there is about John. No chronicler tells us much of John's appearance, his personal habits, or how he bore himself as a man. One surmises that this silence is partly due to the fact that John was an unattractive character and did not capture the imaginations and, as Richard did, the hearts of the writers of the time. No one cared enough about him to record the little details of personal appearance, dress, manners, ways of speech, and foibles that enable us to form a clear picture of Henry or of Richard.

John seems to have been what was, in his time, when the sea of faith was at the full, a rare and, to the monastic chroniclers, an utterly incomprehensible being: a complete skeptic or agnostic. Men were often then as violent and tempestuous in their religion as they were in all the other affairs of their lives. They committed great and spectacular sins, it is true, but they expiated them by great and spectacular penances. One has only to remember Henry before the tomb of the martyred Thomas, being whipped by the monks of Canterbury, or Richard at Messina, clad in a loin-clout, kneeling before his bishops with three scourges in his hand to confess his evil way of life, to realize how foreign such a frame of mind was to John.

He was not even a heretic; he simply cared nothing whatever about religion. If he had had any heretical opinions, the interdict and the teachings of Master Alexander the Mason would have furnished a perfect opportunity to effect the breach with Rome and anticipate, with much less bloodshed and social upheaval, the work of Henry VIII. No one, however, would have laughed more heartily than John at the thought of his setting himself up as "Supreme Head on earth of the Church of England."

This utter indifference must have baffled the monks who were writing the chronicles of their times, and they were repelled by a man who showed no remorse for his sins and never gave an inkling of any desire to mend his ways or to seek godly counsel from priests or spiritual strength from the Sacraments they administered. They recorded his doings, from a safe distance, but they confined themselves to a bare account of his reign and said as little as possible about the character of a man who was an enigma to them and has remained an enigma to succeeding generations.

John inevitably suffers by comparison with his father and his brother Richard. Henry II was one of the greatest kings in English history, and Richard's many faults as a king (if indeed he may be said to have ruled in England at all, so little time did he spend there and so little attention did he give to English affairs) were quite obscured by his dazzling reputation as a warrior and as the pattern of chivalry. There was nothing dazzling about John.

He had the violent temper of his father and brother, without the corresponding bursts of joviality and good nature which made men forget the royal rages. He had his father's interest in the procedures and administration of the law, and he spent a great deal of time in hearing suits in his courts, but he did not have the legal genius that made Henry one of the greatest figures in the history of English law. He had his father's lecherous disposition without any of the romantic tenderness that glows in the story of the Fair Rosamund. What in Richard was a love of all things beautiful degenerated in John into a mere gluttony for good wines and rich food and fine clothes. In contrast to his father, he was neat about his person, and he bathed every fortnight, on an average. He was much involved in military expeditions, but he was without that gift for strategy and leadership that made Richard the greatest soldier of his age. He, like his father, was embroiled with the Church, but he had neither the overwhelming repentance of his father nor Richard's touching regularity of devotion and profound love for the music and liturgy of the Church. He had little of his father's skill as an administrator; if England was well governed during the earlier part of his reign, it was because of Geoffrey FitzPeter and Hubert Walter and a whole school of administrators trained by Henry or brought up in the tradition founded by him.

John was, nevertheless, an energetic, hard-working, and industrious King. In his restless journeys over the length and breadth of England, when he rode as much as thirty miles a day and seldom stayed in one place for more than three or four days, he made his presence felt throughout the whole of his kingdom, and no other ruler has ever known England as thoroughly as he did. For the last ten years of his life he concentrated almost all of his formidable energies upon his kingdom of England, and it may well be that the root of his troubles with the barons lay in their objections to being ruled by a king who stayed in England and supervised every detail of the government, accustomed as they were to kings like Henry, who spent less than half his time in England, and Richard, who was in England less than six months during a reign of ten years.

A faithless husband, a bungling military strategist, a cruel, oppressive, and treacherous lord, and a godless man: John was all of these, yet we in these present days have seen such depths of human depravity that we cannot consider him as the unrelieved villain that he once appeared to be. It is faint praise to say that he was not so bad as he might have been, yet when we consider what men with absolute power have done in later days we are forced almost to admire John's restraint. One has only to compare him with the Tudor tyrants to realize how little he did to deserve his evil reputation. He tried to transmit to his heirs the prerogatives and authority of a King of England, unimpaired by the encroachments of Pope and barons. That was his conception of his duty, and to the best of his ability he did it.

"It is to be hoped," says Matthew Paris, "that some good works that he did in this life may plead for him before the tribunal of Jesus Christ, for he founded a monastery of the Cistercian order at Beaulieu, and on his deathbed he gave the monastery of Croxton land worth ten pounds."

THE GREAT CHARTER

IN THIS appendix, which is based largely on Dr. Mc-Kechnie's *Magna Carta*, it is proposed to discuss the provisions of the Great Charter in the light they throw on the conditions of the time and on the manner in which John governed England.

From the time of the Conquest, England was a feudal society; that is, it was a society based on land tenure, together with the obligations arising therefrom. (It should be emphasized that what follows is a drastic simplification of an extremely complex subject. Every statement should be understood as being qualified by "generally speaking" or "on the whole" or "in many cases," and for every general statement a number of instances directly contrary to it can be quoted. This is not to be wondered at, for even the people living in the midst of what we now call a feudal society did not understand all its ramifications. The King's Court in a number of instances, for example, confessed frankly that it could not decide whether a certain fief was held by knight-service, by sergeancy, or in frankalmoign.)

This society was based on the premise that the king owned all the land of England. William the Bastard apportioned it out among the Crown, the Church, and his followers. Roughly speaking, he reserved two-sevenths of the land for himself and his immediate house-hold; a second two-sevenths he gave to the Church, and with the remaining three-sevenths he rewarded the leaders among his Norman followers. Few indeed of the native English were left in possession of their lands.

The lands reserved to the Crown were known as the royal de-mesne, and the income from these lands was supposed to meet all the personal expenses of the king, to support the royal household, and to defray the costs of the government.

The grants of land to the Church and to the king's followers were not outright gifts. The land was still, fundamentally, the king's. The recipient was merely a tenant, and he had possession of seisin, to use the technical term, only under certain conditions. He had to do hom-age and to place his hands between the king's and swear fealty to him "in life and limb and earthly honor." He was subject to the feudal incidents: he had to pay a relief when he took seisin of his fee (Latin *feodum*, hence "feudal"); the tenant, if a minor, was a ward of the Crown till he came of age; if the fief passed to a woman the king had control over her marriage, and the tenant had to pay the recognized aids when they were demanded.

Most important of all, and this is the keystone of the whole sys-tem, he had to follow the king in battle with a specified number of knights, and in many cases he and his knights had to help guard the king's castles. Fundamentally, then, the system was devised as a means of assuring the king an adequate army when he needed it. Although some land was held on conditions other than that of knight-service, nevertheless the obligation to serve the king in person and with a specified number of knights was the basic condition under which most land was held in mediaeval England.

These tenants, in the uncertain times immediately following the Conquest, at first maintained the specified number of knights in their own households. By the end of the eleventh century, however, the tenants-in-chief, as the men who held land directly of the king were called, had hit upon the expedient of dividing some of their lands among their knights, who then could live on their own holdings and still be ready for military service when it was called for. These tenants in turn swore the same oaths and were under the same obligations to their lords that their lords were to the king. This process of sub-infeudation might be and often was carried still further, but the fundamental obligation that a certain piece of land was held under the condition of furnishing a certain number of knights still remained, as did all the other obligations attached to that piece of land.

Normally, the land passed, under the usual conditions, to the eldest son. In those troubled times, however, when disease, almost constant warfare, and the added hazards of the Crusades made life more than usually uncertain, it occasionally happened that a man died with no heirs at all, in which case the estate returned to the lord, or with no male heirs, in which case it was divided equally among his daughters. This, together with sub-infeudation, led to a further fragmentation of what had originally been estates owing the service of a certain number of knights. Thus it is not uncommon, by John's time, to read of land owing as little as one-sixtieth of a knight's fee. The obvious way out of this anomalous situation was for the tenant owing a fraction of a knight's service to make a money settlement with his lord in lieu of the service.

All this was a complicated scheme, and it was made more complicated by the fact that little of it had ever been put down in writing. Everything depended on what was considered customary or usual, and interpretations of what was customary varied widely. The king was of course interested in getting as much from his barons as he possibly could, and the barons were determined to give as little as possible.

It is not surprising, then, that after the preliminaries of Chapter 1 are out of the way, the Charter proceeds at once to those aspects of

the feudal contract which had proved the sorest points of dispute between the king and his barons.

Chapter 2 establishes the amounts to be paid as reliefs by the various classes of tenants-in-chief, or men holding their land directly of
the king, with no intermediate or mesne lord. It provides that if any
tenant-in-chief holding by military service shall die and his heir shall
be of age, the heir shall have possession of his inheritance by paying
the ancient relief, which was now declared to be a hundred pounds
for an earl or baron and a hundred shillings for a knight's fee.

Earls by this time had been pretty well shorn of any territorial
jurisdiction over the counties or regions from which they took their
titles. They still received a third of the profits of the courts of their
titular counties, but their jurisdiction, like that of any other baron,
was limited to the lands of which they had seisin. Whether by acci-
dent or by design on the part of the king, few of the great men held
their land all in one continuous holding. Their estates were split up
and scattered all over the country, so that one man rarely dominated
a whole county or group of counties, unless he were particularly favored or trusted by the king.

The term baron was an elastic one. Originally it was applied to
all tenants-in-chief of the Crown, so that any man who held his
land directly of the king was considered a baron. By John's time,
however, a loose distinction was being made between the greater and
the lesser barons. The term baron was being restricted to the greater
men, each of whom was summoned to meetings of the Great Council by a writ addressed individually to him. The lesser men were
called knights and were summoned by a collective writ addressed to
the sheriffs of the counties. There was no rigid standard by which
it was determined whether a tenant was to be rated as a baron or as a
knight, although it is obvious that men who held a great deal of
land would be considered barons and those who held little would be

considered knights. In view of the distinction between the reliefs due from baronies and those due from knights' fees, it might seem reasonable to assume as a rough rule-of-thumb that tenants owing the services of more than twenty knights would be classed as barons, and those owing less as knights.

Some men who owed less than the service of twenty knights, however, were classed as barons, and on the other hand some men owing more than that service were not so classed. It would be to the financial advantage of the first man not to be classed as a baron, and to the second man to be classed as one. Consequently, many suits were instituted to clarify the situation, and in almost every case the final proof rested on the wording of the charter by which the man held his land. If the charter said that the land was held as a barony, *per baroniam,* then the man was rated as a baron, regardless of the knight-service due from the estate, and he had to pay a baron's relief.

When the Conquerer distributed his newly won English lands among his followers, he stipulated that the owner of each fief was to furnish in return the services of a certain number of knights when the king demanded them. There was no rigid relationship between the size of a fief and the number of knights it was required to provide. From the time of the Conquest the knight's fee was the established unit of assessment. According to this provision of the Charter, the heir of an estate that was not rated as a barony was to pay a relief of a hundred shillings for each knight's fee at which the estate was assessed.

The payment of relief not only furnished a source of income to the Crown; it also impressed on men's minds the fundamental nature of the contract between the king and those who held land of him. A man did not inherit his father's estates simply by virtue of being his father's eldest son; at a man's death his lands returned to the king, of whom he had held them, and the heir acquired the grant of the lands only upon doing homage, swearing fealty, and paying a sum of money.

The king, by virtue of his right of primer seisin, might occupy the estate, and the heir would then be forced to bargain for it. In such a case, the relief became simply the highest price the heir was prepared to pay in order to gain possession of the lands his father had held.

Through the payment of reliefs, the dependence of the barons upon the king was kept fresh in their minds, and the possibility of their forming the idea that they were absolute masters of their lands with no obligations to their king was prevented.

That this chapter concerning reliefs comes thus early in the Charter is a good indication that John had found them a fruitful field for abuses and that these abuses were one of the chief grievances of the barons. Until a fixed scale of reliefs had thus been drawn up, there was nothing to prevent John from exacting as heavy a relief as he thought he could get.

The modern equivalent of the relief would be the inheritance tax or death duties. A relief was never so heavy as to amount to downright confiscation. John knew quite well the value of all the greater estates in the kingdom, and there would be little point in asking more than the tenant would be able eventually to pay. Furthermore, the Exchequer seems to have been quite lenient in collecting the relief, as well as most other debts to the Crown, over a period of years. So long as the tenant made an occasional payment and seemed to be making an effort to meet his obligations, the Exchequer officials were apparently willing to let the debt run for twenty or thirty years, in extreme cases. On the other hand, when debtors made no effort to meet their obligations, they were often punished by the confiscation of their estates.

· · ·

Chapter 3 provides that if the heir of a Crown tenant was under age when his father died and hence had been under wardship till he reached his majority, he should not have to pay a relief when he comes of age and is given seisin of his inheritance. Men were considered to reach their majority at twenty-one, and women at fourteen.

Wardship was a natural corollary of the feudal contract. Since the king bestowed lands upon a man in return for military service, the bargain could not be kept if the lands passed into the hands of one too young for effective service. During the nonage of the heir, therefore, the revenues of the fief reverted to the king, who was bound only to maintain the heir according to his station in life and was free to keep the remainder. Since the heir thus had no opportunity to accumulate money with which to pay a relief, the barons demanded that John should not require one, which could obviously be paid cnly by borrowing money and pledging future income from the lands.

Chapter 4. Wardship might be a ruinous business for an heir in the grasping hands of John, whose chief and probably sole concern would be to make as much money from the lands as possible, without any effort to maintain the estate in as good condition as it was when the last tenant died. This chapter provides against such abuses of estates. It stipulates that nothing but reasonable produce, customs, and services shall be taken from the estate and its men.

The king might manage estates under his wardship in one of two ways: he might commit them to one of his sheriffs or bailiffs, who would manage them for him and transmit the profits to him; or he might bestow both the management and the profits as a gift on a favorite or sell them to the highest bidder.

The Pipe Rolls abound in records of payments made to the king "for having custody of the land and heir" of N., usually with "and of his marriage" thrown in. A few examples from the Pipe Roll of 1210 will show how common the practice was:

"Richard FitzRichard renders account of 2,000 marks for having custody of the land and heir of William de Rupe, together with the custody of Eva, the wife of the aforesaid William."

"Oliver de Vallibus renders account of 100 marks and 1 palfrey to have custody of the land and heir of Hubert of Munchenesey, together with his marriage."

"And of 30 marks of the fine of William of Meisnilgarin to have custody of the land and heir of Philip of Bodham and to have Alice as his wife."

"Alan Basset, 100 marks to have custody of the daughter and heiress of Ralph of Hastings until she is of age, together with the marriage of the aforesaid girl."

If it was found that the estate was being wasted or destroyed, this chapter provides that it should be committed to the care of two lawful and discreet men of that estate, who would naturally be interested in seeing that it was kept in good condition. If the estate had been committed to a sheriff or other royal agent, he should be fined for damaging it; if the wardship had been given or sold to anyone, he should lose it, and the profits should go to the king.

Chapter 5 lays an obligation on the custodian of the estate to keep up the buildings, parks, ponds, mills, and the like out of the proceeds of the lands and to turn over to the heir when he comes of age all his lands with the instruments of tillage and the standing crops according to the season.

Chapter 6. If an heiress were under the king's wardship, he might marry her to whomever he would. This arose from a sound precaution whereby the king might make sure that the heiress did not marry anyone obnoxious to him, who would by such a marriage become one of his tenants and followers in time of war. Rich heiresses were valuable prizes, and there is plenty of evidence that John married off his female wards to the highest bidder. Marriage was normally a business arrangement and was rarely left to the free choice of the people concerned. The barons had no intention of giving a girl of fourteen liberty to bestow herself and her lands on whomever she pleased.

This chapter confirms the king's right to arrange marriages for his wards, but, in view of his practice of rewarding his foreign favorites with English heiresses, with the limitation that the marriage must be without disparagement; that is, that the man so chosen must be of the same station in life as the heiress. As a further safeguard, it requires that the nearest relations of the heiress shall be notified in advance of the marriage, although it is not likely that their protests would count for much with John. This chapter applies to the marriage of both male and female wards, although it obviously would more often apply to the latter. However, it occasionally happened that the king would, for a price, give a rich young heir to an ambitious father as a husband for his daughter.

Chapter 7. In addition to wards under age, another class of people unable to defend themselves were apt to fall into the king's power. Widows of Crown tenants were peculiarly at the mercy of the king, and apparently John, in his eagerness to profit from his wardship over the lands, paid scant attention to the rights of the widow. This chapter provides that the widow shall immediately, without difficulty and without the need for any payment, have her marriage portion and her inheritance. It further provides that she may remain in her husband's house for forty days after his death and that her dower is to be assigned to her within that time. The marriage portion was the land that had been bestowed upon her by her father at the time of her marriage. The husband thus became the tenant of his father-in-law, but at his death the land reverted to his widow. Her inheritance would be any lands that she might have inherited from any of her relations. Her dower was the widow's share of one-third of her husband's lands, to be enjoyed by her for the remainder of her life. Thus this chapter guarantees to the widow all the lands to which she is entitled and, moreover, provides that she be given possession of them within forty days.

Chapter 8, as a further protection, provides that no widow shall be forced to marry when she wants to live without a husband. As a safeguard against her marrying one of the king's enemies, however, she has to give security that she will not marry without the king's consent, if she holds land of him, or that of the mesne lord of whom she holds land.

John had been in the habit, apparently, of selling the widow and her lands to the highest bidder, unless the widow could bid even higher for the privilege of not being compelled to marry. Thus, from the Pipe Roll of 1210:

"Matilda Luuel renders account of 4 score and 8 pounds and half a mark, in order that she may not be compelled to marry."

"Matilda of Muschans renders account of 200 marks in order that she may not be compelled to marry."

"Robert of Burgate renders account of 700 marks to have as his wife Galiena, who was the wife of John Briewerre, together with her inheritance and dower."

And, from the Pipe Roll of 1212:

"Hadwisa, Countess of Albemarle, renders account of 5,000 marks for having her inheritance and her dowers and in order that she may not be compelled to marry."

(This extraordinary lady, whom Richard of Devizes describes as "a woman who was almost a man, lacking nothing virile except the virile organs," was the daughter and heiress of William le Gros, Earl of Albemarle, who died in 1179. She was married first to William de Mandeville, Earl of Essex, in 1180. When he died in 1189, Richard awarded her and her vast estates to William de Fors, a military adventurer after his own heart. By him she had a son, also called William. William de Fors died in 1195, and Hadwisa was next married to Baldwin de Béthune. After he died, it is quite understandable that Hadwisa had had enough of marriage and was willing to offer the king such an enormous sum for the privilege of avoiding yet another marriage.)

Chapter 9 treats of the procedure to be followed by the Crown in collecting debts from its subjects. In the first place, neither the king nor his bailiffs are to seize a debtor's land or rents when his chattels are sufficient to pay the debt; this is an attempt to preserve a man's means of livelihood whenever possible. Next, a debtor's sureties should not be forced to pay the debt as long as the debtor himself is able to pay it. Finally, if the debtor cannot pay the debt and his sureties have to pay it, they shall have possession of the lands and rents of the debtor till they have had satisfaction for the debt. These provisions are so reasonable that their inclusion would suggest that John had been in the habit of confiscating whole estates in settlement of debts much less than the value of the estates.

Chapter 10. The charging of any interest, however small, was considered usury at this time and was forbidden by the Church. The only time anyone would want to borrow money would be when he was in distress, and the Church forbade a Christian to make a financial profit from his neighbor's misfortune. Hence only Jews served as money lenders, and the precarious nature of their occupation and their monopoly of the trade led them to exact high rates of interest. The normal rate was between fifty and seventy-five per cent a year.

If a man died owing money to the Jews and his heir had a long minority, during which of course the income from his inheritance was enjoyed by his guardian and the interest on the debt continued to pile up at a dizzying rate, the whole estate might be swallowed up in paying off the debt and the accumulated interest when the heir finally took seisin. To guard against this, Chapter 10 provides that a debt should not bear interest while the heir is under age and that if the debt falls into the hands of the king he cannot take anything except the principal of the debt.

This provision was inserted into a compact between the king and his barons and it was extended to all heirs, regardless of whether they held their land of the king or of an intermediate lord, because the Jews and particularly their money affairs were under the direct supervision of the Crown. Furthermore, the money affairs of the Jews frequently became the money affairs of the Crown. John extorted as much money as he could from them, and it was an established custom for the Crown to inherit a third of the estates of deceased Jews. Thus the king might often come into possession of the bonds of which most of the wealth of the Jews consisted. To guard against the possibility that John might attempt to extort the interest on the bonds that had been forbidden to the Jews, this chapter contains the provision that he will require only the principal sum.

Chapter 11. The previous chapter thus forbids the accumulation of interest during the heir's minority; it does not protect the estate itself from being seized to repay the principal of the debt. This chapter repairs that omission by providing: first, that the widow shall have her entire dower and shall not have to pay any of the debt, which removes a third of the security from the possibility of being seized; second, that minor children shall be provided with the necessities of life in accordance with their station; and, third, that the services due to the feudal lord shall be paid. Only after all these claims on the estate have been satisfied may the remainder be used to pay the debt.

Chapter 12. One of the chief grievances of the barons was the king's habit of exacting, arbitrarily, scutages and aids heavier than any they had previously known. Each tenant-in-chief by military service held his lands of the king in return for the obligation to serve him in time of war at the head of a stipulated number of knights. As early as the time of Henry I, the king occasionally found it more convenient to hire mercenary soldiers than to depend on his tenants. They were accordingly allowed to pay the money wherewith to hire the mercenaries rather than to furnish personal service.

This commutation, known as scutage, "shield-money," was levied at a uniform rate for each knight's fee; that is to say, if a baron owed the services of forty knights and the scutage was levied at the rate of twenty shillings on the knight's fee, as it was for the scutage of 1210–11, he would be assessed forty pounds. The king did not offer his barons the choice of personal service or the payment of scutage. If he demanded personal service, they had either to furnish it or to purchase exemption by a heavy fine. If they did neither the one nor the other, they were liable to forfeiture of their lands and could at the least be certain of a heavy amercement.

John relied largely upon scutages to pay for his wars on the Continent and in Scotland and Wales. He levied them more frequently and at a stiffer rate than had either his father or his brother. Henry II levied seven scutages in thirty-five years, and only one of them was at a rate greater than twenty shillings on a knight's fee. Richard, in spite of the great expenses of the Crusade and of his protracted warfare with Philip, collected only four scutages in ten years, and never at a rate greater than twenty shillings. John, however, asked for eleven, and possibly twelve scutages in fifteen years, all but two in excess of twenty shillings, and he would probably have demanded

more if the confiscation of the revenues of the clergy during the interdict had not for the time being furnished him with ample funds. Both
the frequency and the rate of John's scutages drove the barons to
protest. The last scutage, that of 1213–14, at the rate of three marks,
the majority of them refused to pay.

Aids were contributions demanded by the king when circumstances out of the ordinary arose. By custom they were limited to
three occasions: when the king's eldest son was knighted; when his
eldest daughter was married for the first time; and when the king was
captured by his enemies and had to be ransomed. John seems, however, to have levied an aid whenever that appeared to him to be the
easiest way of raising money.

This chapter provides that no scutage or aid may be imposed without the consent of the Common Council of the kingdom, except for
the three recognized aids, which may be levied without the consent
of the Council but at not more than a reasonable rate. This was indeed an innovation; if the Council could give its consent to the imposition of a scutage or an aid, it could also presumably refuse it.
This was no mere attempt to restore the good laws and customs of
the past; it was an effort to impose on the king a restraint the royal
power had never known before and to alter the fundamental nature
of the feudal contract, for it implied that the Common Council,
rather than the king, should be the judge as to when the king might
call on his barons for the knight-service, or the scutage representing
such service, by which they held their lands.

As a sop to the citizens of London, whose support had greatly
strengthened the barons, it was provided that aids from the City of
London should be levied in the same way. This would afford scant
protection to the city, for the Common Council, made up of the barons, would have little reason to moderate the king's demands upon
the citizens.

. . .

Chapter 13 makes fuller though vague concessions to London by affirming that the city shall have all its ancient liberties and free customs, both by land and by water, and grants their liberties and free customs to all cities, boroughs, towns, and ports. This chapter merely confirms such customary rights as they already had; it does not confer any new ones.

Chapter 14 explains the method to be used in calling together the Common Council, whose consent was henceforth necessary for the levying of scutages and aids other than the three recognized ones. Each archbishop, bishop, abbot, earl, and greater baron is to be summoned by an individual letter, and all other tenants-in-chief are to be summoned in general by the king's sheriffs and bailiffs. The meeting is to be held at a fixed date and place, at least forty days after the summons is issued, and all letters must state the reason for the meeting. On the appointed day the business shall be taken up, even though not all who were summoned have come.

This was not a representative gathering; it was simply an assembly of all the tenants-in-chief of the Crown. Its purpose was limited to that of giving consent to the levying of a scutage or of an aid other than the three previously mentioned. It could not make laws; it could not affect the administration; it had no control over the king's ministers; it had no authority over the Exchequer; and it had no power over taxation beyond the specified instances that affected only its own members. Its function was mainly advisory.

Chapter 15. The forces opposed to John were not made up solely of his barons or tenants-in-chief. The barons were in many cases attended by their own tenants and retainers, who may often have had against their lords grievances almost identical with those their lords had against the king. The support of the citizens of London has already been mentioned as being responsible for the concessions granted to them. We may assume that the more moderate clerics, and especially Stephen Langton, helped unite this variegated crowd, moderate the violence of their demands, and ensure that justice was done to the smaller groups.

The support of their tenants was essential to the barons. They therefore included a provision that lessened their own powers in order to retain the good will and help of their tenants. In this chapter the king promises that he will not in the future grant leave to anyone to take an aid from his own free men, except in the three cases previously permitted to the king, and then only a reasonable aid will be permitted.

Just as the king had been collecting aids from his tenants to help him out of his financial difficulties, so the mesne lords had been passing those aids on to their tenants as well as collecting additional aids from them for various purposes, usually in order to pay off their debts. These aids could be collected only by the king's leave, for his sheriffs were the executive authority in the counties and their help would be needed in collecting the money. The following letter is an example of the form in which that leave was granted (to one of John's favorites):

THE KING, to all the knights and free tenants of the LORD PETER, BISHOP OF WINCHESTER, ETC. *Be it known to you that we have given permission to our venerable father in Christ, the Lord Peter, Bishop of Winchester, your lord, to take a reasonable aid from you for the great expenses and labors that he has incurred in preserving our honor and the dignity of the Church. Wherefore we command you to give him such aid, because of this, that we and he may have reason to be grateful to you. And so that you may do this the more freely and better, we send you this our letter patent on the subject.* MYSELF AS WITNESS, at Clarendon, on the 14th day of April [1206].

Apparently John had been selling these licenses to any needy lord who was willing to pay for them, and this provision promises to put a stop to the practice and to limit the aids to the three universally recognized.

Chapter 16. One of the most puzzling aspects of the Charter is the fact that the chapters dealing with the most pressing disputes of the time are the most vague. The chief bone of contention between John and his barons throughout the reign had been their liability to foreign service. John maintained that they were bound to serve him wherever he might call them, and when he returned from Poitou in 1214 he attempted to collect a scutage from those who had not followed him there.

The barons, on the other hand, were not able to agree on just what their undisputed duty to render military service entailed. Some held that they were not obliged to serve outside England, although all precedents were to the contrary. Others, of an antiquarian or legalistic turn of mind, declared that they were bound to follow the king only in the territories over which William the Bastard had ruled when he had conferred fiefs on their ancestors, and Poitou was not among those territories. Still others argued that since John had lost Normandy through his own sloth and cowardice they were not bound to help him try to regain it. They all agreed in objecting to going to Poitou on the grounds that it was far away, the costs of the expedition would be great, and the king had little chance of regaining his dominions in France in any case.

Now if ever would have seemed the time to settle this dispute, and one would expect the barons, who had the upper hand, to force the king to place a limit to their liability to foreign service. Instead, in this chapter the king promises merely that no one shall be compelled to render greater service for a knight's fee or for any other free holding than is due from it. This settles nothing, for the whole dispute was over just that point of what was due from a fee that is here so airily dismissed.

This chapter is the last of those dealing with strictly feudal matters. The next few treat of legal procedure.

Chapter 17. In the time of Henry II, the king's household included all the administrative, financial, and legal machinery of the government. When the king went from place to place, all this moved with him. A man trying to get justice from the King's Court had to follow the king in his restless journeys over the country till he succeeded in getting the Court to hear him. This led to much delay, expense, and confusion. Gradually it came to be recognized that cases in which the Crown was not directly concerned need not be heard before the King's Court but might just as well be heard at one fixed place by his judges. Hence pleas were divided into common pleas and pleas of the Crown, and the former were heard at Westminster, regardless of where the king might be. John rather fancied himself as a lawyer, however, and he seems to have gone back to the old custom of hearing common pleas, in which he was not concerned, and delivering judgments on them. This was recognized to be an abuse, and in this chapter he agreed that common pleas were not to follow his court about the country but were to be held in some fixed place.

Chapter 18. The great legal reforms for which Henry II is best remembered had two principal aims: to replace the jurisdiction of the various local and feudal courts by that of the royal courts and to introduce a more rational spirit into legal procedure in place of the various ordeals and trials by battle that had previously been customary. When Henry came to the throne many estates, as a result of the anarchy and confusion under Stephen, were claimed by two or more men. The customary procedure had been to let the two claimants fight it out in a duel, with the winner gaining the land. To replace this primitive form of justice, Henry had recourse to the assize or sworn inquest as a means of establishing rights of possession.

This chapter provides for the holding of three types of assizes or sworn inquests, known as petty assizes. It states that inquests of novel disseisin, mort d'ancestor, and darrein presentment shall be held only in their own county courts and in the following manner: the king or, if he is out of the country, his Chief Justiciar will send two justiciars to each county four times a year. These judges, together with four knights elected by the county court, shall hold the assizes in the county court on the day and in the place that that court meets.

The three inquests or assizes all had to do with disputed possession of land or rights. The inquest of novel disseisin was devised to hear the claim of a man who stated that he had recently been dispossessed of his land. That of mort d'ancestor was intended to enable an heir to claim possession of his inheritance. The assize of darrein presentment was to settle claims to the right of presenting or appointing an ecclesiastic to a vacant living.

In all three assizes the procedure was the same. Two itinerant justiciars appointed by the king or his Chief Justiciar were to make the circuit of the county courts four times a year. The members of the county court, which was made up of all the free men of the county, were to elect four knights of the county to hear the inquests with the itinerant justiciars. The inquest itself was decided on the oath of twelve landholders of the neighborhood, who would give testimony as to the facts of the case. If it were a case of novel disseisin, they would be asked to tell under oath whether or not the claimant had really had lawful possession of the land of which he claimed to have been dispossessed. In a case of mort d'ancestor, they would establish whether or not the claimant was indeed the rightful heir of the man who had last had possession. Finally, in an assize of darrein presentment, they would under oath state who had made the presentation when the living was last vacant.

This procedure was quick and, depending as it did upon the sworn testimony of reputable men of the neighborhood, certainly more just than the old trial by combat. That it was popular is proved by the insistence of the barons that these petty assizes be held four times a year.

Chapter 19 provides that if all the business of the county court cannot be done in one day, enough knights and freeholders shall remain as are required for making judgments, and by inference allows the remainder of the suitors to return home. Attendance at the county court was obligatory for all free men of the county.

Chapter 20 takes up the question of amercements. At this time, if a man was convicted of a crime, he was said to fall into the king's mercy, and the sum imposed on him in punishment was called an amercement. Today this would be called a fine, but in John's time that term was reserved for contributions, more or less voluntary, to gain the king's favor, to escape his anger, or to secure some privilege. In theory the size of the amercement was proportionate both to the gravity of the offense and to the man's ability to pay. In practice one can be certain that John set the highest sum he thought the unfortunate man could pay, regardless of whether or not the payment might crush him utterly.

To prevent men's being driven to destitution by John's rapacity, the barons forced him to agree that a free man should not be amerced for a petty crime except according to the degree of the crime, and for a grave crime he should be amerced according to the gravity of the crime, with the exception that he must be left enough to live on according to his station in life. In the same way, a merchant must be left enough to carry on his trade, and a villein, if he fell into the king's mercy, must not be deprived of his tools, crops, and livestock. This, incidentally, is the only time the Charter mentions villeins.

To take the matter completely out of John's hands, it was stated that amercements were to be imposed only on the oaths of trustworthy men of the neighborhood, who would know the man's ability to pay and still keep his means of livelihood.

Chapter 21 provides that earls and barons shall be amerced only by their peers, and then only according to the degree of the crime. This chapter deprives John of the right to amerce his nobles at his own pleasure, but it does not provide the machinery for assessing the amercement in the precise way that the preceding chapter does for men of lesser degree. They might be amerced by their peers either at a meeting of the Great Council or by the Barons of the Exchequer.

Chapter 22 extends the benefits enumerated in the two preceding chapters to the clergy, with the further provision that clerks are to be amerced only according to their lay holdings; the benefices they hold by virtue of their ecclesiastical positions are not to be considered in assessing the amercement. This chapter seems to imply that clerics were regularly tried in civil courts for civil offenses without benefit of clergy.

Chapter 23 introduces an abrupt change of subject. No village or man, it provides, shall be forced to make bridges at river banks, unless such an obligation exists legally and from of old. The duty of repairing bridges was one of the threefold obligations in England before the Conquest, bearing first on all free men individually and later on a district as a whole. In view of the limited means of communication, it would seem strange at first sight that the barons should attempt to discourage the king's efforts at improving those means.

John was interested in having bridges built, however, not out of concern for the welfare of his subjects, but in order to facilitate his indulgence in falconry. When the king intended to engage in this sport, he would issue letters to the sheriff of the county he planned to visit, ordering that bridges be made or repaired in the district and that the taking of birds be prohibited till after his visit. The grievance, then, was not against the building of bridges as such but against the unnecessary building of bridges in order to facilitate the king's movements when he went "revaying" and against the prohibition of other people's sport while the king was in the neighborhood. This is made clear by the fact that in the third revision of the Charter, in 1225, this chapter is immediately followed by one providing that no river bank shall be put "in defence"; that is, closed to all hunters save the king, except those that were in defence in the time of Henry II. This prohibition is part of Chapter 47 of the original Charter.

Chapter 24 returns to matter of legal procedure. Chapter 17 dealt with the common pleas; the present section is concerned with pleas of the Crown; that is, of matters in which the Crown was particularly interested. These embraced all serious offenses, in which the king was concerned because they were breaches of his peace. This chapter provides that no sheriff, constable, coroner, or other royal bailiff shall hold pleas of the Crown. The proper persons for trying these pleas were the itinerant justiciars, who visited each county every seven years.

Hubert Walter, as Chief Justiciar, in the "Articles of the Eyre" of 1194, had made the wise ruling that no sheriff could act as justiciar in his own county or any other county in which he had held office since the beginning of the reign. A sheriff would be too intimately concerned in the affairs of his county to act as an impartial judge. This prohibition had continued in effect, in theory at least, during John's reign, but some of his sheriffs and castellans had been attempting to usurp the justiciars' functions. In many cases, furthermore, they were foreigners and lawless characters, and people had reason to dread their intervention and to demand that only the duly authorized justiciars should judge serious cases.

Chapter 25 provides that all counties, hundreds, wapentakes, and tithings shall be at the old farms without increase, except the king's demesne manors. In Anglo-Saxon times it was the duty of the sheriff to collect the Crown revenues, which would come mainly from the king's demesne manors and from the fines levied in the various courts, and transmit them to the royal treasury. Even before the Conquest, however, the expedient was adopted of farming out the county to the sheriff in return for a fixed annual sum. It was then up to the sheriff to collect at least that sum from the county, unless he wanted to make up the difference from his own purse. Anything remaining over went into his pocket. That the surplus was considerable is evident from the amount of money men were willing to pay for the office of sheriff. William de Stuteville, for instance, paid John a thousand pounds in 1201 to be Sheriff of Yorkshire, and this sum is not an uncommon one for the larger counties.

As the expenses of the administration increased, as prices steadily rose, and also as the proceeds from the county, because of the general prosperity that England enjoyed at this time, likewise increased, the old or accustomed farm did not represent a fair return, and the king attempted to increase the farm whenever he could. Each increase in the farm was passed on to the county at large in the shape of increased rents from the royal manors and more numerous and heavier fines in the courts. Since the royal manors were exempt from this provision, the effect intended by this re-establishing of the farm at the old and customary rates was to prohibit the sheriff from increasing his income from the courts by summoning them at frequent intervals and fining those who were bound to attend but did not appear and by levying drastic fines for those offences that came within the jurisdiction of his courts.

Chapter 26 describes the procedure to be followed when a tenant-in-chief dies in debt to the Crown, and it protects his property from the wholesale confiscation that was often practiced by an unscrupulous sheriff. The sheriff or bailiff must first exhibit the royal letters patent summoning the deceased for a debt that he owed the Crown. After this proof has been established, the sheriff or bailiff is to attach and list the chattels to the value of the debt, in the presence of law-worthy men, and nothing is to be removed till the debt has been paid.

After it has been paid, the remainder of the chattels shall be left to the executors of the will of the deceased, after reasonable shares have been given to the widow and the children. Reasonable shares for the widow and the children were fixed by custom at one-third for the widow and one-third for the children. The remaining third was used to fulfill the will, which generally directed that this share be used for pious purposes. All these provisions, of course, relate only to chattels or personal property; the laws regarding succession to land were fixed and could not be altered by a dying man in such a way as to prevent his lawful heir from succeeding to his lands.

Chapter 27. During this period, to die without having made a will disposing of one's chattels was regarded with horror. It was something more than a misfortune; it was considered as almost sinful, since the last testament was made by the dying man in the presence of the priest who had come to administer the Last Sacraments to him, and to die without having made that testament implied that one had died unshriven and cut off from the Christian community. In such a case, the man's lord confiscated all his property.

To prevent this injustice, this chapter specifies that when a free man dies intestate, his chattels shall be distributed by his nearest kinsman and friends, under the supervision of the Church, excepting to each one the debts the deceased owed him. This distribution was placed under the supervision of the Church both because the last testament was normally made in the presence of a priest and because the majority of testators left some of their property to the Church to be given to the poor, to provide for Masses, and for other pious purposes.

Chapter 28 restricts the exercise of the royal prerogative of purveyance, the right of requisitioning the supplies needed by the royal household. This privilege was enjoyed by the constables of the king's castles, who might pre-empt supplies for the garrisons at the market price. As John lost the support of his barons and knights, who would be the proper persons to take charge of his castles, he often entrusted them to his foreign favorites and mercenary captains. These lawless men preyed on their districts and took whatever they needed without paying for it. To correct this abuse, this chapter provides that no constable or other royal bailiff shall take corn or other provisions from anyone without paying money for them immediately, unless the seller voluntarily gives him a postponement. Money is specified because sometimes payment was made in vouchers which could be used only in payments to the royal treasury.

Chapter 29. Another offence of John's constables was connected with the duty of castle-guard. Some fiefs carried with them the obligation to serve in the garrison of a royal castle for a specified number of days every year. John preferred to man his castles with trusted mercenaries rather than with Englishmen, and he and his constables often tried to force men who were obliged to perform castle-guard to make a money compensation instead. This chapter provides that no constable shall compel any knight to give money in place of castle-guard if he wants to stand guard either in his own person or by another trustworthy man, if he himself cannot do it through any reason-able cause; and that if the king has led or sent the knight on military service he shall be quit from castle-guard according to the length of time he was on service. The fact that the barons insisted on perform-ing castle-guard in person rather than on settling for a monetary com-mutation would suggest that John and his constables tried to collect an exorbitant fee, rather than one based upon the daily pay of a hired knight.

Chapter 30 further restricts the right of purveyance by stipulating that no sheriff, royal bailiff, or anyone else may take the horses or carts of any free man for transport service unless the free man voluntarily gives his consent.

Chapter 31. The chapters dealing with purveyance restrict the rights of the royal officers only; this chapter forbids both the king and his officers to take any wood that is not the king's, either for his castles or for any other work, without the consent of the owner, regardless of the compensation. The king's forests were of such great extent that he should have had no reason for augmenting his supply by taking wood from others.

Chapter 32 provides that the king may not keep for more than a year and a day the lands of those who have been convicted of felony, and at the end of that time the lands shall be returned to the lord of the fief to which they belong. When a man was convicted of a felony, he forfeited his lands, and the Crown had the right to occupy them for a year and a day, during which period everything of any value was removed. At the end of this time, the devastated estate should be returned to the felon's lord if the felon was not a Crown tenant. John, however, once he got the land, held on to it, refusing to surrender it to the lord of whom the felon had held it. The purpose of this chap-

ter is to force him to relinquish the lands after he had enjoyed the customary year and a day of occupation and devastation.

Chapter 33. Rivers at this time were a most important means of
communication, and on them barges could transport heavier cargoes
than could be carried in cumbersome carts over wretched roads. The
building of fish weirs across streams obviously would create obstacles
to the free passage of river traffic. This chapter provides that all fish
weirs shall be removed from the Thames, the Medway, and throughout England, except along the seacoasts, where they would not con-
stitute an obstruction.

Chapter 34 illustrates most clearly the efforts of the barons to undo
the legal reforms of Henry II and to regain the powers of which he
had deprived them. It provides that henceforth the writ *Precipe* shall
not be issued to anyone concerning any holding by which a free man
might lose his court.

A fundamental principle of feudal law was that disputes concerning the possession of land should be settled in the court of the lord of
that fief, since the land was held of him and since he and the two dis-
putants were the only people concerned in the matter. Henry II
strove persistently to curtail the privileges and powers of his barons
and particularly to extend the jurisdiction of the royal courts at the
expense of the courts baron. Not even Henry in all his strength dared
so openly to violate custom as to decree that suits concerning the possession of land were to be tried only in the royal courts. He devised
instead the expedient of issuing the writ *Precipe*, which had the intended effect of removing the case into the royal court, but only in
the individual case for which the writ was issued. Thus the general
principle was preserved, while at the same time the way was laid
open for so many exceptions that in practice it was completely un-
dermined.

The writ in question was a direct intervention by the king in a dispute concerning the possession of land. It was addressed to the sheriff, bidding him order (*Precipe quod reddat*) N. to give back the land in question to M. or else to appear before the king or his justiciars to explain why he had not done so. If the order was obeyed and the land was given back, the lord's court was thus bypassed; if it was not obeyed, the case was taken directly to the royal courts.

If the land in question belonged to the royal demesne, the barons had no objection to the use of the writ *Precipe*, for the king as lord of the land in question was the proper person to settle the dispute. If the land was held of a mesne lord, however, the practical effect of the use of the writ would be that the lord, the "free man" of this chapter, would be deprived of his customary jurisdiction over such disputes and hence would "lose his court." John encouraged the use of the writ *Precipe*, both because the fees paid to obtain it increased the royal income and because he was greatly interested in all the details of legal administration and liked to hear cases himself.

Chapter 35 stipulates that there shall be uniform weights and measures, particularly of wine, ale, corn, and cloth, throughout the kingdom.

Chapter 36 returns to the subject of legal procedure. Whereas the barons, in Chapter 34, attempted to undo some of the work of Henry II, the present chapter provides that one of his most important reforms shall be available freely to everyone who asks for it. In the future, it states, no payment shall be given or taken for the writ of inquisition of life or limbs, but it shall be granted freely and not denied.

Before Henry II improved the procedure, a man could accuse another of homicide and thus force him to defend himself against the accuser by engaging, in his own person, in a trial by combat. Henry did not like such a primitive and unjust method of solving so grave a question, in which the verdict depended not upon the guilt or innocence of the accused but upon his physical strength. A strong and ruthless man might accomplish the ruin of a weaker neighbor merely by bringing an unfounded accusation against him.

Henry accordingly devised the writ, here called "of inquisition of life or limbs" but more commonly known as *De odio et atia,* to give the accused man a chance of escaping trial by battle. By declaring that his accuser acted "through spite and hate," he might secure from the king a writ directing that the sworn testimony of twelve of his neighbors be taken. If these men upheld his contention, the accusation was dismissed and there was no necessity for the trial by combat. Furthermore, the accuser would be liable to amercement for bringing false charges. This procedure was so just and rational that the barons insisted that the writ securing it be given without charge to all who asked for it.

Chapter 37 returns to the subject of wardship. Although most tenures were based on knight-service, some lands were held by the payment of an annual rent (fee-farm), the rendering of specified agricultural services (socage or, if the land lay within a free borough, burgage), or the fulfilling of certain nominal services (petty sergeancy). It was just and right that the king should have rights of wardship over an estate held by military service, for a boy could not render the service that was the basis of the contract. John seems, however, to have claimed this right over heirs to lands held by the various forms of non-military service. This was unjust, for the rent or services could just as well be rendered by the heir or his servants, regardless of his age. The barons forced the king, in this chapter, to renounce his pretensions to these wardships to which he was not entitled.

A more complicated case arose when a man held land of the

Crown by one of the non-military tenures and also held of a mesne lord by knight-service. If he died and left a minor heir, John often claimed wardship both over the heir and over the lands that he held of the mesne lord. This was even more unjust than the other claim, and John was forced to renounce it also. Wardship both of the heir and of the land went to the lord of the fief that was held by military service.

Chapter 38 provides that in the future no bailiff shall put anyone to his "law" on his own complaint alone, without trustworthy witnesses brought for this purpose. To be put to one's "law" was the crucial step in judicial procedure at this time. Juries did not have the final word in pronouncing a man innocent or guilty. After hearing the evidence, they merely decided whether or not it was sufficiently weighty to justify putting the accused to his "law," that is, forcing him to undergo the test that would establish his innocence or guilt. The test was by ordeal of fire or water, by trial by combat, or by compurgation.

Usually only women were put to the ordeal by fire, which consisted of carrying a hot iron a specified distance. The burned hand was then wrapped in cloth. After three days the bandage was removed, and if the burn was healing cleanly the accused was considered innocent.

In the ordeal by water, the accused was thrown into a pool of water that had been blessed for this purpose by a priest. If the water received him; that is, if he sank, he was innocent; if the water rejected him, he was guilty. Even though a man had succeeded in clearing himself by the ordeal by water, the Assize of Northampton, in 1176, declared that if he had been accused of murder or other disgraceful crime by the county court and law-worthy knights of his own neighborhood, he had to leave the kingdom within forty days and abjure the realm.

In a trial by combat, the accuser and the accused, or their champions, fought till one or the other was vanquished or killed. That prisoners were allowed to keep themselves in good condition for their approaching ordeal is shown by the following order:

THE KING, to the Constable of Winchester: GREETINGS. *We command you to allow Jordan de Bianney, a knight whom you have in our prison, to go out of the prison twice a day or more to practice swordplay, and in his place hold Oliver de Vaux in prison until he returns, and when he returns then allow the same Oliver to go out and go where he pleases. And see to it, as you value all that you have and your body, that the same Jordan is kept in safe custody.* MYSELF AS WITNESS, at Brook, on the 22nd day of July [1207].

Compurgation was the method normally used in courts christian, although it was occasionally used in civil cases. The accused swore to his innocence, and to his testimony was added that of as many "oath-helpers" as he could find. If a sufficient number of reputable men were willing to swear to his innocence, he was cleared of the accusation.

These ordeals were crude methods of determining a man's innocence or guilt. The Fourth Lateran Council, in 1215, forbade priests, who blessed the water or pronounced the burn to be healing cleanly, to take any part in them. By John's reign, those accused of crime were beginning to be allowed to have their cases heard by a jury who, after hearing the evidence, would pronounce the verdict, without the necessity of an ordeal.

This chapter of the Charter, however, refers to the primitive ordeals. They are not to be inflicted irresponsibly, merely on the unsupported complaint of one of John's agents. He promises that in the future the established procedure will be observed, whereby the accusation must be supported by the oaths of law-worthy men before the accused can be put to the ordeal.

In *Chapter 39*, one of the most famous ones of the Charter, John promises: "No free man shall be taken or imprisoned or disseised or outlawed or exiled, nor will we go upon him or send upon him, except by the lawful judgment of his equals or by the law of the land."

This is commonly thought to guarantee trial by jury to all Englishmen, but a careful reading of the text will show that such is not the case. In the first place, it applies only to free men, who made up probably a fourth of the population, the remainder being villeins. In the second place, trial by jury in criminal cases, as we understand the term, was a new, rare, and expensive procedure. The Pipe Rolls for 1210 and 1211 record eight payments in each year, ranging from half a mark to a hundred shillings "for having a jury," and only one such payment is recorded for 1212.

What were called juries in John's day were sworn inquests or fact-finding commissions that settled such matters of fact as the ownership of land, and juries of presentment or accusing juries, whose functions are described above. Trying juries as we understand the term were just beginning to be used in criminal cases. One had to buy a special writ for the privilege, and no one could be forced to submit to "the verdict of twelve." Since no distinction was made, apparently, between the accusing jury and the trying jury and the witnesses could sit on the jury, it could not have been a satisfactory device in many cases.

The legal rights granted to every free man by this chapter were that the accusation against him was to be heard by men of station equal to his, who would then decide whether or not he should be put to the proof or "law," what form that "law" should take, and, when he had submitted to it, whether he had succeeded. "The law of the land" may mean either that the "law" or proof should be one of the conventional and recognized ones, or it may have the wider meaning of the generally accepted body of legal principles current at the time.

In any case, the effect of this provision was to force John to abide by the established legal procedure rather than to take the law into his own hands in dealing with those he considered his enemies, as he did when he imprisoned and starved Maude de Braose and her son in 1210 and as he had attempted to do in the summer of 1213, when he started to "go upon" his barons and was dissuaded by Stephen Langton.

Chapter 40 is equally famous and perhaps equally misunderstood. In it John promises: "To no one will we sell, to no one will we deny or put off right or justice." This does not mean that justice was to be had for nothing in John's courts. Going into the courts has always been an expensive business. To be sure, John sold writs, in the sense that fees were collected for writs that obtained some special and speedy procedure that put the members of the royal courts to unusual trouble, but to charge for these writs was not the same thing as selling justice. In many cases, however, John exacted such heavy fees that it looked for all the world as though he were selling justice.

The king in his ceaseless peregrinations through the country heard many cases, and it would seem that occasionally he allowed handsome gifts to influence his decisions. It was within his power also to refuse to hear certain pleaders and to postpone cases to his advantage, and these are the abuses that he renounces.

Chapter 41 enumerates the privileges accorded to foreign traders. There was no need to treat of native merchants, for their affairs were regulated by their guilds and by the various city and borough charters. In time of peace, merchants are to be allowed to enter and to leave England and to tarry there and to move about in safety, and to buy and sell according to the ancient and rightful customs, free from all evil tolls. In time of war, merchants of the enemy country are to be detained without injury to themselves or their wares till the king can learn how English merchants are being treated in the enemy country.

The king had direct supervision over foreign trade, and it was a recognized practice for him to receive a toll of a fifteenth or a tenth part of a foreign cargo landed in England. John's rapacity, however, led him to increase the exactions and lay heavier and thus "evil" tolls. This both discouraged the foreign merchants from coming and led them to increase the price of their wares to reimburse themselves. Since the foreign merchants dealt in luxuries and hence catered to the wealthier classes, it was to the barons' interest as consumers to see that the merchants were allowed all possible freedom and protected from high tolls, which they would pass on to their customers.

Chapter 42 permits anyone, except prisoners, outlaws, and, in time of war, natives of an enemy country, to leave England and to return safely and securely. Few Englishmen, except the clergy, could have had any reason for leaving the country at this time. Since the loss of Normandy, nobles who had estates on both sides of the Channel had either divided them among different branches of their families or forfeited their lands in one country or the other, and hence the barons would have little occasion for foreign travel. Neither would the merchants, for the foreign trade of the country was conducted almost wholly by foreigners. The clergy, however, with the increasing complexity of the procedure of the Papal Curia and the ever-widening field of jurisdiction that it claimed, would have ample reason to go to Rome, both in connection with cases in which they were concerned and in efforts to advance themselves.

Henry II, in the Constitutions of Clarendon in 1164, had ruled: "It is not permitted to archbishops, bishops, and 'parsons' of the kingdom to go out of the kingdom without the permission of the Lord King." The practical effect of this chapter of the Charter, then, was to repeal this provision of the earlier document and allow the clergy to carry their appeals to Rome without the necessity for the royal permission. This chapter was no doubt put in at the suggestion of Stephen Langton and his bishops, and John, in his role of Crusader and Vassal of the Holy See, was pleased to give his consent.

Chapter 43 clears up a fine point of feudal law regarding land tenures. When a tenant-in-chief forfeited his lands to the Crown, all those who held land of him now moved up one rung on the ladder and became tenants-in-chief. In cases where their feudal dues and obligations as sub-tenants had been less than those normally required of tenants-in-chief, John tried to increase their dues to conform to their new status, which brought them, however, no increase in land or income with which to meet his demands. This section accordingly provides that if anyone holds land that has been part of a forfeited estate, he shall pay no other reliefs and perform no other services than he would if the estate had not been forfeited.

Chapter 44 is the first of those dealing with the forest laws. "Forest" is a technical term applied to those areas set aside for the king's hunting. There "the beasts of the forest," deer and wild boars, were protected by the stringent forest laws, and the common law of the country did not run. Almost a third of the country, including the whole of Essex, was under the forest law. A forest might and often did include populous districts with much arable land. Free men dwelling within the boundaries of the forest were obliged to attend the forest courts, just as those living outside had to attend the various courts in which the common law was administered. The obligation to attend the forest courts was extended to those dwelling in the neighborhood of a forest but not within it, which worked a severe hardship upon them. In addition to attending the ordinary courts, they were faced either with a second loss of time in attending the forest courts or with the necessity of paying a fine for not attending sessions of a court in which they were not concerned.

This abuse was corrected by this chapter, which provides that men who live outside the forest need not attend the forest courts unless they are accused of offences against the forest laws or are pledges for anyone so accused.

Chapter 45. Most of the provisions of the Charter propose definite and specific remedies for the evils they seek to correct. Chapter 45 departs from this standard, however, for in it the king promises that he will appoint as his justices, constables, sheriffs, and bailiffs only those men who know the law of the kingdom and truly wish to keep it. This promise is so vague that it has little force. It provides no standards by which the fitness of John's officers is to be determined and sets up no authority to pass on their fitness.

One class of officials, nevertheless, is debarred even by these vague qualifications: John's foreign favorites, who were becoming increasingly powerful as they were appointed to responsible positions. They knew nothing of the laws of England and showed no desire to keep them. Some of these men are mentioned by name in Chapter 50, as though the barons recognized that Chapter 45 might be too vague to secure their removal.

Chapter 46 provides that barons who have founded abbeys or who have succeeded to the right of wardship over them shall have the right of wardship over them when the office of abbot is vacant. Both the Kings of England and their barons had founded abbeys and endowed them with lands; even John founded an abbey, that of Beaulieu. In return for this endowment, the founder exercised the right of wardship over the abbey's lands when the office of abbot was vacant, just as the king exercised the right of wardship over the lands of a bishopric when the episcopal chair was vacant.

The intention of this chapter was not to assert a right that the Church denied but rather to provide that the founder or his successor should have that right, in spite of the king's efforts to take over the wardship of all vacant abbeys, whether they had been founded by his royal ancestors or by another.

Chapter 47 returns to the subject of forests by providing that all areas that had been made forests in John's time should immediately be disafforested and that a similar course should be followed concerning river banks that had been put "in defence" in that time.

Forests could be made or extended by the king's sole word. This would inflict great hardship on the people affected, for they were brought under the rigorous forest laws and deprived of many of their customary rights, in the interests of preserving the king's game. Although John created no new forests, he extended the boundaries of some of the existing ones. The barons forced him to agree that the forests should be restored to the boundaries obtaining when he came to the throne.

River banks might also be put "in defence" for a period of time when the king wanted to go hawking, and during this time no one else might practice the sport in that area. John agreed to restrict his exercise of the right to those river banks that were customarily placed "in defence" at the beginning of his reign.

Chapter 48 is a sweeping condemnation of all "evil customs" pertaining to the forests, the river banks, and the sheriffs and their administration, and it sets up the machinery whereby they are to be extirpated. The honest men of each county are to elect twelve knights of that county, who are to inquire into all the "evil customs" practiced both within the royal forests by the foresters and within the counties by the sheriffs and their officers. Such evil customs as the knights condemn are to be abolished utterly, so that they may never be restored, within forty days of the inquest, provided that notice is given to the king or to his Chief Justiciar, if the king is out of the country.

Chapter 49 promises to redress one of the worst abuses of John's reign, the taking of hostages and charters. The taking of hostages to secure the fulfillment of a treaty or as a guarantee of good behavior from a recently conquered rebel was a normal practice. John, however, early in his reign began to take as hostages the children or other near relations of such of his nobles as he suspected of disaffection, in order to guard himself against their rebelling. This cowardly but cunning device culminated in his demanding hostages of all the nobles of the kingdom in 1208, when the imposition of the interdict had made him doubtful as to how much support he might receive from them. The fate that might befall his hostages is illustrated by the hanging of the young Welsh hostages in the summer of 1212.

When he took hostages from them, John usually required his nobles to give him at the same time a charter pledging him their faithful service and confirming their oaths of fealty. As a further precaution, he sometimes forced them to surrender to him the charters whereby they held their lands, so that their tenure henceforth depended wholly upon his good will and might be terminated by him at any time, leaving them with no documentary proof of their claims. Men went to great trouble and expense to secure written evidence of their rights to lands and privileges and to obtain the king's confirmation of these charters. In some cases, they even instituted fictitious suits, in order that the "final concord" might be made a matter of record.

In this provision of the Charter, John undertook to restore all hostages and charters immediately.

. . .

Chapter 50 promises to remove from their offices a group of Frenchmen, mentioned by name, "and all their brood." All those named came from the vicinity of Tours and had been made sheriffs, forest wardens, or constables of royal castles by John. They were his willing agents, knowing and caring little about the laws of England, and their extortions were a source of bitter complaint.

Chapter 51. In addition to these outstanding foreigners, there remained the mercenary troops that John had brought from abroad to man his castles. In this chapter he promised that as soon as peace was restored he would remove from the kingdom all foreign knights, crossbowmen, sergeants, and mercenaries.

Chapter 52 provides that if John had dispossessed or removed anyone from his lands, castles, liberties, or rights, without the lawful judgment of his equals, he will restore them to him immediately. If any dispute arises, it is to be settled by the committee of twenty-five barons called for by Chapter 61. If, however, it is claimed that such wrongs were committed by John's father or by his brother Richard, the King is to enjoy the Crusader's respite of three years before the matter is decided and restitution effected.

Chapter 53. John had already agreed to disafforest the lands he had made forests and to relinquish wardships to which he was not entitled. This chapter modifies that renunciation to some extent. Lands that John had made forests are to be disafforested immediately, but he is allowed the Crusader's respite in dealing with lands made forests by Henry II and Richard and in restoring wardship to their proper owners.

Chapter 54 provides that no one shall be taken or imprisoned upon the appeal of a woman for the death of anyone except her husband. Although, according to ancient English custom, a woman was allowed to bring accusations only of the rape of herself or of the murder of her husband, in these two cases she enjoyed a special privilege because of her sex. If a man accused another of murder, both the accuser and the accused had to submit to the ordeal of battle in their own persons. If the accuser were a woman, however, she was allowed to choose a champion to fight in her place.

This reaffirmation in the Charter of the customary limitation upon a woman's right of appeal would seem to indicate that women had been allowed to bring accusations of murder not only of their husbands, as was their right, but also of their male relatives. In July 1212, for example, John ordered the Sheriff of Buckingham to deliver to Geoffrey FitzPeter for safekeeping Samuel FitzRichard and Philip his brother, whom Alina, the wife of William of Poitou, had accused of the murder of her son William. Furthermore, as a letter close of May 28, 1207—in which John tells the Sheriff of Lincoln that three of his justices are coming there to hear the appeal that Agnes, the daughter of Richard the Clerk, has made against a group of people, accusing them of breach of the peace and robbery—would indicate, the latitude allowed female appellants had been greatly extended.

This would allow women who enjoyed the friendship of particularly strong and warlike men a great deal of irresponsible freedom in making accusations against people they did not like. The solution devised by the barons, whose chivalric feelings had apparently been sorely tried, was to reaffirm the limitation of a woman's right to appeal to the sole case of the murder of her husband.

Chapter 55 is one of the most sweeping provisions of the Charter. In it John promises either to remit entirely all fines and amercements made by him unjustly and against the law of the land or to submit them to arbitration. Disputed cases are to be decided by the committee of twenty-five barons or by a majority of them, together with Stephen Langton and such others as he may want to bring with him. If any of the twenty-five barons is interested in a similar suit, his place shall be taken by another.

John had found in the levying of unjust amercements and the imposition of excessive fines a profitable means of replenishing his treasury and at the same time punishing his enemies, and he exercised great ingenuity in this field. Amercements were out of all proportion to the gravity of the offenses, and fines were exacted in accordance with the wealth of the victim and the ill will that John bore him.

Especially noteworthy about the composition of the board of arbitration to pass on the justice and legality of the fines and amercements is the fact that Stephen Langton was given authority to join it and to bring as many men with him as he wanted. This concession indicates the confidence the barons placed in his judgments.

Chapters 56, 57, and *58* extend to the Welsh the promises John had made to restore immediately all illegal disseisins that he had made, to restore after the Crusader's respite those made by his father and his brother, and to return the hostages and charters he had taken as securities. Included among the Welsh hostages was a son of Llywelyn ap Iorwerth.

Chapter 59. Having thus placated the Welsh, the barons inserted a chapter dealing with Scottish affairs. The young Alexander had succeeded his father as King of the Scots in the preceding December, and he favored the barons in their struggle. This chapter strikes a balance between placating Alexander and preserving the claims of the English Crown to the homage of the Scottish king. It provides: "We will do to Alexander, the King of the Scots, concerning the returning of his sisters and hostages, and his liberties and his right, according to the way in which we shall do to our other barons of England, unless it should be otherwise through the charters we have from his father William, the former King of the Scots, and this shall be by the judgment of his equals in our court."

Alexander's sisters were Margaret and Isabel. They are not to be confused with William's two bastard daughters of the same names, who were married, respectively, to Eustace de Vesci and Robert de Ros. The two legitimate daughters had been given to John as wards and virtual hostages by their father in June 1209, and were being kept in Corfe Castle.

John promised to restore Alexander's liberties and rights in the same way that he would do to his other barons, for Alexander, while King of the Scots, was also a baron of England by virtue of holding the counties of Northumberland, Cumberland, and Westmorland of the English King. Thus Alexander's equals in an English court would be John's other barons. No mention was made of the feudal lordship over the whole of Scotland that Henry II had wrested from the defeated William the Lion in 1174.

Chapter 60 was probably the price the barons had to pay to their tenants for their support. It provides that all the customs and liberties that John has conceded to his barons shall in turn be observed by them, whether clerics or laymen, in their dealings with their tenants. The barons themselves were a small group, and for their military forces they had to depend upon their feudal tenants. It was both just and discreet, then, that the agreements covering the relations between the king and his tenants-in-chief should be extended to the relations between the mesne lords and their tenants, who made up the greater part of the barons' army.

The concluding chapters, which set up the means for enforcing the Charter, are discussed in Chapter XII.

· · · ·

The Charter as issued in 1215 had little practical effect, for its nullification by the Pope, the outbreak of civil war, and the death of John prevented most of its provisions from being put into practice. It was, however, universally recognized as a remedy for all the evil ways into which the government had fallen since the days of Henry II and as a statement of the rights and privileges of free men. Henceforth it was to take the place in men's minds of "the good laws of King Edward" and "the laws of Henry I" as the ideal that should guide the king and his ministers in their government of the country and that should protect men's rights against the encroachments of the king.

The barons attached such importance to the Charter that shortly after the young Henry was crowned, in order to draw them away from Louis and to assure them that their liberties would be respected, William Marshal, as *Rector regis et regni*, and the Legate Gualo issued, under their seals, a slightly revised version of the Charter on November 16, 1216. Those chapters referring specifically to John or for which the necessity had already passed were of course omitted.

The barons deserted Louis in ever-increasing numbers and returned to their rightful allegiance. Louis recognized that he had no chance of winning the crown of England. By the Treaty of Lambeth, in September 1217, he agreed to withdraw from England with his troops. The nation was at last reunited, and in recognition of that fact a second revision of the Charter was issued on November 6, 1217. It was accompanied by a Forest Charter, setting forth the laws that dealt with the king's forests. The name Magna Carta was apparently applied to the Charter for the first time in the following year, to distinguish it from the Forest Charter.

Henry III did not reach his majority till October 1, 1228, but as he approached that age he began to take an active part in the government. In December 1224, the regents asked for the grant of a fifteenth of all movable property to meet the expenses of the administration. The Great Council set a precedent for almost all succeeding

Parliaments for several centuries when they were presented with a similar demand. They made the grant conditional upon the confirmation of the Charter. Accordingly, on February 11, 1225, the third and final revision of the Charter was issued, in the form in which it was known to succeeding generations. It was issued under the king's seal, and Henry specified that he was acting *spontanea et bona voluntate.*

This confirmation of the Charter was a most solemn occasion, and Stephen Langton and the assembled bishops pronounced a sentence of excommunication against all who violated it. Throughout the Middle Ages, this sentence was solemnly proclaimed in all the churches of England twice a year. In the latter years of Henry's reign and for many years thereafter, the Charter was commonly referred to as *Magna Carta communium libertatum Angliae*—"the Great Charter of the common liberties of England."

Gradually a document that was originally devised to provide specific remedies for the specific complaints of a group of feudal barons concerned to protect their feudal privileges against the encroachments of a grasping king became the safeguard of the liberties of the subject against the arbitrary will of the sovereign. With each age the interpretation of the Charter varied, and at times its provisions were violently twisted to meet situations for which they were not devised and which could not possibly have been in the minds of the men who framed it.

Underlying all these varying interpretations and the changes wrought by succeeding centuries, however, is the fundamental concept upon which the Charter and the Constitution of England, of which it is the cornerstone, rest: that the king is subject, not superior, to the law.

A NOTE ON THE AUTHOR

JOHN T(ATE) APPLEBY was born in Fayetteville, Arkansas, on June 10, 1907. He is a graduate of Harvard University, Class of 1928. In 1948 the East Anglian Publishing Company, Ipswich, Suffolk, England, published *Suffolk Summer*, an account of the author's experiences as a member of the 8th Air Force during the war. Mr. Appleby turned over the royalties to the Borough of Bury St. Edmunds for the upkeep of the Abbey Gardens. The book sold some 10,000 copies, and with the revenue the Borough made a rose garden in a corner of the Abbey grounds—on the site of the great Abbey where the barons met in 1214 and swore their oath to force King John to grant them the charter that in due course became Magna Carta. The garden is dedicated to the memory of the British and American airmen who lost their lives in World War II. The Rose Society of Great Britain has several times named it as the best of the municipally kept rose gardens in England.

Mr. Appleby lives in Washington, D.C., and is currently engaged on a biography of King John's father, Henry II.

A NOTE ON THE TYPE

THE text of this book was set on the Linotype in a face called *Eldorado,* so named by its designer, WILLIAM ADDISON DWIGGINS, as an echo of Spanish adventures in the Western World. The series of experiments that culminated in this type-face began in 1942; the designer was trying a page more "brunette" than the usual book type. "One wanted a face that should be sturdy, and yet not too mechanical. . . . Another desideratum was that the face should be narrowish, compact, and close fitted, for reasons of economy of materials." The specimen that started Dwiggins on his way was a type design used by the Spanish printer A. de Sancha at Madrid about 1774. Eldorado, however, is in no direct way a copy of that letter, though it does reflect the Madrid specimen in the anatomy of its arches, curves, and junctions. Of special interest in the lower-case letters are the stresses of color in the blunt, sturdy serifs, subtly counterbalanced by the emphatic weight of some of the terminal curves and finials. The roman capitals are relatively open, and winged with liberal serifs and an occasional festive touch.

THE BOOK *has been composed, printed, and bound by* THE PLIMPTON PRESS, *Norwood, Massachusetts.* PAPER *manufactured by* P. H. GLATFELTER COM-PANY, *Spring Grove, Pennsylvania.* TYPOGRAPHY *by* CHARLES FARRELL. BINDING *design by* GUY FLEMING.